# THE TIME
## *is at*
# HAND

A Wake-Up Call To The Church

*By Angela Barbut Peiris*

*[handwritten signature: Angela Peu]*

John 1: 1-5, 14

Love you Lindsey
God Bless You —

## xulon PRESS

# DEDICATION

꘎

T his book is lovingly dedicated to my gracious Heavenly Father, my awesome Lord and Savior, Jesus Christ, and the precious Holy Spirit, who led and guided me through the writing of this entire book. To You my God, be blessing, and honor, and glory and power, forever and ever. Amen.

To my precious grand-children, Michael Keenan Kelly, Micah Joshua Kelly, Israel Jordan Kelly (who is with the Lord Jesus Christ), Noah Judah Kelly, baby Kelly (who is soon expected), and to Zachary Michael Kelly my dear step-grandson. This is my prayer for you.

May God himself, the God of peace, sanctify you through and through. May your whole spirit, soul and body be kept blameless at the coming of our Lord Jesus Christ. The one who calls you is faithful and he will do it. 1 Thessalonians 5:23-24

I love you all very much.
Nani

# ACKNOWLEDGEMENTS

I want to thank my precious daughter Carol Kelly and her husband Michael Kelly for their love and support during the writing of this book. Thank you, my much loved grand-son Keenan Kelly, for your thoughts for the cover design. Also my dear friend and partner in ministry, Amy Fischer, who took time to read and encourage me, all the way, thank you with all my heart. Pastor Tony Krishack, thank you so much for your time, and for prayerfully directing me to write this book. Dr. Ray McMurtry, I am so very grateful to you for your time, and for writing the foreword. Thank you my beloved friends: Linda Torres, Steve and Amy Steeves and Martha Pena, for all your prayers and support.

May God bless you all richly, always.

# TABLE OF CONTENTS

———⊗≋⊗———

# FOREWORD

———∞∞∞———

Recommendation to Readers:

My name is Dr. Ray McMurtry and I was asked by Pastor Angela Peiris to read the manuscript for the forth coming book entitled: "THE TIME IS AT HAND" She is such a spiritually inspiring person, I was glad to go through her manuscript. As a full professor at a Christian University I had an opportunity to read a number of book and article manuscripts. I was at Azusa Pacific University, located in, Southern California, where I retired as a professor Emeritus and administrator after having served there for fifteen years.

I want to highly recommend, Pastor Angela's book to any Christian Church pastor, elder or church member. In her book, she has taken the Holy Bible and used it as God's revealed truth to guide and direct our lives on a daily basis. She has received a great number of revelations from the Lord Jesus and the Holy Spirit. These revelations have inspired and directed her in the writing of many of the chapters in the book. I found every chapter in this book to be very informative and inspirationally challenging. This is not a book that will make you feel good. This is a book that can and will change your life. "GOOD READING."

Ray McMurtry, Ph. D,
Professor Emeritus

# PREFACE

⸺ ⧉ ⸺

T his book could be best prefaced in the words of Psalm 55. There is nothing I can personally say that will reveal its purpose and intent better than the Words of the Lord. This book is a loving invitation from the Lord Jesus Christ to an awesome relationship with Him, that culminates in a certain seat at the Marriage Supper of the Lamb. So dear reader, receive His invitation:

> Come, all you who are thirsty, come to the waters; and you who have no money, come, buy and eat! Come, buy wine and milk without money and without cost. Why spend money on what is not bread, and your labor on what does not satisfy? Listen, listen to me, and eat what is good, and your soul will delight in the richest of fare. Give ear and come to me; hear me, that your soul may live. I will make an everlasting covenant with you, my faithful love promised to David. See, I have made him a witness to the peoples, a leader and commander of the peoples. Surely you will summon nations you know not, and nations that do not know you will hasten to you, because of the LORD your God, the Holy one of Israel, for he has endowed you with splendor."

> Seek the LORD while he may be found; call on him while he is near. Let the wicked forsake his way and the evil man his thoughts. Let him turn to the LORD,

and he will have mercy on him, and to our God, for he will freely pardon.

"For my thoughts are not your thoughts, neither are your ways my ways," declares the LORD. "As the heavens are higher than the earth, so are my ways higher than your ways and my thoughts than your thoughts. As the rain and the snow come down from heaven, and do not return to it without watering the earth and making it bud and flourish, so that it yields seed for the sower and bread for the eater, so is my word that goes out from my mouth: It will not return to me empty, but will accomplish what I desire and achieve the purpose for which I sent it. You will go out in joy and be led forth in peace; the mountains and hills will burst into song before you, and all the trees of the field will clap their hands.

Instead of the thornbush will grow the pine tree, and instead of briers the myrtle will grow. This will be for the LORD's renown, for an everlasting sign, which will not be destroyed." (Isaiah 55:1-13)

# INTRODUCTION

—⚬⚬⚬—

*"Behold, I am coming quickly! . . . the time is at hand"*
*(Rev 22:7-10).*

July of 1998 was another steamy, summer month in Houston. The day was Saturday and the sun blazed down with unrelenting heat. Fortunately it turned out to be a day I had to myself, so I decided to spend it with the Lord. As usual I went to Him in prayer, but this time things were somewhat different. The Lord began speaking to me in a rather unusual way.

As I knelt in prayer, amazing events began to unfold before me like a slide presentation. Each individual slide would pause just long enough to make a mental impression upon me. As I tried to make sense of what all this meant, the Lord said. "Write down what you are seeing."

"Lord, if I stop to write I'll miss what You're showing me!" I answered.

"I am in control, my child," He gently replied, "Just do as I say."

"Certainly, Lord" I said, as I quickly grabbed a notebook and a pen.

I really couldn't understand much from the pictures I was seeing at the time, but I followed the Lord's instructions and simply began recording the exact details of each frame. These slides kept showing up for next several minutes. I am not exactly sure how long I was in the presence of the Lord as He continued to show me what I am now about to write.

Later as I scanned through the notes I had made on each picture, I knew I needed to ask the Lord the meaning and the reason for this vision. He answered by leading me to this Scripture.

*"Once again, the kingdom of heaven is like a net that was let down into the lake and caught all kinds of fish. When it was full, the fishermen pulled it up on the shore. Then they sat down and collected the good fish in baskets, but threw the bad away. This is how it will be at the end of the age. The angels will come and separate the wicked from the righteous and throw them into the fiery furnace, where there will be weeping and gnashing of teeth. (Matthew 13:47–50)*

As I prayerfully studied these verses I began to see that this was an alert from the Lord to all of us who call ourselves the Church—a wake-up call if you may.

As Jesus walked me through this Scripture, I noticed that when He told the disciples the parable of the "good fish and the bad," He was explaining to them things that would happen at the end of the age. When He had finished He asked them, *"Have you understood these things?* They answered, *"Yes Lord."* Then Jesus said to them:

*"Therefore **every teacher** of the law who has been instructed about the Kingdom of Heaven is like the owner of a house **who brings out of his storeroom new treasures as well as old."** (Matthew 13:51–52)*

Suddenly these Scriptures began to take on a deeper and clearer meaning to me than they had in the past. I knew now that I had to know exactly what the Lord wanted me to do with the information he was giving me, so I began fervently seeking His direction.

The Lord reminded me that His Word alone is *treasure* that endures forever. It is only His Word that contains great riches of truth, wisdom, revelation knowledge, and blessings, which become available to all who care to seek them.

This rich and vast storehouse of everything that *pertains to life and Godliness* remains etched on the pages of both the Old and New Covenants, otherwise known as the Bible. As such, it is the Lord's desire that anyone who teaches His Word should both respect and present it in its totality.

The Lord told me that people were using select portions of His Word, while choosing to deny the truth of the rest of it. This certainly did not meet with His approval. The Lord also made it very clear that He holds *everyone* who teaches His Word responsible for how they deal with it. *The Word is by no means to be toyed with, distorted, manipulated, added to or taken from.* God requires His Word to be honored, upheld, and taught with great accuracy. Hearers must be urged to study the Word while prayerfully seeking the direction and instruction of the Holy Spirit. As knowledge and understanding grow, it becomes essential that we live in accordance with the Word.

I was now led by the Lord to yet another passage in the Book of Matthew. This time, speaking of His return, Jesus said,

*When the Son of Man comes in his glory, and all the angels with him, he will sit on his throne in heavenly glory. All the nations will be gathered before him, and he will separate the people one from another as a shepherd separates the sheep from the goats. **He will put the sheep on his right and the goats on his left.** "Then the King will say to those on his right, 'Come, you who are blessed by my Father; take your inheritance, the kingdom prepared for you since the creation of the world. For I was hungry and you gave me something to eat, I was thirsty and you gave me something to drink, I was a stranger and you invited me in, I needed clothes and you clothed me, I was sick and you looked after me, I was in prison and you came to visit me.' "Then the righteous will answer him, 'Lord, when did we see you hungry and feed you, or thirsty and give you something* *to drink? When did we see you a stranger and invite you in, or needing clothes and clothe you? When did we see you sick or in prison and go to visit you?' "The King will reply, 'I tell you the truth, whatever you did for one of the least of these brothers of mine, you did for me.' "Then he will say to those on his left, 'Depart from me, you who are cursed, into the eternal fire prepared for the devil and his angels. For I was hungry and you gave me nothing to eat, I was thirsty and you gave me nothing to drink, I was a stranger and you did not invite me in, I needed clothes and you did not clothe me, I was sick and in prison and you did not look after me.' "They also will answer, 'Lord, when did we see you hungry or thirsty or a stranger or needing clothes or sick or in prison, and did not help you?' "He will reply, 'I tell you the truth, whatever you did not do for one of the least of these, you did not do for me.' "Then they will go away to eternal punishment, but the righteous to eternal life. (Matthew 25:31–46)*

Many times we relate the words of this Scripture to sharing of literal food, water and clothing with those who are sick, in need, or in prison, and so we should. While this is true and must always be done, there is a greater form of hospitality and kindness we shouldn't overlook. This is of course sharing the Word of God, with those who are perishing from spiritual hunger and thirst, those who are strangers to the Kingdom of God, those imprisoned by Satan, and those who are spiritually naked and desperately sick. Jesus said, *"I am the bread of life. He who comes to me will never go hungry, and he who believes in me will never be thirsty (John 6:35).* Jesus said again, *"Whoever believes in me, as the Scripture has said, streams of living water will flow from within him" (John 7:38–39).* What we have freely received of the Lord we must freely give.

The Lord then said to me that the time of His return is very near, and the day of our reckoning at hand. Everyone who loves Him and obeys His Word will receive the blessing of eternal life, but the disobedient and those who disregard or treat His Word and commands lightly will be eternally separated from Him. Jesus warned, *"He **who rejects Me** and does not receive My sayings, has one who judges him; **the word I spoke is what will judge him at the last day** (John 12:48). Jesus also said, I tell you the truth, **if anyone keeps my word, he will never see death"** (John 8:51).*

I was now directed by the Lord to *Revelation 22:16: "I, Jesus, have sent my angel to give you this testimony for the churches . . ."* While reading this Scripture given to John so long ago, I was able to deduct that the Jesus was using it to instruct me to share with the Church what He was revealing to me.

At this point I decided to go to my Pastor, Tony Krishack, the senior pastor at Victory Christian Center, in Houston, Texas, where I was attending at the time. He graciously took time out of his busy schedule to sit down with me for a while. As I shared with him what the Lord had revealed to me, he listened carefully and said, "Angela, this is what I am receiving in my spirit from the Lord right now, He has given you this information for the Church, and you must put it in a book for the Church to read."

This explained the very large pencil I had seen Jesus placing in my hand, at the end of all the things He revealed to me. I knew then that Jesus had just confirmed what He wanted me to do.

A mix of inadequacy and reverent fear flooded my being. It hadn't been too long since I had received the baptism of the Holy Spirit, and I found it hard to comprehend that the Lord would consider me for a task such as this. As I struggled with myself, Jesus reminded me that He had used fishermen, tax collectors, and a host of other very ordinary folk all throughout history to do His work, and so He could very easily use me, as well. It is nonetheless with much humility and submission to Jesus Christ my Lord and Savior that I now report to you, my beloved brothers and sisters, what He instructed me to say. It is my fervent prayer that those who read this book will recognize the voice of Jesus and heed His loving and urgent call.

Since this message was given for the Church, it is obviously intended for all who consider themselves to be Christians, regardless of whether they are pastors, leaders, teachers, or those who sit in the pews. Those who call themselves believers but seldom or never frequent a church are addressed as well. This word from the Lord Jesus Christ is a wake-up call to all of us, and the urgency of this message should in no wise be missed or taken lightly.

With that said, let me begin to share what Jesus revealed.

The Lord began by addressing the shepherds and leaders of the churches with some rather startling questions.

"Are you awake?" He asked.

"Are your own storehouses—your hearts, filled with the treasures of My Word to the extent that they overflow from you to your flock?"

"By the way, what about your sheep, are they filled with the Word so that from their fullness, the lost and those in darkness are being touched and led to me?"

"What exactly are you preaching and teaching? Is it the same message that my apostles and I taught?" Are your sheep really being nourished with the wonderful treasures from both the Old and the New Covenants? Or are you leaving some of it out?"

With that, the Lord turned His attention to all believers. "Take a close look at your personal lives, He said. Where would you find yourself if you were to face me today?"

"Would you be counted a sheep or a goat; a good fish or a bad one?"

"What actually *is* the true condition of your heart and life?"

"How obedient are you to my Word? Do you study it, search it, and live by its instructions? Or does your Bible simply decorate a table or shelf in your home?"

My heart began to pound rather uncomfortably, and my thoughts began rapidly scanning my own habits! Where did I stand in my knowledge, understanding, and obedience to

God's Holy Word? What about my family and friends, my church family; where did they stand? Where exactly does the Church at large stand? Who and what dominates our lives, our thoughts, our energies, and our hearts? Somehow the words spoken by the Apostle Paul in the following Scripture seemed to apply rather loudly to our modern-day church.

> *. . . there will be terrible times in the last days. People will be lovers of themselves, lovers of money, boastful, proud, abusive, disobedient to parents, ungrateful, unholy, without love, unforgiving, slanderous, without self-control, brutal, not lovers of good, treacherous, rash, conceited, lovers of pleasure, rather than lovers of God—having a form of godliness, but denying its power . . . (2 Timothy 3:1–5)*

As harsh as that may sound, somehow, this picture appears to describe the Church of today rather accurately. To compound this bleak scenario, a large number of those who claim to believe in Jesus Christ don't even seem to be aware that Paul's words are speaking directly to them.

In the light of this Scripture, it becomes hard to miss that the Church today has begun to look much like the world! Desensitization in the lives of believers is the direct result of waltzing too closely with the world. The ways of the world have very effectively rubbed off on the Church instead of the other way around, and the difference between the two has blurred. The Apostle John gave us this warning.

> *Do not love the world or anything in the world. **If anyone loves the world, the love of the Father is not in him. For everything in the world—the cravings of sinful man, the lust of the eyes and the boastings of what he has and does—comes not from the Father but from the world.** The world and its desires pass away, but the man who does the will of God lives forever. (1 John 2:15–17)*

Time as we know it is rapidly running out! If we know what the Bible says, we will also understand from the daily news or newspaper headlines, how close we really are to the coming of the Lord.

If each of us was to seriously study ourselves in the mirror of God's Holy Word, we might be amazed at what would be revealed. Would your reflection be one of a sheep or a goat, a good fish or a bad one? What would mine be? Direct scrutiny from the Holy Spirit is something that each of us should welcome and be more than willing to submit to; but this comes only from faithful prayer and time in the Word.

Jesus Christ is coming back for His Church very soon, He loves us so very much, and we His people must wake up. We must be ready to meet Him.

It is time to *watch, pray,* and *obey* for *the time is at hand!*

# Chapter 1

# DEEP, DEEP DARKNESS

---∞---

M y visual journey with Jesus began when He showed me a huge expanse of extreme darkness. From directly above, a giant shaft of light beamed down upon this dark area, but amazingly, the light seemed to bounce off this heavy darkness instead of penetrating it. The density of the black fog was so great that it gave the appearance of a thick granite wall. I watched closely as this great heavenly light tried persistently to pierce this immense darkness, but not with much apparent success.

I must explain that from the outset of this carefully imaged expedition to its finale, the Lord brought Scriptures to my mind to substantiate and explain what He was showing me. He then explained what I saw, in the light of the Scriptures He chose to use. This is why I have used so many Scriptures throughout the book and I make no apology, for no one can say it better than God.

As I tried to make sense of the heavenly beam of light seeking to penetrate the massive darkness, the following Scripture came to mind.

*In Him (Jesus) was Life, and the Life was the **Light** of men, **the Light shines in the darkness, and the darkness has not comprehended it.** (John 1:4–5)*

The Lord Jesus said to me, "The picture you saw, describes not only the very great spiritual blindness in the world, *but also an enormous lack of understanding within the church.*"

I could sense the Lord's pain, as my mind sped to the numerous church bodies so deeply ensnared in man-made traditions, legalism, and multitudes of other false doctrines combined with a huge lack of knowledge of the Word of God. ' Consequently, there is ritual but no relationship with the Lord. The words Jesus spoke so long ago now became especially significant.

> *These people honor me with their lips, but their hearts are far from me. They worship me in vain: Their rules are but rules taught by men. (Matthew 15:8–9)*

This Scripture makes evident the many furtive ways in which Satan has infiltrated the churches. The Lord went on to explain that varying degrees of pride, passivity, complacency, apathy, false doctrine, and false security all rolled into one, have successfully lulled the Church into a very dangerous spiritual stupor.

We are told in God's Word,

> *. . . Our struggle is not against flesh and blood, but against the rulers, against the authorities, against the powers of this dark world, against the spiritual forces of evil in the heavenly realms. (Ephesians 6:12).*

As is obvious, we are up against a formidable enemy, but alarmingly, our own state of alert is nowhere near high. Much of the Church is asleep in enemy territory with their front doors wide open.

Peter cautioned us,

> *Be self-controlled and alert, your enemy the devil prowls around like a roaring lion looking for someone to devour. (1 Peter 5:8)*

As we look around we see that too many churches have become fair and easy game for the enemy. Scores of "believers" metaphorically serve as Satan's breakfast, lunch, and dinner as well, because they choose to ignore the warnings of God's Holy Word. Too many Christians have their plates filled with much to do, and not enough time to spend with the Lord.

Peter makes it abundantly clear that if we are to avoid being devoured by Satan, then *we* personally should do something about it. Peter goes on to spell this *'something'* out for us; he says we are to *"be self-controlled and alert."* Unless we take God at His Word, and become vigilant we will be ensnared in traps of the enemy.

Too great a part of the Church goes about its daily life, not even realizing that the common mindsets of selfishness, pride, complacency, self-focus and so on, are wide-open doors to the devil. Satan does not wait for an invitation; he accesses every door he can get through, and of course his intentions are far from cordial.

Peter instructs us, *"Resist him,* [Satan] *standing firm in the faith . . ." (1 Peter 5:9).* If we are to be able to do as Peter instructs however, we should remember where faith comes from. The Bible tells us, *"...Faith comes by hearing and hearing by the Word of God" (Romans 10:17).* To be able to resist the devil, we must know God's Word and believe and obey it. We must also appropriate it and use it effectively as Jesus did. It is safe to say that *where there is no Word, there will also be no faith.*

The Scriptures—*the Sword of the Spirit,* is our God-given weapon against the enemy; but it is only when we know the Word that we can use it as intended. God's Word is to be used skillfully, accurately, and deliberately against the enemy of our souls. If we don't know God's Word, nor choose to carefully live by its principles, we will soon find that we are defenseless in the face of the diabolical schemes of the devil. One of the greatest pitfalls we face comes from attempting to live our lives, handling things in our own strength. Whenever we attempt to skip the instruction of the Bible, prayer, and careful attention to the *voice of the Holy Spirit,* we will find that we have walked directly into the dangerous trap of presumption and pride.

The Bible tells us very simply where this bumpy road leads; *"Pride goes before destruction, and a haughty spirit before a fall" (Proverbs16:18).* James adds, *". . . God opposes the proud but gives grace to the humble" (James 4:6).*

This is definitely not a pleasant place in which to be. Peter reminds us, *"Humble yourselves therefore, under God's mighty hand, that He may lift you up in due time" (1 Peter 5:6),* but the problem most of the time, is that we do not recognize pride within ourselves.

Jesus the Son of God—the Living Word, walked this earth in humble obedience to the Father, and if we ever hope to prevail against the devil, we must choose do the same thing. God's Word provides everything we need to know so that we can live victoriously and in obedience to Him. However, despite God's amazing gift to us, much of the church population doggedly chooses to remain in blind ignorance of the countless treasures etched on the pages of His Holy Word.

The "do-it-yourself" road is a much-too-dangerous one to traverse. Pride says "I can handle my life." Humility says, "I can't, but God can, and I need Him to guide me every step of the way." *"Your **Word** is a Lamp to my feet, and a Light to my path" (Psalm 119:105).*

There is an interesting passage of Scripture found in the Book of Amos, listen to it:

*The days are coming," declares the Sovereign Lord, "when I will send a famine through the land—not a famine of food or a thirst for water, **but a famine of hearing the words of the Lord.** (Amos 8:11)*

This Scripture is being fulfilled before our very eyes. Today very little of the Bible is shared from the pulpits, and a dearth of knowledge exists in the lives of too many believers because they take no time for it, as well. Pastors and teachers seldom encourage personal time in the Word, and so the famine of hearing God's Word is upon us.

We commonly see thousands of well-dressed people attending church each Sunday, and Wednesday nights too. Much of the time, everyone looks just great on the outside, but on the inside, many are hurting, angry, prideful, confused, and pretty miserable. This is a very sad state of affairs, and it gets even worse; most of these people leave the assemblies of their choice exactly the same as they entered. *This simply isn't the church that Jesus gave His life to build!*

There is immense darkness within the churches today, even though the light of Jesus Christ is strongly beaming down. The acts of singing, giving, and listening to the preacher as part of a church day experience are great, but something simply isn't right when multitudes of desperately hurting people leave the assemblies, never once having encountered the glorious light and presence of the Savior or the blessing of His healing love.

In some gatherings it would be quite unthinkable for people to get on their faces before the Lord, humbling themselves in brokenness and prayer. It would also be unheard of for people to acknowledge and repent of their sins, calling out to the Lord for His forgiveness, mercy, and blessing.

Unfortunately there exists a scripted venue in most churches to which both the Lord and all the people must strictly adhere: a certain number of songs and a set time for everything. Yet we should permit the Holy Spirit to lead. The Bible tells us:

*Humble yourselves, therefore, under God's mighty hand, that he may lift you up in due time. Cast all your anxiety on him because he cares for you. (1 Peter 5:6–7)*

God cares so very much for all the multitudes of spiritually ill and hurting people who walk in and out from these weekly services. They are never once given the opportunity to be touched or healed by His loving outstretched hand, and so many weary folks simply wear a mask to hide their pain. These dear people have never learned how to receive God's kindness and mercy. This *is a state of dense spiritual darkness.*

The Church is to be the light-bearer, but the Church desperately lacks the light of *Jesus the Light Giver.* The Church today does not resemble the Church Jesus built. Something has changed, and the Church must go back to what it was originally intended by Jesus to be! Jesus said, ". . . *If then the very light in you [your conscience] is darkened, how dense is that darkness! (Matthew 6:23, AMP)*

Is this not what needs to change? Shouldn't there be more light in our hearts?

The Lord says,

> *If My people, who are called by My name, will humble themselves and pray and seek My face and turn from their wicked ways, then will I hear from heaven and forgive their sins and heal their land. (2 Chronicles 7:14)*

Humility and obedience to God's Word go hand in hand, and when they are coupled with complete trust and dependence upon Him, forgiveness and peace prevails. However, this will only happen when the Church starts to fully yield to God. Then hurting multitudes will learn to receive from Him.

Yet amidst all of this, there is a *remnant Church* that seriously seeks the face of the Lord. All of us as believers should make certain that this is the church to which we belong. We should be passionately seeking the presence of the Lord. A church that is desperate for God truly belongs to Him. We should all make sure of our own spiritual condition, through a deep and sincere soul search. Our hearts must open to Almighty God in true humility and honesty. John the apostle tells us,

> *This is the verdict: Light has come into the world, **but men loved darkness instead of light because their deeds were evil.** Everyone who does evil hates the light, and will not come into the light for fear that his deeds will be exposed. **But whoever lives by the truth***

*comes into the light, so that it may be seen plainly
that what he has done has been done through God.
(John 3:19–21)*

More than ever before, the time has come for all believers
to run to Jesus Christ and permit the powerful light of His Word
to penetrate even the minutest areas of our lives. It is time to
truly humble ourselves and invite the Holy Spirit to lead and
illuminate our understanding. If we really know what is good
for us, we would cry out to God for the light of His Word to
shine deep into our hearts. We would then choose to live in
and through the power of the light of the written Word, keeping
in mind that Jesus Christ is the Living Word.

Apathy comes from no real understanding or care about
what is available to us in the Lord. Apathy means the absence
or suppression of passion, emotion, or excitement. Look
around you, how excited is your church about Jesus?

Jesus is coming back for a *"...radiant Church, without
stain, wrinkle, or blemish, but holy and blameless" (Ephesians
5:27)*. He is coming for a Church that is excited about His
return—a church that is faithful and active in obeying His will
and commands.

Without doubt, this would be the Church that passionately
nourishes itself with generous helpings of the life-giving Word
and Living Water that the Bible offers. In a world that is crazed
with diets of all sorts, it is worth noting that this amazing *Word
diet* is guaranteed not to add a single ounce of body fat. It will
in fact provide eternal health to the eater and life to the drinker.

How could we not be excited about the imminent return of
the Messiah?

The Lord is coming for a Church that overflows with desire
to serve Him by generously dispensing the Bread of Life and
Living Water to multitudes of lost and dying people in the
world. *In other words this would be the Church that executes
the Great Commission with zeal.* Surely, the Lord is returning
for an overflowing Church that clothes the naked, feeds the
hungry, gives drink to the thirsty, heals the sick, casts out

demons, and sets the prisoners free. This exuberant Church would also be the one that welcomes strangers to the wealth and glory of God's Kingdom. Jesus described this kind of living, as the *abundant life*.

It is time that we wake up and start living in the fullness of the life that Jesus offers. This is what He said: *"...I have come that they may have life, and that they may have it more abundantly" (John 10:10).*

The Lord's abundance is available to everyone who will receive it. The *they* Jesus was referring to in the (John 10:10) Scripture, are His children—the faithful remnant church.

As the Lord kept speaking to me, bringing Scripture after Scripture to mind and explaining how they defined the Church, He brought me to the story of the woman at the well, discussed in John, chapter 4: *"Sir, give me this [Living] Water..."* she cried. Somehow this hurting, sinful woman caught the vision Jesus was trying to impart. Something changed within her and she ran to bring her whole village to Jesus the healer and Savior. Friends, that was overflow!

The words the Lord spoke to the Samaritan woman regarding His bountiful supply of Living Water caused her to desire it, receive it, and then pour it out to her entire village. This should be our style, but many of us have missed this great offer from the Lord.

We have become a complacent, over-satisfied, do-nothing Church that escapes the instruction of the Life-giving Word entrusted to us by Almighty God. Consequently, thousands strive to live by the cheap standards of the world, and in doing so they plod an empty road, oblivious to the impending danger of being caught in this lackluster condition at the return of Lord.

With reference to the living water of the Word of God, many believers who ought to know better are "running on empty." They have not chosen to fill up their tanks, and as a result they cannot give what they do not have. Remember the five foolish virgins? They had no oil!

Friends, what kind of Church are we—you and I, sheep or goats? The Lord's final words to us before He left this earth were:

> **All authority in heaven and on earth has been given to me. Therefore go** *and make disciples of all nations, baptizing them in the name of the Father and of the Son and of the Holy Spirit, and teaching them to obey everything I have commanded you. And surely I am with you always, to the very end of the age. (Matthew 28:18–20)*

What each of us chooses to do with this instruction, should give us a pretty good idea of which category we personally fall into—sheep or goat. Didn't the Lord say, *"My sheep hear My voice, and I know them, and they follow Me"* (John 10:27).

Is the Church truly following Jesus? To follow Jesus is to do what He did. Don't we remember the children's game of "Follow the Leader?" What did you do when you played the game?

The Church is intended by God to be the Body of Christ—Jesus, of course, being the Head. If we were to analogize the Church to the physical body of a human being, how healthy would this individual be if only the head and a few parts of it functioned efficiently? What if the hands and legs of this person were paralyzed or went off in directions not dictated by the head? What if the heart was sluggish and malfunctioning? Would this individual truly be considered healthy? The answer obviously is "No." Every part of the human body must function at maximum best for it to be in optimum health. If the church, the body of the Lord, continues to remain in a sluggish, atrophied, or self-directed condition, then needless to say, we have a major malfunction in the body, and it is a heart issue.

A church in this spiritually impoverished state could hardly be described as the unspotted and radiant Bride Jesus is coming back for. It simply does not compute! The time is short and it is time to wake up and change course! As surely as unhealthy physical conditions produce physical death, spiritual death becomes the inevitable outcome for those who will not rise up and do what Dr. Jesus, the Great Physician, has prescribed.

Jesus answered the devil's every temptation by replying, **"It is written."** He said, *"It is written Man does not live on bread alone but on **every word that comes from the mouth of God**" (Matthew 4:4).* Jesus not only said this, but He lived by every word that came from the mouth of God. Through Jesus this should be our goal as well. There is no way to survive on anything less.

It is of vital importance to do as Jesus did! We should begin each day by eating several helpings of the Bread of Life—God's Word, and while we're at it, we should also wash it all down with many daily drinks of the Living Water of God's Holy Word.

For physical well-being, we are counseled that our daily intake of water should equal in fluid ounces, half the weight of our bodies. Just think if you weighed 150 pounds and applied this principle to your Scripture intake, by equating one fluid ounce of water to a verse from the Bible, you would be ingesting at least seventy-five verses of Scripture daily. If you faithfully followed this routine and then chose to obey the Word you received, sooner rather than later, you would easily be living by every Word that proceeds from the mouth of God, just as Jesus did.

The time is most certainly here for all of us to get off our comfortable pews and stop being entertained spectators or spiritual couch potatoes. It's time as never before, to get up like the Samaritan woman and begin exercising spiritually, by reaching out to the lost with the Gospel. Remember this woman first dealt with herself, she then ran and brought her entire village to Jesus.

Multitudes are dying and souls are being lost every day because we—the twenty first century Church—carry on in the comfort of our uncaring, self-absorbed, unconcerned mind-sets. We sit as spoiled spectators in our plush sanctuaries, not doing one thing to help the cause of Jesus Christ.

The Lord was once amazed at His own earthly parents' lack of understanding. He had stayed behind in Jerusalem at the Temple instead of returning to Nazareth with Mary and Joseph. Jesus had done this to listen to the leaders discuss the deep things of God and ask questions of them. When his concerned parents found him, He asked them this question, *"Why did you seek me?* **Did you not know that I must be about My Father's business?"** *(Luke 2:49)*

By the way, He was only twelve years old when this happened. Friends, do we measure up? No we don't! We remain deeply involved in our own pursuits and so very uninvolved in our Heavenly Father's business. It is time friends; it is time to return to the Lord's final commission to all believers. *It is a matter of eternal life and death! How could we be so complacent?* Jesus commanded:

> . . . *Go and make disciples of all nations, baptizing them in the name of the Father and of the Son and of the Holy Spirit and teaching them to obey everything I have commanded you. And surely I am with you always, to the very end of the age. (Matthew 28:19–20)*

Let's pause here for a brief moment.
- Did you read your Bible today?
- Did you share Jesus Christ with someone today?
- Did you even think about it at all today?
- If not, will you start today?

The Apostles and the first century believers simply couldn't be contained. They shared the Good News of the Gospel at great cost to their lives. Why? They were filled with the Word. They had just spent three and a half years with the Living Word, Jesus Christ, and consequently, out of their innermost beings rivers of Living Water gushed forth. They couldn't hold back the Word even in the face of certain death. Jesus said, *"If anyone thirsts, let him come to Me and drink. He who believes in Me, as the Scripture has said, out of his heart will flow rivers of living water" (John 7:37–38).*

The Church of today is starved of Life-giving Bread and very dehydrated from the lack of Living Water. A Church so deeply malnourished cannot give *what it does not have.* So dispassion and disinterest abound in the lives of believers, much to the empowerment of the enemy.

The devil once tried to tempt Jesus to make bread out or stones. Of course, the tempter failed quite miserably! However, too many people who claim to be followers of Jesus today, have fallen into the trap of desperately trying to make bread out of the stones of life, instead of following the example set by the Lord.

The urgency of the Great Commission has dimmed because of the countless other things believers would rather be doing instead—things that gratify the self-indulgent appetites of our twenty-first-century Christian mentality. Regrettably, much of the Church has become consumed by the world instead of the other way around, and the Word is overwhelmingly ignored.

It is surely time we all wake up to the Bible and start obeying Jesus. It is time to begin living in submission to the Holy Spirit, permitting Him to lead and guide us in to *all Truth* as the Lord promised.

As we discussed earlier, unlike in the days of the Apostles, a great part of the Church does not receive the Truths of God's Word at the hands of pastors and leaders. So the vast treasures of both the Old and the New Testaments are lost to the hearers. The Scriptures are glossed over, distorted, or watered down by many of today's preachers. Many times the Word is fudged and minimized because it would not be financially feasible for the Truth to be heard. Someone important might just be offended! So time and time again, the Personhood, the life and ministry, the death and resurrection of the Lord Jesus Christ is denied or held in question, while politically correct statements spew forth from pulpits around the globe. Jesus asked a simple but profound question: *"Why do you call me 'Lord, Lord' and do not do what I say?" (Luke 6:46)*

34

The Bible tells us:

*All scripture is given by inspiration of God, and is profitable for doctrine, for reproof, for correction, for instruction in righteousness: That the man of God may be perfect, thoroughly furnished unto all good works. (2 Timothy 3:16–17)*

When pastors manipulate the Scriptures to titillate the ears of the hearers, there is no way the church is being taught, rebuked, corrected, trained in righteousness, or fully equipped for every good work. A feel-good Gospel is by no means the one Jesus and His disciples preached. They taught, they exhorted; they boldly emphasized that which is right and wrong in eyes of God. Very simply, they taught The Word and they lived by what the Word taught.

We are urged to *"Work hard so God can approve you. Be a good worker, one who does not need to be ashamed and who correctly explains the word of truth"* (2 Timothy 2:15). We are called to be diligent workers who rightly divide the Word of Truth so that we might be approved by God. *"All Scripture is **God Breathed.**"* In the natural, a person is not able to live more than six or seven minutes without air. God breathed His life-giving oxygen into Adam and he became a living soul. Considering that we are Adam's descendants, it is God's Breath that keeps us spiritually alive as well. Why then do we presume to be able to live without the Scriptures—the Breath of God?

How very careful every preacher should be regarding what he or she teaches! A gospel different to the one Jesus and the Apostles preached cannot produce life, because any other gospel is not "God Breathed." In fact Paul stated, *"But even if we or an angel from heaven should preach a gospel other than the one we preached to you, let him be eternally condemned!"* (Galatians 1:8)

We should never forget that the Lord will call each person into account for reward or loss, based upon the accuracy of his or her ministry of His Word.

Paul said to Timothy:

*In the presence of God and of Christ Jesus, who will judge the living and the dead, and in view of His appearing and His Kingdom, I give you charge; Preach the Word; be prepared in season and out of season; correct, rebuke, and encourage with great patience and careful instruction. For the time will come when men will not put up with sound doctrine. Instead, to suit their own desires, they will gather around them a great number of teachers to say what their itching ears want to hear. They will turn their ears away from the truth and turn aside to myths. But you, keep your head in all situations, endure hardship, do the work of an evangelist, discharge all the duties of your ministry. (2 Timothy 4:1–5)*

Friends, let me suggest to you that the *"itching ear"* era has arrived with a bang. People only want to hear things that make them feel good. Paul's instructional words to young Timothy can benefit all of us greatly if they are heeded and obeyed.

Paul strongly advised Timothy to do seven things:
- Preach the Word.
- Be prepared in season and out of season.
- Correct, rebuke, and encourage with great patience and careful instruction.
- Keep your head in all situations.
- Endure hardship.
- Do the work of an evangelist.
- Discharge all the duties of your ministry.

This sound instruction from Paul should be a beacon for everyone who sets out to teach or preach. James gave us a warning that every Biblical pedagogue should take very seriously. *"Not many of you should presume to be teachers,* *my brothers, **because you know that we who teach will be judged more strictly**" (James 3:1).* Taking into consideration this word from James, every teacher should pause and take an inward look before the Spirit of God. Don't the Scriptures say our bodies are temples of the Holy Spirit? Are we really honoring the Holy Spirit with the word we teach?

Ezekiel was once taken by the Spirit of the Lord to the Temple at Jerusalem. The Lord showed him the idolatry and sin that was present within. He said to Ezekiel,

> *Son of man do you see what they are doing, **the utterly detestable things the house of Israel is doing here, things that will drive Me far from My Sanctuary? But you will see things that are even more detestable.** (Ezekiel 8:6)*

God watches what goes on in sanctuaries around the world, both personally and in places of worship. The deepest yearnings of our hearts should be for the Presence of the Living God in our sanctuaries, in our homes and in our lives. We should be consumed with desire to please Him, not ourselves. When we find that we are becoming consumed by self-indulgence, a red flag should immediately go up. The Hebrew letter tells us, God does not change, and His standards remain immutable. The last thing we want to do is to drive the Lord far from us— His sanctuaries. So let's keep in mind that, *"Jesus Christ is the same yesterday, today and forever" (Hebrews13:8).*

In the Book of Revelation, the Lord Jesus described to John the condition of the seven churches in Asia.

What the Lord said should wake up the sleeping giant— the Church. We should bring everything we teach, together with our motives for what we say, into submission to the Holy Spirit. How important it is to keep in mind the grave warnings that Jesus gave to five of those seven churches. Perhaps we should get in the habit of asking ourselves "What if the message I teach today is the very last one I get to do before I meet the Lord, what would I hear Him say?

Would it be?

*Well done good and faithful Servant!"(Matthew 25:23)
or, 'I never knew you; depart from me, you who practice
lawlessness! (Matthew 7:23)*

No doubt the Lord would want so very much to say, *"Well
done!"* However, it is *our* responsibility to make certain that
we remain passionately faithful to Him so that we can receive
this blessed reward. It will be too late to make any changes
for willful neglect of His Word once we find ourselves face to
face with the Lord.

The Lord greatly loves us and wants this great reward to
be ours, but now is the time to make sure we will receive it, for
the Time is very near at Hand.

Wake up!

# Chapter 2

# THE DOOR OF DARKNESS

—◦∞◦—

T he Lord now showed me an extremely dark, circular door that was rock-like in appearance and gigantic in proportion. In the middle of this door there was a large round knob which could be grasped so as to roll the door away.

I wondered what this could mean. Then the Lord directed my mind to the stone that sealed the entrance to His tomb. I began to understand that the large, dark, rocky door I had seen was somehow connected to the one that stood between Jesus and all humanity during the seemingly endless hours in which His body lay in the tomb. The cold, hard rock at the entrance of the tomb of Jesus served briefly as an ostensibly impassable barrier between God the Savior and all mankind, even those who loved Him most.

Separation was the key word of this picture.

I could feel the Lord directing my attention to the fact that the massive stone at the grave of Jesus was not only one that had put God and man on opposite sides in the physical realm, but it was also a portrait of a condition of much greater spiritual significance. As the Lord further nudged my understanding, the deeper meaning began to emerge more clearly.

I now began to see that while the tombstone was a physical barricade at the grave of Jesus, it more significantly symbolized the spiritual separation that had taken place between the Almighty and His beloved children so long ago in the Garden of Eden. Ever since that dismal day, stony mindsets of dis-obedience and rebellion have been the cause of immense spiritual darkness within the hearts and souls of all mankind, barring them from the presence of God.

On the terrible day Adam and Eve chose to take a bite of sin, the rock-like condition of pride and rebellion was birthed within their hearts and consequently in the hearts of all their descendants. Ever since then, sin has been the reprehen-sible boulder that stands between every human being and Almighty God.

The actions of our first parents not only plunged the entire human race into total spiritual darkness, but also sealed our own inability to change or reverse the terrible consequences. God's gracious answer to this hopeless situation came in the form of His beloved Son, Jesus Christ. Now in the tomb, atoning for the guilt and sins of every human being, from creation to the end of time, was the Son of God, lying cold and dead while eternity itself seemed to have come to a screeching halt!

What would happen next?

Jesus had discussed this coming event with His disciples, and all His words had come true thus far. He had actually fore-told with great accuracy everything that was going to happen to Him. He had also added that on the third day He would rise from the dead. Would this last part come to pass as well? These were His exact words.

> *We are going up to Jerusalem, and the Son of Man will be betrayed to the chief priests and the teachers of the law. They will condemn him to death and will turn him over to the Gentiles to be mocked and flogged and crucified.* ***On the third day he will be raised to life!*** *(Matthew 20:18–19)*

Needless to say, the stone at the tomb would bear varying significance to different ones that day.

What could this stone mean to Satan and his minions? Surely for them, it must have spelled immeasurable anxiety.

Jesus had clearly stated that He would rise again on the third day.

Could this really happen? Would the Lord actually rise up from the dead? Would the stone really be rolled away? If so, the door of division which had been Satan's best success thus far would be completely destroyed. Until now, the devil had actually been quite effective in maintaining the rift between God and His children, but the schism that he had managed to establish so early on in creation now appeared to be in grave danger of being eliminated.

Would Jesus actually emerge from the grave with great and mighty power, shattering the efficacy of all Satan's diabolical schemes and efforts? If so, would the Lord also set the captives free? To the devil and all his cohorts this had to be quite unthinkable, one would imagine.

On the other hand, what about those who loved the Lord? How did they see this stone?

From all biblical accounts, to them it was an emblem of great grief and pain mingled with fear, doubt, and unbelief. They had trusted Jesus with all of their hearts. They had believed him to be their deliverer, and now suddenly, He was dead! They had seen Him die, and unbelievable as it seemed, there He lay, silent in the grave behind that huge rock. Sorrow and disillusionment racked their very beings.

Then there were those who hated the Lord, surely, they must have seen the stone as a symbol of resounding victory. Undoubtedly the Roman guards could keep that motley crew of rag-tag disciples from stealing the body and promoting their cause.

What a relief! The political positions of the High Priests would now finally be secure, or so it would seem. To them it must have all appeared to be just perfect. One could almost see their smirks, as they stroked their beards and rubbed their hands together in smug satisfaction.

How about the indifferent onlookers? What could this stone possibly have meant to them? Not much, not much more than any other tombstone perhaps. To them this stone merely sealed off the grave of a dead carpenter, an insurrectionist, or whatever else they chose to call Him. The Roman soldiers who gambled for His clothes certainly fit this category of thinkers.

Basically everything remained quiet: agonizingly quiet, after that first mighty earthquake rocked the earth rending the curtain of the temple from top to bottom as the Lord drew His last breath.

Now hours had rolled by, and minutes persistently ticked on. Perhaps the Cross and the Tombstone had actually silenced forever the Lord of all creation. The stillness at the grave must have been deafening! Nothing changed; nothing at all, as hour after hour crept slowly by. The Roman guards mildly bored, sat around waiting for their watch to finally come to an end.

The devil however, was probably chewing his ugly fingernails by this time, and the demons most likely shuddered with fear as the dawn of third day steadily approached. Minutes ticked on, and then seconds.

In the grayness of the early hour, a few faithful women cautiously advanced towards the tomb of their beloved Lord and Master. Spices in hand, they were ready to anoint His precious body. Quietly they crept along, nervously discussing in whispers who might roll the stone away for them.

Then suddenly, an explosion of brilliant light punctuated by the deafening rumble of a powerful earthquake shattered the silence. The earth rocked and reeled, and with an ear-shattering crash, the great stone thundered to the ground revealing the empty tomb. Matthew's description of this scene is riveting. He said:

*After the Sabbath, at dawn on the first day of the week, Mary Magdalene and the other Mary went to look at the tomb.* **There was a violent earthquake, for an angel of the Lord came down from heaven and, going to the tomb, rolled back the stone and sat on it.** *His appearance was like lightning, and his clothes were* *white as snow. The guards were so afraid of him that they shook and became like dead men. The angel said to the women,* **"Do not be afraid, for I know that you are looking for Jesus, who was crucified. He is not here; he has risen, just as he said. Come and see the place where he lay. Then go quickly and tell his disciples: 'He has risen from the dead and is going ahead of you into Galilee. There you will see him.' Now I have told you."** *So the women hurried away from the tomb, afraid yet filled with joy, and ran to tell his disciples.* **Suddenly Jesus met them. "Greetings," he said. They came to him, clasped his feet and worshiped him. Then Jesus said to them, "Do not be afraid. Go and tell my brothers to go to Galilee; there they will see me.** *(Matthew 28:1–10)*

Stamped indelibly upon the stone in God's own hand, would be the proverbial words *"Paid in full."* Without a doubt, the amazing power of those three mighty words, unseen by human eye, but surely visible to the entire spiritual world, would have dealt a stunning blow to Satan and all his cohorts. Then to top it all, out of the blinding light stepped Jesus, the Lord and Master of all.

The satanic host obviously had no alternative but to plunge to their detestable knees, groveling in the dust and grudgingly declaring that Jesus Christ is Lord. The deafening crescendo and clarity of the Words from the Holy Writ would have reverberated their defeat.

*Therefore God exalted him to the highest place and gave him the name that is above every name, that at the name of Jesus every knee should bow, in heaven and on earth and under the earth, and every tongue confess that Jesus Christ is Lord, to the glory of God the Father. (Philippians 2:9–11)*

Hallelujah! It was done! The price for sin was completely paid through the precious Blood of the spotless Lamb of God!

As all these amazing things transpired, the fallen grave-stone served as a seat for the mighty angel of the Lord, and the Roman guards—the ultimate hope of the chief priests and Pharisees—lay sprawled as dead men on the ground.

From now and throughout all eternity, the empty tomb would always triumphantly trumpet the music of the greatest victory ever! *Jesus the Messiah is Risen and He lives forever and ever!* The celestial choirs would explode with magnificent praise to the Risen Lord. John described a heavenly praise scene in the following words.

*Then I looked and heard the voice of many angels, numbering thousands upon thousands, and ten thousand times ten thousand. They encircled the throne and the living creatures and the elders. In a loud voice they sang: "Worthy is the Lamb, who was slain, to receive power and wealth and wisdom and strength and honor and glory and praise! (Revelation 5:11–12)*

Then just as abruptly as glorious salvation emerged from the tomb in the form of the Risen Savior, the free offer of forgiveness and mercy became instantly available to any and all who would receive it. The unseen stone that had once stood between God and man for thousands of years was now gone forever and *the only thing* that would keep a person from Almighty God would be his or her own self-will.

Meanwhile, the loving voice of the Savior continues to gently invite whosoever will, to come to Him. Hear His beautiful invitation:

*Come unto me, all you who are weary and burdened, and I will give you rest. Take my yoke upon you and learn of me, for I am gentle and humble in heart, and you will find rest for your souls. For My yoke is easy and My burden in light. (Matthew 11:28–30)*

All who hear His call and accept His invitation will forever find rest in His loving arms.

Jesus once told a parable describing four types of hearts upon which His words fall as he beckons the nations to Himself. He described these hearts in terms of soil.

- **The Wayside heart**—depicts the heart of one who hears but does not receive. Satan and his demons—the birds, very easily whisk away the life-giving Word from the wayside heart of this individual, and the heart of this hearer *does not receive* the Savior who gave His Life for him or her.

- **The Rocky-ground heart**—is the person who hears the Word and quickly responds to the Lord, but sadly, is of a *very shallow nature.* Such a person retains control of his or her heart. Circumstances dictate the degree of this individual's loyalty to Christ. No sooner than a tenuous situation arises, so goes the faithfulness of this person, and he *turns back to the world.* Jesus said, a plant with no deep root system is soon scorched by the sun.

- **The Thorny-ground heart**—describes the one that acknowledges Jesus as God but never submits to Him as Lord. This person gets smothered by trying to handle life in *his or her own strength.* Sooner or later the cares of the world and the deceitfulness of riches arrive. The devil makes sure of that. This person *gets choked by the concerns of this life,* and becomes totally useless in the Kingdom of God. Blessed is the one who casts his cares on the Lord in accordance with His advice.

- *The Good-ground heart*—is the one who receives the Lord and *totally surrenders* his or her heart to Him, serving Jesus with diligence and truth. This person permits Jesus to be both Lord and Savior of his or her life and *produces a harvest* of thirty, sixty, or a hundred fold.

The Lord said,

*Behold I stand at the door and knock, if anyone hears my voice and opens the door, I will come to him, and will dine with him and he with Me. (Revelation 3:20)*

Listening to this statement one might think Jesus was speaking to unbelievers, but amazingly, He was actually addressing the Church at Laodicea. This church was luke-warm and their love and zeal for the Lord was exceedingly low. Unfortunately, this tepid, indifferent attitude has become ever increasingly evident in our postmodern churches. The lack of genuine love and passion for the Lord and His word causes Jesus much disgust; He warned the Laodicean church that He would spit these unfaithful ones out of His mouth unless they changed their ways. Thorny-ground–hearted people resemble the Laodicean congregation more than a little, and the church at Laodicea seems to vividly describe a great part of the professing Church today.

The words of Revelation 3:20 should bring our attention to a very significant door; one that each of us should personally focus on with great acuity. This is the very personal door to each of our hearts. Jesus stands and patiently and knocks, but it is only a few who answer. Ask yourself, am I listening, am I responding to His call? The door to an indifferent heart hinders the owner's proper response to the Messiah, because this door has etched upon it only one name—self. Sadly it is the word *self* that locks the Savior out of an individual's life.

The destructive door that divides and destroys, first made its appearance when Lucifer said, "I will," in defiance to Almighty God. His prideful words immediately destroyed his relationship with the Almighty and eternally separated him from his Creator. This same dreadful syndrome became the lot of the human race when Adam and Eve said, "I will" to Satan. Pride and rebellion continue to be the rock that stands between God and every person who chooses to say to Him, "My will" instead of, *". . . Yours be done."*

It is very important to note, that under the most difficult circumstances ever, Jesus declared to His Father, *". . . not*

*My will, but **Yours**, be done" (Luke 22:42).* This should be our response in every circumstance as well, if we are to have a right relationship with the living God.

Jesus mercifully and patiently stands outside the door to each of our hearts and knocks and we must keep in mind that the door-knob is exclusively on our side. We alone, can unlock the door, throwing it open to invite Him in. He went to His tomb so that we might be set free from ours. Will we open the door and permit Him to come in and be the Savior, Deliverer, and Lord of our lives? Unless we hear His voice, roll the stone of self-will and pride away, and invite Jesus into our hearts, we will never meet Him as Savior and Lord. Heartbreakingly, many a religious soul will remain locked away behind the prideful, darkened doors of its own constructing just as the Pharisees and Priests did. They were pridefully religious, and religiously prideful, and so they missed the knock of the Savior.

Jesus in His goodness and mercy continues to shine His light onto the dark, dark doors of the hearts of many. He waits patiently for the invitation to enter and bring in His great Salvation.

If you have never asked Jesus into your heart, no matter how long you've been in a church, then please do it now. Simply say, *Lord I am sorry for my sins. Thank you for dying in my place. Please forgive me, come into my heart, and be the Lord of my life. My heart is Yours from this moment on; please use me as you will.* If you prayed that simple prayer, you just rolled away the great stone that has thus far separated you from God. From now on the Lord and you will be on the same side forever, unless you roll the stone back again to shut Him out once more.

Jesus offers us a salvation so great and complete that it includes a continued deliverance from ourselves. This offer goes way past initial Salvation. It enters the zone of requiring from us a willingness to die daily to ourselves and permit the Lord to live through us. Listen to Paul,

*[I assure you] by the pride which I have in you in [your fellowship and union with] Christ Jesus our Lord, that I die daily **[I face death every day and die to self]**. (1 Corinthians 15:31, AMP)*

When we first invite Jesus into our lives we allow Him to enter and take up residence in the home of our hearts. His presence brings peace with God and incredible joy. However, it often turns out that not long after the first glorious experience of His abiding presence, things start slipping. Cares, frustrations, familiar habits, and sins begin to creep back into our lives reclaiming surrendered territory. We feel the loss of that first great intimacy with the Lord but don't know how to get it back. We have accepted Jesus, so what would be causing this problem now?

At the moment of salvation we completely surrender to Jesus, but with time and carelessness, we slowly begin to take back what we have given to Him. This is the re-emergence of self-will. Soon the Lord becomes no more than a guest, when at first we had invited Him to be the owner of our hearts.

The more heart territory we take back from the Lord, the greater the feelings of emptiness and defeat we begin to experience. No doubt the devil makes this his top priority with every believer and problem after problem begins to emerge in our lives. This is actually the time to surrender more deeply to the Lord and not take back from Him even a speck of surrendered territory.

As Lord and Savior, Jesus must be given the full right to shine His light into every nook and cranny of our hearts, and we should get in the habit of asking Him to do just that. As we surrender to Him, all the filth of pride, self-will, and sin that we have so carefully begun to sweep under the rug will now become clearly visible. At this point we should be willing to humbly accept and submit to His great scrutiny. The brilliant illumination of God's Word will reveal us as we really are, and we must become willing to let go of the encrustations of everything in our lives that is displeasing to the Lord. We should be willing to get on our knees before the Savior in repentance.

It is important to confess each revealed sin and allow His precious blood to wash away every spot and blemish that is disclosed by the radiant beam of His Holy Light. This is true repentance, and He is faithful and just to forgive.

> *We must pay more careful attention, therefore, to what we have heard, so that we do not drift away. For if the message spoken by angels was binding, and every violation and disobedience received its just punishment, how shall we escape if we ignore such a great salvation? This salvation, which was first announced by the Lord, was confirmed to us by those who heard him. (Hebrews 2:1–3)*

It is vitally important to permit the holy cleansing of the Word to continue throughout our lifetimes, thus keeping our hearts abundantly pure. It is crucial to also work at living in obedience to the Lord while submitting to His grace and mercy. This most certainly will take a lifetime, but we will learn more and more to allow Jesus to not only be Savior, but Lord of our lives as well.

Where better could we spend our lives than on our knees, both physically and spiritually, in the presence of the Lord? As we start practicing humility we will soon find it to be a wonderful place in which to live. Paul urges us to *"Pray at all times and on every occasion in the power of the Holy Spirit"* (Ephesians 6:18). It is also written,

> *Therefore God exalted him to the highest place and gave him the name that is above every name, that at the name of Jesus every knee should bow, in heaven and on earth and under the earth, and every tongue confess that Jesus Christ is Lord, to the glory of God the Father. (Philippians 2:9–11)*

49

Beloved it is better to bow *now*, than later for this is certainly something that will transpire. Jesus said:

*Everyone who does evil hates the light, and will not come into the light for fear that his deeds will be exposed. But whoever lives by truth comes to the light so that it may be seen plainly that what he has done has been done through God. (John 3:20–21)*

When all is said and done, we will find that it is only when we are willing to receive the perfect work of salvation offered to us by Jesus Christ, and become ready to be conformed to His Image, that we will receive true freedom from ourselves. *"So if the Son sets you free you will be free indeed" (John 8:36).*

Too many churches are packed with people who have never really come into the cleansing light of Jesus Christ. Countless people believe that they are Christians simply because they were born into a family who has membership in some particular denomination. Unfortunately those who trust in any given religious institution for their salvation, live by the dictates of their own desires. They have no idea that the ugly door of self-will and sin separates them from the Lord. They simply don't know that they must throw open the doors of their hearts and invite Jesus in. The Lord loves them so much that He died for them and yet they don't know this great truth because their churches never teach them this vitally important fact.

Occasionally, some of these people may catch a glimpse of their spiritual condition when some bold disciple of the Lord proclaims the Word of truth, but all too often they slide back to the "itchy-ear doctrines" that they have grown accustomed to. Unfortunately as they continue to live by false doctrines they also shut their ears to the gentle knock of the Savior saying to them once more, "Open."

*Open up, ancient gates! Open up, ancient doors, and let the King of glory enter. Who is the King of glory?*

*The Lord of Heaven's Armies—he is the King of glory.
(Psalm 24:9–10)*

At this point the Lord led me to the Book of Ezekiel. God commanded Ezekiel to say to the leaders of his day, the same thing He is saying to many leaders of Churches today.

> *. . . This is what the Sovereign LORD says: Woe to the shepherds of Israel who only take care of themselves! Should not the shepherds take care of the flock? You eat the curd, clothe yourselves with wool and slaughter the choice animals, but you do not take care of the flock. **You have not strengthened the weak or healed the sick or bound up the injured. You have not brought back the strays or searched for the lost. You have ruled them harshly and brutally. So they were scattered because there was no shepherd, and when they were scattered they became food for all the wild animals. My sheep wandered over all the mountains and on every high hill. They were scattered over the whole earth, and no one searched or looked for them.** (Ezekiel 34:1–6)*

Churches today are filled with people who are both spiritually and physically ill. There is no solution available to them because not much differs between the spiritual leaders of Ezekiel's time and those of today. In the meantime, desperately sick, weak, and hurting people receive no answers to their problems. The churches have no answers because the leaders themselves have not believed the Truth. Yet Jesus began His Church with an invitation which is also *the* answer to all our woes.

> *Come to me all you who are weary and burdened, and I will give you rest. Take My yoke upon you and learn from Me for I am gentle and humble in heart, and you*

*will find rest for your souls. For My yoke is easy and My burden is light. (Matthew 11:28–30)*

Because too many preachers take incredible liberties with the Scriptures, disbelieve, twist its commands, deny, and add to the written Word, they are devoid of the Truth. So they teach their flock an empty and confused gospel leading the people astray. Consequently, great numbers of these misguided sheep end up looking for help in all the wrong places. Instead of inviting the hurting and disabled to run to the Good Shepherd—*the only One who can heal, strengthen, and bind up the brokenhearted,* these leaders deal wrongly with them through legalism and various other forms of false doctrine, even weaving into the Word of God teachings from pagan religions. Needless to say the results are disastrous, and the people scatter becoming prey to every wild beast, proverbially speaking. Thousands end up in the offices of hardened and atheistic professionals who provide them with answers diametrically opposed to the Word of God, thus moving them from the frying pan to the fire.

People who have been raised all their lives in so-called Christian homes and have grown up in the church atmosphere continue to attend lifeless, ritualistic services each week. Disillusioned and disheartened scores of these folk plunge headlong into the camp of the one who comes to *"steal kill and destroy"(John 10:10).* The Lord warned us about this predator, the devil, who systematically proceeds to provide a plethora of enticements designed for total destruction: drugs, alcohol, sex, false religions, and suicide, to name a few. The enemy provides whatever gives a broken person a temporary fix and then consequent eternal death.

We need relationship with the Lord, not religion. Hosts of people, who are exposed to the religious approach to God, remain empty but searching. These are the ones who are so easily lured into eastern religions, the occult, new age philosophies, and doctrines of demons. Paul spells out the results of this rather clearly.

*For although they knew God, they neither glorified him as God nor gave thanks to him, but their thinking became futile and their foolish hearts were darkened. Although they claimed to be wise, they became fools and exchanged the glory of the immortal God for images made to look like mortal man and birds and animals and reptiles. (Romans 1:21–23)*

Jesus is so very close and his love so great, yet vast numbers of people have lost their way and become prey to the deadliest enemy of all—the devil. In the meantime, few shepherds go out to look for these sheep who have fallen away, nor do they seek to lead them back to the *"Way, the Truth and the Life" (John 14:6)*.

All a hurting person has to do is to call on the Lord and He will answer and the stones that obstruct their aching hearts will instantly roll away. Jesus Christ—*"the WAY, the TRUTH and the LIFE,"* will enter and gently lead the bruised, the hurting, and the lost, home. People, please turn to Jesus. He is the only way to eternal life and peace. Joy and love will be your lot. It is as easy as asking Him; that's all it takes. Won't you do it today?

Ezekiel fearlessly declared the words of the Lord to the shepherds of his day. He said:

*Therefore, you shepherds, hear the word of the LORD: As surely as I live, says the Sovereign LORD, you abandoned my flock and left them to be attacked by every wild animal. Though you were my shepherds, you didn't search for my sheep when they were lost. You took care of yourselves and left the sheep to starve.* ***Therefore, you shepherds, hear the word of the LORD. This is what the Sovereign LORD says: I now consider these shepherds my enemies, and I will hold them responsible for what has happened to my flock. I will take away their right to feed the flock, along with their right to feed themselves. I*** *will rescue my flock from their mouths; the sheep will no longer be their prey. "For this is what the Sovereign LORD says: I myself will search and find my sheep. I will be like a shepherd looking for his scattered flock. I will find my sheep and rescue them from all the places to which they were scattered on that dark and cloudy day . . . I myself will tend my sheep and cause them to lie down in peace, says the Sovereign LORD. I will search for my lost ones who strayed away, and I will bring them safely home again. I will bind up the injured and strengthen the weak. But I will destroy those who are fat and powerful. I will feed them, yes— feed them justice!* (Ezekiel 34:7–16)

While this Word primarily applied to the leaders of Israel, it should also serve as a strong wake-up call to every church leader today. Leaders who are unfaithful, those who spiritually neglect the flock should wake up and heed the strong words of warning that came from the prophet of the LORD so long ago. If you don't, God Himself will make the changes that Ezekiel mentioned. Jesus the Good Shepherd, will gather the flock that has been assigned to you, and it will soon become apparent that the sheep who are sincerely seeking the Lord will begin moving to places where there is good pasture. We must remember that judgment always begins at home.

Thank God for pastors who remain worthy of their calling; true shepherds who are faithful to God and the Lord Jesus Christ. Every believer fortunate enough to have one of these faithful men or women of God in leadership over them, should give thanks to the Almighty for their obedient service. We should make it a point to love and support them by lifting them up in daily prayer and petition. Paul counseled,

*Dear brothers and sisters, honor those who are your leaders in the Lord's work. They work hard among you and warn you against all that is wrong. Think highly of*

*them and give them your wholehearted love because of their work. And remember to live peaceably with each other. (1 Thessalonians 5:12–13)*

Someday these men and women who have taught the Truth and been loyal to God, will enter glory to hear the awesome voice of the Master saying,

*Well done, good and faithful servant! You have been faithful with a few things: I will put you in charge of many things. Come and share your Master's happiness! (Matthew 25:23)*

At this point we should not forget that the sheep too will also have to give an account for themselves to the Lord. The Righteous Judge will decide with great precision and accuracy between the sheep and the goats, the fat sheep and the lean ones, the ones who push with their legalistic and prideful horns, driving away the weak ones. Jesus said: *"My command is this: Love each other as I have loved you" (John 15:12).*

Ezekiel once again had the unenviable task of bringing this word of warning to the believers regarding the Lord's impending judgment between one sheep and another.

*And as for you, my flock, my people, this is what the Sovereign LORD says: I will judge between one sheep and another, separating the sheep from the goats. Is it not enough for you to keep the best of the pastures for yourselves? Must you also trample down the rest? Is it not enough for you to take the best water for yourselves? Must you also muddy the rest with your feet? All that is left for my flock to eat is what you have trampled down. All they have to drink is water that you have fouled. "Therefore, this is what the Sovereign LORD says: **I will surely judge between the fat sheep and the scrawny sheep. For you fat sheep push and butt and crowd my sick and hungry flock until they are**

**scattered to distant lands. So I will rescue my flock, and they will no longer be abused and destroyed. And I will judge between one sheep and another. And I will set one shepherd over them, even my servant David. He will feed them and be a shepherd to them. And I, the LORD, will be their God, and my servant David will be a prince among my people. I, the LORD, have spoken!** *(Ezekiel 34:17–24)*

Just as with the nation of Israel, the principle of this message applies strongly to the Church. As followers of the Lord Jesus Christ, we should be very careful in our relationships one with another! We certainly need to be careful not to hurt or drive away those who are weaker than we are by our words and actions. The Apostle Paul tells us, *"Accept him whose faith is weak without passing judgment on disputable matters" (Romans 14:1).* We should be very careful to accept those in our midst whose faith we might consider weak. We should love our brothers and sisters into a closer relationship with Jesus, instead of judging them into separation from the Lord. Paul says again,

> *You then, why do you judge your brother? Or why do you look down on your brother? For we will all stand before God's judgment seat. (Romans 14:10–11)*

We mentioned before that when Jesus said, *"Here I am! I stand at the door and knock. If anyone hears my voice and opens the door, I will come in and eat with him, and he with me"* He wasn't addressing the world, but the church in Laodicea—the lukewarm church. Here are some synonyms for lukewarm—tepid, showing little ardor, zeal, enthusiasm, indifferent, half-hearted, cool, apathetic. If this is what lukewarm means, then lukewarm rather vividly describes a large section of the today's church. A great lack of zeal, love, or desire for the Lord exists among scores of modern-day believers. Passion for Jesus in the Church of the first century was very apparent by their devotion to the Lord. Their unrestrained desire to share the Gospel was a high indicator of their love and devotion to Him. This cannot be said of many believers today.

Friends, let's face it; too many church-goers are half-hearted, indifferent, and complacent! As we take a look at the vast majority of those who claim to belong to Jesus Christ, we will find that they are quite content to live their own lives, doing their own things like eating and drinking, marrying and giving in marriage, buying, selling, planting, and building. Not much thought is given to the warning signs of the times, given to us by Jesus. Yet we mustn't fail to see that it is the Lord's great love for us that caused Him to give us this clear alert:

*Just as it was in the days of Noah, so also will it be in the days of the Son of Man. People were eating, drinking, marrying and being given in marriage up to the day Noah entered the ark. Then the flood came and destroyed them all. "It was the same in the days of Lot. People were eating and drinking, buying and selling, planting and building. But the day Lot left Sodom, fire and sulfur rained down from heaven and destroyed them all. **"It will be just like this on the day the Son of Man is revealed.** (Luke 17:26–30)*

The coolness of the average Christian today, the vigorous pursuits of their own desires and goals, and their lack of ardor and enthusiasm for the things of the Lord, all seem to echo the mindset of the people who lived in the days of Noah and Lot.

Friends, it is time to wake up and invite God's light to shine in our hearts to reveal everything that we should let go from our lives. We must throw open the doors of our hearts and invite Jesus to come in and dine with us. He promised to do so *(Revelation 3:20).* When He enters, His light will reveal the cobwebs, rust, and junk hidden deep within the recesses of our hearts.

As we ready up for a date with the most distinguished of guests—the Lord Jesus Christ, indescribable joy and gladness will fill our hearts and souls. Soon we will want Him to be the owner of the sanctuary of our hearts once more. We will gladly hand Him the key so that He could simply walk in and fellowship with us whenever He chooses to. This was exactly what He used to do in the Garden of Eden before Adam and Eve chose to sin, thereby shutting the doors of their hearts to Him. In fact after they fell, they hid as they heard Him walking in the garden. How sad!

The question each one of us should ask ourselves is, "What have I allowed myself to become?" Am I a sheep who feeds on good pasture and stomps on the rest of it? Am I one who drinks clear water but muddies up the rest of it for the others? If we find that we have to answer "yes" to any or all of these questions, we should also ask ourselves if this is what we want to continue to be. Surely the answer is "no," so please let's do a one-eighty through the power and blood of Jesus, and then steer clear of bringing reproach to His name through our behavior and lifestyles. How careful we should be that no one turns away from the Lord and blames Him because of something we did. Those of us who think ourselves to be beyond reproach, should take a look at God's Word. Paul advises, *"Therefore, let him who thinks he stands take heed lest he fall"* (1 Corinthians 10:12).

What an immense blessing we have received through our loving Savior! He has given us the right to enter boldly into the presence of the Heavenly Father. Our own request of the Lord each day should agree with the heart-cry of the Psalmist,

> *Search me, O God, and know my heart: try me, and know my thoughts: And see if there be any wicked way in me, and lead me in the way everlasting. (Psalm 139:23–24)*

There really is no way to stress strongly enough that the *day is near*, and the *time is at hand*.

Let us diligently pray that we will not be caught off guard. Jesus counseled,

> *Be careful, or your hearts will be weighed down with dissipation, drunkenness and the anxieties of life, and that day will close on you unexpectedly like a trap. For it will come upon all those who live on the face of the whole earth.* **Be always on the watch, and pray that you may be able to escape all that is about to happen, and that you may be able to stand before the Son of Man.** *(Luke 21:34–36)*

Please wake up while you still have time, and shake free from the bondages of sin and the world; open the doors of your heart to the Lord who loves you so much, and invite Him to enter and dine with you. He will be more than willing to do just that. Make it a point to be thankful that the Lord knows all your thoughts and ways. He will reveal any wicked thing hidden in your heart so that you can repent, be cleansed, and walk in the Way of life everlasting.

Wake up beloved, the time is at hand.

# Chapter 3

# THE NEGLECTED WORD

———∞∞∞———

T his time I found myself looking at an old printing press and wondering what this broken-down machine could possibly mean; so I asked the Lord about it.

He answered by directing my mind to the overabundance of printed material that floods our modern world. We enjoy the benefits of being able to acquire every imaginable type of printed material we could ever want. The Bible is no exception. We have Bibles of every kind and by the millions. Also available to us are the zillions of books relating to the Bible. Consequently, we have come to take all this for granted.

However, people were still using quills and reeds as the only instruments to write with until the fifteenth century. Writing was slow and laborious, and reading material was not voluminous at all. Bibles were hard to come by. In fact prior to the invention of the printing press, we are told, it took a whole year's wages to purchase a single Bible.

When Johannes Gutenberg built his movable-type printing press in the 1400s, amazingly the very first book to roll off it was the Bible. This, clearly, was no accident but the work of the mighty hand of God. Obviously it was God who arranged the means for an abundant supply of His Word. People would now be able to purchase a Bible at a much lower price. In spite of the huge blessing the world had suddenly received by way of this great invention, the people of Gutenberg's day began to be afraid that the printing press was some form of black art which came from the devil.

Always a liar! Always a thief! The devil never ceases in his quest to steal the glory that belongs to God. Fear is one of Satan's most effective means of oppressing human beings, and he uses it to deprive us of God's richest blessings. History proves that the devil did not spare any time or effort in his attempts to get rid of the Bible. Although His schemes to destroy the written Word have been numerous and his tactics daunting, through lies, oppression, and murder, he has not been successful, nor will he ever be able to eliminate God's Holy Word. Many people used by the devil have relentlessly attacked, denied, burned the Bible, and done everything within their power to squelch and suppress the spread of the Holy Word of God, but they have never been able to attain their desired goal.

God made certain the Bible would be available to all, but it is we who have chosen to neglect it. Unfortunately, there are people who, to their own detriment, believe the lies and deception that Satan continually levels at the Bible. Among them are those who even describe themselves as Christians. People suffer tremendously in various and diverse ways, and they have no idea that the prophet Hosea declared many centuries ago, *"My people are destroyed from lack of knowledge"* *(Hosea 4:6).*

Adam and Eve experienced the terrible taste of a diabolically modified account of God's Word—*"You will not surely die."* This lie was spoken by a serpent! Much to the loss of all mankind, the first man and woman believed that lie. Regrettably, when Adam and Eve chose to act upon this great untruth, they and all their offspring were plunged into a state of separation from God. Spiritual and physical death became the legacy of our first parents.

We are told *"The tongue has the power of life and death and those who love it will eat its fruit" (Proverbs 18:21).*

The literal and metaphoric truth of this Scripture is evident. The titillation of Adam and Eve's taste buds through a spoken lie from the devil, brought both physical and spiritual death to them and to all mankind. God's Word is life, so it only stands to reason that any word that rolls off Satan's forked tongue would be nothing other than a death sentence to whoever receives and acts upon it.

The evil one's ability to effectively operate against us comes directly from the amount of access we allow him. Unfortunately, we often permit him to speak lies into our lives. Just as Adam and Eve did, we too, often accept the deceitful words of the devil and act upon them while rejecting the truths of God's holy Word. Once we receive and believe the lies of the enemy, we automatically give voice to them. We then act upon fears that accompany the deception, and thereby open mighty doors in our own lives to sickness, poverty, anger, death, or whatever else the enemy might wish to throw at us.

Everything Satan says, is and will always continue to be a lie, because his words always go contrary to God's Word and His divine will and purpose for our lives. Most times the reason we accept the devil's junk, is because we lack knowledge of the Scriptures and the desire to obey it. Jesus said of Satan: *When he lies, he speaks his native language, for he is a liar and the father of lies (John 8:44).*

As is a common trap for all believers, Moses' anger level had to be tested by the devil. Perhaps it would be a very good vehicle to use depending upon how he would react to extreme injustice. Moses' blood pressure rose as he watched the Hebrew slave being mercilessly beaten by the taskmaster. The devil struck, "Kill the Egyptian!" Moses did, and consequently spent forty valuable years of his life paying for it in the Median desert. However, the Scriptures tell us,

> . . . all things work together for good to those who love God, to those who are the called according to His purpose. (Romans 8:28)

God has a remarkable way of taking the dross of our lives and turning it into gold.

Having once been successful in manipulating Moses' anger management skills or the lack of them, perhaps the adversary figured he could trip up this mighty servant of God once again; only with greater consequences this time. Just maybe, two birds could be killed with one stone this time around! Perhaps Moses could be rendered totally unusable to the Lord and the Commandments written in God's own Hand could be destroyed forever at the same time. Surely it would be worth a try on the part of Satan, to prod Moses' tendency to swift anger and see what would happen.

The Bible tells us, *"The LORD is compassionate and gracious, slow to anger, abounding in love" (Psalm 103:8).* No wonder the devil loves to irk believers into irritation and anger. It is a sure way of getting us to behave in ways very unlike our Heavenly Father. It is also the surest way to render a Christian powerless, because anger and strife go hand in hand. We are told, *"For where envying and strife is, there is confusion and every evil work" (James 3:16).*

Moses descended the mountain at the Lord's instruction, carrying the stone tablets upon which the Law was inscribed by the very finger of God. The time was ripe for the enemy to strike. The riotous pagan sounds of lasciviousness and debauchery blared upwards reaching the deeply concerned ears of Moses. Israel had turned her back on God, and returned to the pagan worship and idolatry of Egypt. Aaron, Moses' trusted brother, the one he had left in charge, had not only failed to be faithful to God and Moses in his oversight of the Israelites, but he had actually sculpted the golden calf that all Israel now bowed down to in worship.

Wham! It worked! Just as the devil planned, Moses was beside himself with rage and the stone tablets flew out of his hands like missiles, shattering on the desert floor several feet below. Had the enemy succeeded in his mission? Well! Not quite so fast! This time Satan had God's written Word to contend with, and the echo of this resounding defeat would be one that he would hear again many hundreds of years later from the lips of the *Living Word, Jesus Christ.* Three times the

Lord answered the devil's temptations with the words, *"It is written."* Satan had no alternative but to flee.

Forty days of prayer, fasting, and intercession later, Moses was back up on the mountaintop, in the presence of Almighty God. The LORD once more graciously inscribed His Word upon new tablets of stone. The children of Israel now had the instruction of God's Word to live by.

One would think the devil would eventually get smart and give up. Instead he has only continued on with ever increasing diabolical fervor, as he races incessantly toward his ultimate destination; the final destruction reserved exclusively for him and his cohorts by God Almighty.

As we can see Satan has one pressing mission and goal that consumes him. This is his overwhelming desire to obliterate the Word of God.

Herod the Edomite, Satan's pawn, sought relentlessly to take the life of the infant Jesus—the "Living Word," but God had other plans. Since then, at the instigation of the devil, thousands of Bibles have been burned and dishonored and people have been tortured and killed for merely possessing one. Despite the continuing onslaught, the precious Word of God has remained indestructible. The Bible is the number one bestseller of all times, and more copies of it have been distributed than any other book upon the face of the earth.

Statistics reveal that the Bible is the most widely read book in the history of mankind, and this sounds very good at first take. I really wondered what the Lord was trying to make me understand when He showed me a dilapidated old printing press. I certainly didn't get it until He brought home to me the fact that despite all the good statistics, there is a tremendous lack of the knowledge of His Word. Regardless of the many Bibles that are printed and purchased, the Word simply isn't being read, studied, or understood, as God intended it to be.

It would seem logical to believe that Christians read the Bible, but how does one accurately estimate how widely read the Bible actually is? Does the number of copies sold really determine this? Just because Bibles are purchased in great numbers doesn't necessarily mean that the Word is actually being read, studied, meditated upon, understood, or lived by. Couldn't this be why God says? *"My people are destroyed from lack of knowledge" (Hosea 4:6).*

Obviously from God's viewpoint the answer is "yes." Bibles sit untouched year after year on dusty old shelves and tables. Sadly, the LORD'S many instructions to His people about how to live blessed, victorious, and prosperous lives remain untapped and unknown by many, and the countless negative things people encounter by willful neglect of God's Holy Word are very great.

So the Lord says, *"My people are destroyed from lack of knowledge" (Hosea 4:6).* This was as true of Hosea's day as it is now.

Even though Satan can never rid the earth of God's Word, believers unknowingly play into his hands by giving him varying degrees of victory over their personal lives, because they do not know that the Word is our greatest defense against the enemy. The Bible tells us to, *Take the helmet of salvation **and the sword of the Spirit, which is the word of God** (Eph 6:17).*

The unbelief of the worldly and the sluggish attitudes of believers toward the Scriptures are the devil's greatest opportunities to bring destruction and havoc into the lives of many. Jesus said,

> *Therefore whoever **hears these sayings of Mine, and does them,** I will liken him to a wise man who built his house on the rock. (Matthew 7:24)*

The Lord warned us that *"the thief comes only to steal, kill and destroy. . ." (John 10:10).* The devil has certainly achieved this stealing, killing and destroying strategy against a great many people, believers and unbelievers alike. He has managed to do this by providing a glut of distractions to the Church in the form of television, the Internet, entertainment of various sorts, endless recreational activities, sports and a host of other things that erode precious time that should be spent with the Creator.

One of the most common phrases believers use is, "I don't have enough time to read my Bible." Yet, somehow these very people find more than enough time to do almost everything else. Why is today's church so blind to the fact that God's Word, the Sword of the Spirit, is our only weapon against the devil?

The Lord has been wonderfully faithful in preserving and providing for us an abundance of His life-giving Word, but far too many believers do not give it the honor it deserves. Many think the Bible is a book that can be read casually like a novel or glanced at for catchy phrases; they miss the fact that *it is God's handbook for life. The Bible is God's power and His love revealed.*

We must study the Scriptures. We also must memorize the Word, believe it, speak it, live it, and always act on its instructions if we are to truly lead successful and prosperous lives.

God has some powerful instructions on how we are to regard the Scriptures.

*And these Words which I command you today shall be in your heart. You shall teach them diligently to your children, and shall talk of them when you sit down in your house, when you walk by the way, when you lie down and when you rise up. You shall bind them as a sign on your hand, and they shall be as frontlets between your eyes. You shall write them on the doorposts of your house and on your gates. (Deuteronomy 6:6–9)*

When we neglect the wisdom of God's Word we also reject the true answers to life's problems. Those who do so usually end up embracing the knowledge and ways of the world. We quite commonly find that many Christians walk, talk, and live no different than the world. Consequently, they also suffer the same defeats and miseries that the unbelieving world falls prey to. This certainly is not God's plan for the lives of believers in

Jesus Christ. The Lord intends us to be different. He wants us to be strong in His Mighty Power, and to overcome whatever the devil throws at us. Jesus prayed this prayer for all who would believe in Him:

> *I have given them the glory you gave me, so that they may be one, as we are—I in them and you in me, all being perfected into one. **Then the world will know that you sent me and will understand that you love them as much as you love me.** (John 17:22–23)*

As we can see from this prayer, Jesus prayed all the mighty blessings that He himself walked in, upon those who believe in Him. These great blessing are not given for the benefit of believers alone, but so that the unbelieving world will begin to understand that God loves the believers as much as He loves Jesus. The believer's victory in Jesus through the power of His Word is intended to provoke the unbeliever into recognition of the tremendous blessings that come from living in harmony and obedience to the Lord. If we allow these abundant blessings from God to permeate our lives and flow through us, those in the world will know we are truly different and they will desire what we have. This in turn will provide us the opportunity to lead them to the Jesus Christ.

If we are to operate in the abundant life that Jesus has made available to us, we should first have knowledge that this abundant life actually exists. The Bible tells us *"So then, faith comes by hearing and hearing by the Word of God" (Romans 10:17)*. If we prayerfully read the Scriptures aloud to ourselves, great deposits of faith will enter into our spirits. One good way to accomplish this would be to read along with a good audio version of the Bible. The more we do this, the more Scriptures we will commit to memory and steady changes will begin to occur within our lives. Consequently, instead of speaking defeat and dread, we will automatically speak the power of God's holy Word in times of trial, trouble and victory. David said, "*I have hidden your word in my heart that I might not sin against you*" *(Psalm 119:11).*

The Bible makes this very clear,

> *Without faith it is impossible to please God, because anyone who comes to Him must believe that He exists and that He rewards those who earnestly seek Him. (Hebrews 11:6)*

As the deposits of Scripture within us increase, the more we will believe that God really does exist and we will be able to trust Him implicitly. As we mix God's promises with faith and act upon them, He is pleased and the blessings and favor of His gracious hand will manifest in our lives. Unless we choose to receive the truth and power of God's Word, His blessings will remain ineffective for us.

All too often believers rely on the resources of the world, and live as if the Word of God doesn't even exist. Dear friends, for all intents and purposes, this attitude renders the great blessing of the printing press of no effect as far as the Bible is concerned. It might just as well be a ramshackle piece of junk that brought us no benefit. The abundance and availability of the Holy Script will not profit anyone who does not seek true knowledge and understanding.

Lack of knowledge of the Word will surely lead a person down the path of destruction. There are only two choices before each of us, even as there were only two trees of choice in the Garden of Eden. Adam and Eve had to make a decision between God's Word—the Tree of Life, and the Tree of the knowledge of good and evil—the other word, also known as worldly wisdom, or Satan's lies.

Each of us must at some point decide whether the Word of God is true and living and worth obeying. If we turn to the world and its teachings, *we will ultimately become our own gods*. We will inevitably come to trust our own opinions and judgments instead of God's Word. This is exactly what Satan's wants.

Jesus said, *"My sheep listen to my voice; I know them, and they follow me" (John 10:27).*

God is calling us to separate ourselves from the world and be joined to Him through His Word. This is holiness—God focused. When we choose to walk, talk, and behave in ways contrary to the instructions of the Bible, we chart our descent into idolatry because this puts us in submission to a system that is clearly opposed to God. Listen to what He has to say about this.

*Do not be yoked together with unbelievers. For what do righteousness and wickedness have in common? Or what fellowship can light have with darkness? What harmony is there between Christ and Belial? What does a believer have in common with an unbeliever? What agreement is there between the temple of God and idols?* **For we are the temple of the living God. As God has said: "I will live with them and walk among them, and I will be their God, and they will be my people." "Therefore come out from them and be separate, says the Lord.** *(2 Corinthians 6:14-17)*

It is alarming to note that the only bits of Scripture many people ever hear, come almost entirely from the teachings of their pastors. They then go on to either believe or reject what they have heard but do not prayerfully read or study the Bible for themselves. They do not meditate on the great and powerful truths contained in the Bible, and so they remain very ignorant of God's Word. One day when God spoke to Hosea the prophet, about the lamentable condition of His people, He said:

*My people are destroyed from lack of knowledge.* **Because you have rejected knowledge I also reject you as my priests. Because you have ignored the Law of your God I will also ignore your children. The more the priests increased the more they** *served against me. They exchanged their glory for something disgraceful. They feed on the sins of My people, and relish their wickedness and it will be like people, like priests. I will punish both of them for their ways, and repay them for their deeds.* They will eat but not have enough, they will engage in prostitution and not increase, because they have deserted the LORD to give themselves to prostitution, to old wine and new which take away the understanding of my people. They consult a wooden idol, and are answered by a stick of wood. A spirit of prostitution leads them astray; they are unfaithful to their God. (Hosea 4:6–12)

The answers that come from ungodly leaders today are about the same as the answers that came from priests who consulted wooden idols. They are just as worthless and as false as an answer that might come from a stick of wood.

Spiritual prostitution happened in Hosea's day, and it has continued to happen down through the ages. It is rampant today. Many present-day leaders consult intellectual idols that they elevate above God's instruction to mankind. Their answers to life do not come from the Truth of the Scriptures but from their own vain and prideful imaginations. Through the deception of humanism and intellectualism, these ungodly people believe and teach things that are untrue; they have believed a lie and their understanding has been darkened. Instead of guiding the fold by the Way of Truth—God's Holy Word, they tell people whatever they want to hear. They are people- pleasers; leaders who tolerate and condone ungodly lifestyles.

Some denominations have gone so far as to ordain as ministers and bishops, men and women whose lives are in brazen opposition to God's Word. The people of their congregations are not provoked to recognize their sin, neither are they led to repentance and humility before God. Therefore both the leaders and those being led by them stand guilty before the Lord. They are greatly unfaithful to the Almighty. The Word of God tells us:

*The weapons we fight with are not the weapons of the world. On the contrary, they have divine power to demolish strongholds.* **We demolish arguments and every pretension that sets itself up against the knowledge of God, and we take captive every thought to make it obedient to Christ.** *And we will be ready to punish every act of disobedience, once your obedience is complete. (2 Corinthians 10:4–6)*

The Holy Spirit brings the truths and the functions of the Word, home to us very clearly through this Scripture:

*For the word of God is living and active. Sharper than any double-edged sword, it penetrates even to dividing soul and spirit, joints and marrow; it judges the thoughts and attitudes of the heart. (Heb 4:12)*

As we are told the Scriptures penetrate and judge the thoughts and intents of our hearts, and this could be quite uncomfortable for many people. Might this be the reason why so many Christians avoid reading and studying God's holy Word? Could it be that they don't like the conviction that comes from the Holy Spirit, because they do not want to change their lifestyles?

The Word of God is alive and active because *Jesus is the Word.* Those who call themselves by His name shouldn't have much difficulty understanding that to spend time in the Word, is to actually spend time with Jesus. There is no way to get to know the Lord intimately unless we spend time with Him.

John the Apostle saw Jesus standing among the Seven Churches of Asia with a double-edged sword in His mouth. It is obvious that Jesus was speaking the Word to the Churches because He was standing in the midst of seven of them. You can find this account in the Book of Revelation. Since "seven" is the number for completion or perfection, it could well be that every church body throughout all ages, is represented by one or another of those seven churches in Asia.

Jesus said *"Out of the overflow of the heart the mouth speaks" (Matthew 12:34)*. Therefore, the words that come from the mouth of Jesus would of necessity be the overflow of His own heart. Jesus said, *"My sheep listen to my voice, I know them and they follow me" (John 10:27)*. The only way to know the Master's voice and listen to His heart, is to spend time with Him in His Word—the Bible. Jesus repeatedly said, *"He who has an ear, let him hear what the Spirit says to the churches" (Revelation 2:11)*.

Everything we think God speaks to us either directly or through someone else, *must* line up with the written Word. We are warned that*. . . Satan himself masquerades as an angel of light" (2 Corinthians 11:14)*. Therefore, it only stands to reason that we must know the voice of the Lord Jesus Christ, if we are to be able to distinguish His voice from the voice of the adversary—the devil.

Believers so often run around saying, "God told me to do this, and God told me to do that." What they don't realize is that God doesn't constantly change His mind about things. Could it just be that they are mistaking the identity of the speaker? It is not necessarily what *sounds good* that comes from the Lord, *but that which is good*. Anything God speaks to us will accurately line up with the written Word, but we will only be able to tell if it is from God based upon our own knowledge of the Scriptures. It is vitally important for every Christian to wake up and diligently fill themselves with the knowledge and wisdom of the Word of the God. *Wisdom is supreme; therefore get wisdom. Though it cost all you have, get understanding (Proverbs 4:7)*.

The time of the Lord's return is very near at hand. Wake up; please do not take the chance of missing His call because you don't recognize His voice!

# Chapter 4

# THE INACTIVE CHURCH

❦

The Lord now showed me a woman who was sitting in an office type chair. I could see this person only from her waist down. Even before I could ask the Lord what this meant, He explained it. Very simply Jesus said, "Many who believe they are the Bride of Christ are not at all ready to receive the Bridegroom. The woman you saw is the Church."

From the Lord's explanation, I could now understand why the woman was dressed in ordinary, everyday clothes instead of bridal attire. She was wearing a nice fitted black skirt that came to her knee and smart black high-heeled shoes.

One thing about this well-dressed woman stood out rather strongly to me. It was the fact that she was doing absolutely nothing. She was just sitting with her hands neatly folded in her lap, extremely still, and not moving a muscle.

I sensed pain in the Lord's statement about the Church, and suddenly the parable of the ten virgins came to mind.

*At that time the kingdom of heaven will be like ten virgins who took their lamps and went out to meet the bridegroom. Five of them were foolish and five were wise. The foolish ones took their lamps but did not take any oil with them. The wise, however, took oil in jars along with their lamps. The bridegroom was a long*

*time in coming, and they all became drowsy and fell*
*asleep. (Matthew 25:1–5)*

As we know, oil in the Bible represents the anointing or the presence of the Holy Spirit. Those who spend little or no time with God in His Word would be categorized by the five foolish virgins that Jesus spoke of. They have a very casual attitude towards the things of the Lord and are grossly lacking the oil—or presence of the Holy Spirit. Very simply put, these people are not in a deep and loving relationship with the Lord. By contrast, the wise virgins were careful to take extra oil in their jars. We might ask what this extra oil really is. It could mean only one thing—the supernatural strength that comes from great intimacy with God the Holy Spirit. It is total dependence and abandonment to God's abiding Presence.

*Then you will call upon me and come and pray to me,*
*and I will listen to you. **You will seek me and find me***
***when you seek me with all your heart. I will be found***
***by you, declares the LORD** . . . (Jeremiah 29:12–14)*

We must note that the Savior isn't lacking in either love or desire for a close relationship with us. It is we who fall short of an adoring and sold-out response to Him, and under such circumstances it becomes extremely hard to live for Jesus or do what He commands.

*If you love me, you will obey what I command. And I will*
*ask the Father, and he will give you another Counselor*
*to be with you forever-the Spirit of truth. (John 14:15–17)*

Notice, it is only those *who love Jesus and obey His commands* that receive the Counselor, the extra oil—the Spirit of truth, to be with them forever. Jesus gave us this command:

*All authority in heaven and on earth has been given to*
*me. **Therefore go and make disciples of all nations,***

*baptizing them in the name of the Father and of the Son and of the Holy Spirit, and teaching them to obey everything I have commanded you. And surely I am with you always, to the very end of the age. (Matthew 28:18–20)*

Too many believers are unconcerned with this mandate however, because instead, they are deeply consumed by their own pursuits, rather than the desire to please the Lord. As we stated before, the most common excuse given by lukewarm people for not sharing the Gospel, is the lack of time and an inadequate knowledge of the Bible.

How does this not resemble the story Jesus told of the foolish virgins, who didn't bring any extra oil? Prayerful submission, roots that go deep down into God's Word and the fervent desire for revelation knowledge from the Holy Spirit would be descriptive of the mentality of the wise virgins. These people carried *oil in their jars.* Jars would represent their total beings. Their lamps would be their spirits. *"The spirit of a man is the lamp of the LORD, Searching all the inner depths of his heart" (Proverbs 20:27).* In other words, these virgins were filled with God's Word. They were submissive and in tune with the Lord. *"Your word is a lamp to my feet and a light for my path" (Psalm 119:105).*

By contrast the ones who lacked oil were those whose laziness and lack of desire for the Word of God and the presence of the Holy Spirit, had left them with a light that was dying out. This speaks of the very large section of the Church that continues to walk in spiritual blindness. They are blind to the great blessings that God has placed at our disposal. Fear and ineffectiveness thrive where there is no Word; fear controls those who don't know the Word, rendering them powerless. Paul the Apostle prayed for the Ephesian Church,

*I pray also the eyes of your heart may be enlightened in order that you may know the hope to which He has called you, the riches of His glorious inheritance in the*

*saints, and His incomparably great power for us who believe. (Ephesians 1:18)*

If those of us who refer to ourselves as Christians would take time to know, trust, and act on the promises of God's Word, fear would become nonexistent and we would walk in faith and boldness like the first Church did two thousand years ago. Because so many are not obeying the commission of the Lord, and sadly are not even aware of it, no change of heart or behavior can take place and deep complacency prevails. It is imperative that the Church wakes up. The Church must know, believe, and act upon the promises of God's Word!

There is a very significant Scripture in the Book of Luke.

*One day as he [Jesus] was teaching, Pharisees and teachers of the law, who had come from every village of Galilee and from Judea and Jerusalem, were sitting there. And the power of the Lord was present for him to heal the sick. (Luke 5:17)*

In the days when Jesus was on earth, the Pharisees were respected for their knowledge of the Scriptures. The Bible however, sheds some interesting light on the degree of their actual knowledge and understanding. One would expect these Pharisees to have been the ones eager to support the Lord and help Him in every way to lead the hurting and brokenhearted to God. Instead they were simply *sitting there,* much like the Church of today. They did not participate in the Lord's work, but remained sitting idly by on the sidelines, with their hearts and minds full of doubt and unbelief. They did absolutely nothing to help the cause of Jesus, but instead they did much to hurt what He was doing.

Thank God for all faithful sold-out believers who work hard to get the Gospel to as many as possible! These soldiers of Christ will certainly receive a great reward from the Lord. Yet while a lot of work is being accomplished by a relatively small number of faithful servants, the vast majority of lukewarm sit-arounders remain uninvolved. Sadly, these same people fill up their time living exactly as the world does!

Jesus Christ gave His Life for us, and yet well dressed, tepid pew warmers do nothing by way of serving alongside Him. Jesus said: *"The harvest is plentiful but the workers are few" (Matthew 9:37).*

The Lord Jesus indicted the Laodicean Church of being lukewarm. Unless they changed, He declared, He would spew them out of His mouth. These words of the Lord should serve as a clarion call to all of us, but a whole lot of churchgoers today do not realize that the term "lukewarm" might very aptly describe them. Multitudes of today's believers are oblivious to the fact that they are actually very much a part of the Laodicean Church that Jesus so strongly addressed.

This blindness comes from only one place—a despairing lack of knowledge and indifference to the Word of God.

Jesus said to the Church at Laodicea,

*You say, 'I am rich; I have acquired wealth and do not need a thing.' But you do not realize that you are wretched, pitiful, poor, blind and naked. I counsel you to buy from me gold refined in the fire, so you can become rich; and white clothes to wear, so you can cover your shameful nakedness; and salve to put on your eyes, so you can see. (Revelation 3:17–18)*

So what should those who are strong in the Lord do? We should do as Jesus commanded: *Ask the Lord of the harvest, therefore, to send out workers into his harvest field" (Matthew 9:38).* We should pray that those who simply sit in the pews, will wake up, be strengthened in the Lord, and go into the fields or at least pray for those who will go.

We could also do as Paul did; we could come together to pray and intercede for those who remain unconcerned. We should care a little bit more about the ones who are weak and stumbling. Paul carefully prayed this for the Church at Ephesus.

*I keep asking that the God of our Lord Jesus Christ, the glorious Father, may give you the Spirit of wisdom and revelation, so that you may know him better. I pray also that the eyes of your heart may be enlightened in order that you may know the hope to which he has called you, the riches of his glorious inheritance in the saints, and his incomparably great power for us who believe. That power is like the working of his mighty strength, which he exerted in Christ when he raised him from the dead and seated him at his right hand in the heavenly realms, far above all rule and authority, power and dominion, and every title that can be given, not only in the present age but also in the one to come. And God placed all things under his feet and appointed him to be head over everything for the church, which is his body, the fullness of him who fills everything in every way. (Eph 1:17–23)*

Jesus said, *"I lay down my life for the sheep" (John 10:15)*. How about us? Would we be willing to lay down our lives in fervent prayer and intercession for our brothers and sisters who have lost their zeal? Perhaps you and I could be more diligent in carrying out our Father's business even as Jesus constantly was.

The Lord didn't say, my sheep know about me or of me, but *"My sheep know me" (John 10:14)*. The one indispensible element in getting to know someone well is time; time spent with that person. It is probably safe to say that only a minimal number of Christians spend time with Jesus through prayer and study of the Scriptures on a daily basis. He paid a huge and terrible price to redeem us from death, hell, and the grave. The least we could do in return is to spend time getting to know Him better and love Him more, so that we could accomplish what He so greatly desires us to do.

Jesus needs us to be His hands and feet, His ambassadors. Every opportunity we miss to share the Gospel is an opportunity lost, and with it perhaps a soul, too.

It is quite amazing to watch the fervor of those in multi-level marketing. They take every opportunity to share their business; they never miss a meeting, and think nothing of keeping late hours daily. They drive many miles to make one contact. If they are rejected they remain undaunted and try all the harder the next time, and all this for a dollar. Perhaps we should learn a thing or two from them, and translate it into our own efforts at sharing the Gospel.

We frequently see the disciples of different cults, tirelessly knocking doors and stopping folks to share their fake gospel. What would happen if every true follower of Jesus Christ acted with as much zeal in spreading the Good News, as those in their marketing or cultic ventures? Perhaps just a few more people in the world would be saved and the Church would start looking a lot more like the one that was raised up and empowered on the day of Pentecost.

You can hear the voice of Jesus pleading,

*Do not store up for yourselves treasures on earth, where moth and rust destroy, where thieves break in and steal. But store up for yourselves treasures in Heaven, where moth and rust do not destroy, and where thieves do not break in and steal. For where your treasure is there your heart will be also. (Matthew 6:19–21)*

It is time for the church to wake up and make a Scriptural evaluation of what real treasure is. What exactly was Jesus referring to? Are we storing up treasures in Heaven? If so, we would be diligently doing the Lord's work, because our hearts would be where our treasure is.

God's Word states that we are *"heirs of God and co-heirs with Christ if indeed we share in His sufferings in order that we may also share in His Glory"* (Romans 8:17). Christians today leap to stake claim in Christ's glory, but few are willing to share in His suffering. This part certainly does not attract us. Even the mere thought of suffering is much too hard for our twenty-first century minds to wrap around. No doubt there is a big difference between the Church of today and the one of the first century.

The disciples of Jesus were willing to lay down their lives to spread the Gospel, what about us? What are we willing to do?

What are some of the things the disciples did that we are **not** doing? For one, they spent every possible moment they could in prayer, petition, and worship to the Lord. We must too, but it takes love, discipline, and commitment to obtain the awesome relationship they had with Jesus. If we cultivate this type of relationship with the Lord, it would inevitably cause us to act just as fearlessly and unashamedly as the disciples did for the cause of Christ. Paul wrote,

*I am not ashamed of the gospel of Christ, for it is the power of God to salvation for everyone who believes, for the Jew first and also for the Greek. (Romans 1:16–17)*

As they faced charges before the authorities for preaching the Gospel, Peter and the other apostles boldly declared, *"We must obey God rather than men!" (Acts 5:29)* Dear friends, we too must obey God rather than men. Those of us who profess to be God's children must realize there is a cost. It costs to know and abide in Christ, but let us never forget, it cost Jesus His life to save us, but He didn't flinch.

With His very last words on earth, Jesus commissioned the Church to go out to the unsaved of the world even as He and His disciples did. He promised that miracles, signs, and wonders would follow believers as they obey His commission, but the Church today simply isn't moving.

*Go into all the world and preach the good news to all creation. Whoever believes and is baptized will be saved, but whoever does not believe will be condemned. And these signs will accompany those who believe: In my name they will drive out demons; they will speak in new tongues. (Mark 16:15–17)*

Nowhere are believers told to behave like the world. In fact Jesus said *"You do not belong to the world, but I have chosen you out of the world" (John 15:19)*. We are also told, *"Do not be overcome by evil, but overcome evil with good" (Romans 12:21)*.

The Church needs to be out on the front lines, clothed in the power and strength that come from a deep and abiding relationship with Jesus Christ our Lord; but bruised and helpless people sit on pews or stand in prayer lines again and again, weeping over their own problems while needing someone to pray for them just one more time. Their worldly counterparts sit on barstools and weep their woes into one more beer. The beer drinkers are truly helpless because they do not know God, and there is certainly no comparison at all being made between prayer and the results of beer. However, what is being called into question is the defeated attitude of the people who refuse to rise up in their God-given authority and stand in the power the Word of God.

When did you see a broke, busted, and defeated Peter, John, Paul, or any of the other apostles standing in someone's prayer line? Sure, they asked the church to pray for them because the "Prayers of the righteous avail much," but what they did not do was to hop from one prayer line to another each Lord's Day, in defeat, seeking someone to pray for them over and over again. They were not powerless, and so they did not act powerless. Instead they went out in the full authority of Jesus Christ and served on the frontlines. This determination is what is grossly missing in many Christians today.

There is something enormously wrong with this picture! The Church has a mighty God who answers prayer, and He is also a mighty God who must be believed and trusted.

> *And without faith it is impossible to please God, because anyone who comes to him must believe that he exists and that he rewards those who earnestly seek him. (Heb 11:6)*

If Christians would believe with all their hearts that God *is,* and that He rewards those who earnestly seek Him, they would be confident of His answers to their prayers. They would not always be looking for someone else to pray for them, thinking that perhaps God would shower some great favor upon them through this other person. Lack of confidence comes from a lack of intimate relationship with the heavenly Father, which in turn comes from lack of knowledge of the written Word. The Scriptures state, *"faith comes by hearing and hearing by the word of God" (Romans 10:17).* Without the Word there can be no power! It is the Word that generates faith because *Jesus is the Word.*

Jesus said to the disciples,

*Peace be with you! As the Father sent me, I am sending you. And when He had said this, He breathed on them, and said to them, Receive the Holy Spirit. (John 20:21–22)*

We must learn to receive God's peace and walk in it regardless of all physical circumstances. This peace comes only from the Holy Spirit. Prayer and intimacy with God should be our lifestyle.

Sometimes believers who are unfamiliar with the Scriptures wonder off onto the dangerous trail of using Biblical passages or parts of them inaccurately in attempts to get God to do what they want. In doing this they use the Word irreverently. Consequently, when they do not receive what they desire, they begin to confess doubt and unbelief. Some whine and complain and even try to make excuses for God, instead of going back to the Bible and prayerfully checking to see where they went wrong.

Then there are Christians who express complaints and excuses for God in the presence of unbelievers. How terrible a careless tongue can be on top of all the lack of faith!

The Bible tells us,

*Do your best to present yourself to God as one approved, a workman who does not need to be ashamed and who correctly handles the word of truth. (2 Timothy 2:15)*

One thing we should keep in mind is that God always keeps His Word. If things don't look right, it is not God who is doing something wrong; we are. We should go back to the Word and prayerfully check the Scriptures to find out where we went wrong.

We are told, *"The tongue has the power of life and death and those who love it will eat its fruit" (Proverbs 18:21).* Isn't it curious that this Scripture says "those who love it will eat its fruit?" It takes us back to the garden where Adam and Eve *received a twisted version of God's Word and literally ate its fruit—the fruit of death.*

Not only could faithless words cause our own spiritual demise, but they could also keep others from ever entering into the salvation of Jesus Christ. The unsaved are always watching those who claim to be Christians either for the sake of making fun of them, or more importantly, to see if what they believe will actually come to pass.

After Jesus had returned to heaven, His disciples always spoke with power that came from the Holy Spirit of God. The Holy Spirit descended upon them, empowering them as they prayed together.

*On the day of Pentecost, seven weeks after Jesus' resurrection, the believers were meeting together in one place. Suddenly, there was a sound from heaven like the roaring of a mighty windstorm in the skies above them, and it filled the house where they were meeting. Then, what looked like flames or tongues of fire appeared and settled on each of them. And everyone present was filled with the Holy Spirit and began speaking in other languages, as the Holy Spirit gave them this ability. (Acts 2:1–4)*

The Lord had promised His disciples this would happen, and just as He promised it came to pass. In order to receive the coming of the Holy Spirit and His power, the disciples and followers of Jesus had to obey the Lord's command and remain in Jerusalem. It must be noted that only those who obeyed this vital instruction from the Lord received the amazing blessing of the baptism of the Holy Spirit.

Those who chose not to obey the Lord's command missed the coming of the Holy Spirit. After His resurrection Jesus appeared to five hundred of His followers (*1 Corinthians 15:6),* but on the Day of Pentecost there were only one hundred and twenty in the upper room (*Acts 1:15).*

This goes to show that it is only when we do things God's way that we will *surely* receive His blessings. God always does His part.

> *. . . so is my word that goes out from my mouth: It will not return to me empty, but will accomplish what I desire and achieve the purpose for which I sent it. (Isaiah 55:11)*

The Lord does not change, so we must change to agree with Him. We should be eager to allow God's Word to abide in us, and we must use it in faith in Him. Jesus promised,

> *If you remain in me and **my words remain in you, ask whatever you wish, and it will be given you.** This is to my Father's glory, that you bear much fruit, showing yourselves to be my disciples. (John 15:7–8)*

We cannot live victorious lives if we only grab onto parts or sections of God's promises with the hope of changing the negative circumstances of the moment, and then plummeting into depression and incorrect speaking when things do not instantly turn out as we wish.

Praying, studying, believing God, and being rooted in desire to please Him should be our lifestyle. We definitely should not try to use Scripture as a formula to achieve some selfish end. If we truly love God and trust Him, we will understand that His Word always works for those who know it, believe it, and accurately and consistently confess it.

Listen to Jesus, here is what He said,

> *So Jesus answered and said to them, "Have faith in God. For assuredly, I say to you, whoever says to this mountain, 'Be removed and be cast into the sea,' and does not doubt in his heart, but believes that those things he says will be done, he will have whatever he says. Therefore I say to you, whatever things you ask when you pray, believe that you receive them, and you will have them." And whenever you stand praying, if you have anything against anyone, forgive him, that your Father in heaven may also forgive you your trespasses. But if you do not forgive, neither will your Father in heaven forgive your trespasses. (Mark 11:22–26)*

To get the results Jesus promised, we must do exactly what He says.

Key # 1. Say *and don't doubt,* regardless of the circumstances.

Key # 2. *When you pray, believe that you have received* (past tense). This means that God does it for us at the moment we pray and not when the answer becomes manifest. We should remember, that in God's Kingdom "Believing is seeing" and not the other way around.

Key #3. *When you pray,* if you hold anything against another *forgive.* Many pray for help while harboring unforgiveness and anger in their hearts.

If we keep in mind that "*It is impossible for God to lie*" *(Hebrews 6:18),* we will have faith that indeed moves mountains.

Jesus said this to His disciples before He ascended to His Father,

*All authority in heaven and earth has been given to me. Therefore go and make disciples of all nations, baptizing them in the name of the Father and of the Son and of the Holy Spirit, and teaching them to obey everything I have commanded you.* **And surely I am with you always to the very end of the age.** *(Matthew 28:19–20)*

If Jesus is truly the Lord of our lives, it is imperative that we walk in His authority, and in obedience to His commands. We must be overcomers. The Bible informs us that the saints *"Overcame him* (the enemy) *by the blood of the Lamb and the word of their testimony" (Revelation 12:11).*

If we do not set aside a daily time to read, study, and meditate on the Word of God in subjection to the Holy Spirit, it will be absolutely impossible to be strong in faith and service to the Lord. The Word is spiritual food, and a lack of it starves and weakens our spirits to the point of death.

There is no way to *"go and make disciples"* when we are personally starving, spiritually weak and sick, even to the point of death. If we will not diligently spend time with God in His Word, we will end up being, not much more than churchy duplicates of the world—powerless.

Each one of Jesus' disciples endured more problems than perhaps all of ours put together. Not many of us have been imprisoned, beaten, stoned and left for dead, shipwrecked, snake bitten, or whipped as they were. Yet these faithful servants of God kept their eyes steadfastly focused on the Lord with the ultimate priority of preaching the Gospel to as many as possible.

Every one of the twelve [not counting Judas Iscariot] died violent deaths for the sake of the Gospel, with the exception of John. History tells us John was thrown into boiling oil in an attempt to kill him, but he survived through the protection of God. He was then exiled to the isle of Patmos where he received the visions which comprise the Book of Revelation. John later died naturally. There is a cost for being a disciple of Jesus Christ; He forewarned us,

*If anyone desires to come after Me, let him deny himself, and take up his cross daily, and follow Me. For whoever desires to save his life will lose it, but whoever loses his life for My sake will save it. For what profit is it to a man if he gains the whole world, and is himself destroyed or lost? For whoever is ashamed of Me and My words, of him the Son of Man will be ashamed when He comes in His own glory, and in His Father's, and of the holy angels. (Luke 9:23–26)*

Paul's life was always in danger but that didn't stop him from proclaiming the Gospel. He said,

*I only know that in every city the Holy Spirit warns me that prison and hardships are facing me. However, I consider my life worth nothing to me, if only I may finish the race and complete the task the Lord Jesus has given me-the task of testifying to the gospel of God's grace. (Acts 20:23–24)*

The mountains of difficulty we face are usually nothing other than hoards of demons assigned by Satan to tear down and destroy our faith and service to God.

Goliath was Israel's mountain. His clear assignment was to demoralize and destroy the faith of God's people. Goliath taunted the Israelite army day after day, and blasphemed the God of Israel, until little David, a teenager, who had an awesome relationship with the living God, came along. This young man, who both knew his God and trusted Him implicitly, rose up to face this mighty giant with nothing more than five smooth stones and a slingshot. *David never saw Goliath as a giant but merely an uncircumcised Philistine, because he kept his eyes on almighty God.* David kept his mind steadfastly on the God who had delivered him from the paw of a lion and a bear. Listen to what David said to Goliath.

> *You come against me with sword and spear and javelin, but I come against you in the name of the LORD Almighty, the God of the armies of Israel, whom you have defied. This day the LORD will hand you over to me, and I'll strike you down and cut off your head. Today I will give the carcasses of the Philistine army to the birds of the air and the beasts of the earth, and the whole world will know that there is a God in Israel. All those gathered here will know that it is not by sword or spear that the LORD saves; for the battle is the LORD's, and he will give all of you into our hands. (1 Samuel 17:45–47)*

We all know the rest of the story; David was victorious, and Goliath was history. The mighty and awesome God, whom David loved, trusted and served with all his heart, came through for him and for all Israel in undeniable victory.

We too can slay the giants that taunt us, but we must also do it through implicit faith in the power of the mighty name of the Lord Jesus Christ. If we choose to spend as much time with Jesus as David did with God, we will also implicitly believe His Word straight into victory. Jesus said, ". . . *I have come that they may have life, and that they may have it more abundantly" (John 10:10).*

Paul advises us,

> *Let the word of Christ dwell in you richly as you teach and admonish one another with all wisdom, and as you sing psalms, hymns, and spiritual songs with gratitude in your hearts to God. (Colossians 3:16)*

Let's make it a point to encourage other believers with the Word of God rightly spoken. When we praise and give thanks to God in the form of singing and worshipful adoration, we both acknowledge that God is, and that He indeed rewards those who diligently seek Him. In an atmosphere of faith-filled praise, the mountains of demons that manifest in the form of financial or medical problems, marriage situations, or any other type of problem, will end up being cast deep into the sea as we command them to, through the magnificent power of the name of Jesus Christ our Lord. It is written:

> *. . . at the name of Jesus every knee should bow, in heaven and on earth and under the earth, and every tongue confess that Jesus Christ is Lord, to the glory of God the Father. (Philippians 2:10–11)*

When we elevate the One who alone is able to give us abundant life, the works of the evil one who comes to steal, kill and destroy, is demolished. Hear the words of the Holy Spirit: *"I tell you, now is the time of God's favor, now is the day of salvation" (2 Corinthians 6:2).* We have every right to walk in God's awesome favor right now!

Without doubt, now is the time for the eyes of our hearts to be,

> *. . . enlightened in order that we may know the hope to which He has called us, the riches of His glorious inheritance in the saints and His incomparably great power for us who believe. (Ephesians 1:18)*

Now is the time for us to believe that God's power,

> *. . . is like the working of his mighty strength, which he exerted in Christ when he raised him from the dead and seated him at his right hand in the heavenly realms, far above all rule and authority, power and dominion, and every title that can be given, not only in the present age but also in the one to come. (Ephesians 1:19–21)*

Now is the time for us to act with boldness, keeping in mind that,

> . . . *God placed all things under his* [Jesus'] *feet and appointed him to be head over everything for the church, which is his body, the fullness of him who fills everything in every way. (Ephesians 1:22–23)*

Now is the time for the Church to rise up and act in accordance with the mighty power of the name of the Lord Jesus Christ. It is time to hasten to the work He commanded us to do. The Bridegroom is coming for each one of us, and we will then find out if we belong with the wise virgins who kept their lamps filled, trimmed, and ready to meet Him, or with the foolish ones who let their lamps die out, and heard His final frightening words, *"I tell you the truth, I don't know you."* As they frantically called, *"'Sir! Sir!' . . . 'Open the door for us!'"* (Matthew 25:11-12)

What will you and I be wearing when Jesus comes? Will we be dressed in glorious wedding attire or will our clothes be that of a regular business day?

The time to choose our garments is now! It will be too late to decide when He arrives.

Remember, there were ten virgins, five wise and five foolish. Half of the total number was unfaithful. This scary statistic could mean, only half of what is known as the Church will be found faithful and ready at the return of Jesus Christ. Which half will you belong to?

Wake up dear ones! Awake! The Lord lovingly calls to you, the hour is late, and today is the day of salvation.

# Chapter 5

# THE LEG BRACE

———∞∞∞———

I wish the word the Lord had given me about the inactive Church symbolized by the sedentary woman had been all He had to say about it, but it wasn't. Once again, I was shown the same woman sitting exactly as I had seen before. She had on the same clothes, hands in her lap, and just as previously, she was doing absolutely nothing. One thing had changed however, this time she had a brace on one of her legs.

The interpretation Jesus gave me regarding this picture was twofold. In the first case, the woman's inactivity spelled indifference, but in the second instance, her indolence had actually caused her leg muscles to atrophy. In other words, her ability to go and spread the Gospel was now seriously impaired through long disuse.

Whether it was grief or impatience or a mixture of both that I sensed in the Lord was hard to accurately say, but it wasn't difficult to miss His displeasure.

As I mentioned before, this woman symbolized the Church. If in the Lord's eyes the Church appears listless and lethargic, not adorned in bridal array, unprepared to receive Him, lame and sitting down on the job He entrusted to us, then the Church is really in pretty bad shape. We had better wake up and do something about it fast.

Heaviness filled my heart as I considered this distressing picture. Then the Lord directed my attention back to the

Scriptures and His own ministry. Jesus said to His disciples and to us, *". . . As the Father has sent me, I am sending you" (John 20:21).* We are to go as Jesus went, because it is He who is sending us. He went because His Father sent Him. He also achieved all that His Father entrusted him with. It wasn't difficult to see that the Lord was saying, "Look carefully at what I did; then go out and do the same."

The Lord Jesus opened His ministry in Nazareth by reading the scroll in the synagogue.

> *The Spirit of the Lord is on me, because He has anointed me to preach good news to the poor. He has sent me to proclaim freedom for the prisoners and recovery of sight for the blind, to release the oppressed, to proclaim the year of the Lord's favor. (Luke 4:18–19)*

Jesus used the Word to show God's plan for Him on earth. He then went on to faithfully execute and complete His Father's every assignment. We the Church should be diligently doing the same thing. *"As the Father has sent Me, I am sending you" (John 20:21).* His Words should spur our hearts and our bodies to action, but for some reason it doesn't.

How disappointing this must be to Him! The Church—no bridal attire, but merely a woman dressed in everyday clothes sitting idly by, hands folded, and wearing a leg brace! How could we, the ones He bled and died for be so cold, so unmoved, so uncaring? Does His enormous sacrifice really mean so little to us that we barely think about it at all in terms of what He instructed us to do?

> *The Lord Jesus in the night in which He was betrayed took bread; and when He had given thanks, He broke it and said, "This is My body, which is for you; do this in remembrance of Me." In the same way He took the cup also after supper, saying, "This cup is the new covenant in My blood; do this, as often as you drink it, in remembrance of Me." **For as often as you eat this***

**bread and drink the cup, you proclaim the Lord's death until He comes.** *(1 Corinthians 11:23–26)*

In the covenant of the communion we can see that Jesus wants us to remember the price He paid to redeem us from death, hell, and the grave. In remembering His death we should also remember that He died not just to save us, but to save a lost and dying world. The Lord commanded us to go and share, but many of us go the other way. We never venture further than the doors of our individual church buildings, while many perish in their sins not but a few feet away.

Could a clue to our inactivity be gleaned from these words of the Lord?

*Yes, I am the vine; you are the branches. Those who remain in me, and I in them, will produce much fruit. For apart from me you can do nothing. Anyone who parts from me is thrown away like a useless branch and withers. Such branches are gathered into a pile to be burned. But if you stay joined to me and my words remain in you, you may ask any request you like, and it will be granted! My true disciples produce much fruit. This brings great glory to my Father. (John 15:5–8)*

If we are not bearing fruit, a red flag should immediately go up. According to the words of Jesus this means that we have grown distant from Him. Bearing fruit is a natural part of being a live branch that is attached to the vine. Jesus said, *"My true disciples produce much fruit. This brings great glory to my Father"* *(John 15:8).* Very obviously, according to the Lord, the degree of a person's fruitfulness is directly linked to being one of His true disciples.

So what then are we all about? Apparently our own personal desires have overtaken the Lord's purpose for our lives. Referring to this exact frame of mind Jesus said,

*But seek first the kingdom of God and His righteousness and all these things will be given to you as well. (Matthew 6:33)*

Why don't we take Him at His Word? Listen to His promise,

**"But if you stay joined to me and my words remain in you, you may ask any request you like, and it will be granted!** *My true disciples produce much fruit. This brings great glory to my Father." (John 15:7–8)*

The Lord left us with only one instruction, *"Go and make disciples of all nations" (Matthew28:19).*

We can make every day count for the Lord if we are willing to. We can turn everything into an opportunity to share the Gospel with those around us if we are so minded. This is exactly what the Apostles and early Christians did; the difference between them and us is that they were totally in love with the Bridegroom. They thought about Him constantly and so they couldn't stop talking about Him.

Sharply accusing the disciples the High Priest declared, *"We gave you strict orders not to teach in this name, yet you have filled Jerusalem with your teaching . . ." (Acts 5:28).* The Apostles boldly answered, *"We must obey God rather than men!" (Acts 5:29)* For this they were flogged and ordered once more not to speak in the name of the Jesus. The Apostle's amazing response was to leave rejoicing that they were counted worthy to suffer disgrace for His name.

What about us? What is the Church of today willing to do for Jesus? Or would "unwilling" be the more accurate term to use to describe much of the current church population?

Didn't the Master warn that the *"love of most will grow cold?"* Haven't we already reached this point?

There is yet hope for those whose inactivity has made them sluggish, but much less for those whose leg muscles have atrophied along with their hearts.

Friends, this is not a message that many will want to hear or agree with, and it is definitely not an easy one to deliver. However, the Lord is trying to convict each one of us regarding the fearsome state of the Church. If we would only listen with open hearts, we will see that it is because of His great love and concern for all of us who are called by His name that He is trying to wake us up, to get on the right track before it is too late.

The Messiah said,

**You are the light of the world. A city on a hill cannot be hidden.** *Neither do people light a lamp and put it under a bowl. Instead they put it on its stand and it gives light to everyone in the house.* **In the same way let your light shine before men, that they may see your good deeds and praise your Father in Heaven.** *(Matthew 5:14–16)*

In the Book of Revelation, Jesus referred to the Seven Churches of Asia as lampstands. The purpose of a lampstand is to elevate the source of light so that in turn it will illuminate the darkness around it. Churches are required to be lampstands that uphold the light of the Gospel of Jesus Christ, so those in darkness might see and come to Him. Jesus constantly went to those in darkness. Matthew says of the Lord, *"The people living in darkness have seen a great light; on those living in the land of the shadow of death a light has dawned"* *(Matthew 4:16)*.

The Messiah is a continuous light to those in darkness and we His people must allow His light to shine through us into the dark, dark world around us. Jesus extended an amazing invitation first to his disciples and then to all of us, *"Come, follow me,"* Jesus said, *"and I will make you fishers of men"* *(Matthew 4:19)*.

We might ask how we could do this and where we would start. Let's find out where Jesus started.

One day the Lord was in the Temple, He had just declared His Messiahship by quoting from Isaiah 61. The Pharisees were offended because Jesus declared that He was the Messiah. Suddenly a man possessed by evil spirits began screaming in a loud voice, declaring that Jesus was the Holy One of God. Jesus immediately commanded the demons to be quiet and come out of him, and the man was set free.

We might learn a lesson from Jesus and start working with the people closest to us. Notice how Jesus related to the oppressed. Let's do the same.

Few of us ever reach out to people who are weak, sick, and in bondage to the enemy. We find them right inside the four walls of our church buildings. How do we deal with them? Do we usually avoid them or discuss them with our friends? We might sometimes refer to the oppressed as being weird. Doubtless, many of us have been guilty of this. Maybe we think these hurting individuals are the pastor's responsibility; or perhaps the deacons, ushers, or someone else's problem, but our love for Jesus should compel us to reach out to them in love.

The truth is, Jesus has called each one of us to do as He did. We could always say a kind word, share the love of the Lord, or offer the strength of the Scriptures to these people. Who knows, it may be the last chance a person like this has, before he or she totally turns away from God because of our coldness and lack of love. It could also be the very last opportunity we ourselves have to share Jesus with someone before we step into eternity to stand before Him.

Not too far into His ministry, Jesus chose twelve men to be His disciples; eleven of the original twelve formed the core group that became the first Church. Among these men was also one from the enemy's camp who later betrayed the Lord with something as intimate as a kiss.

Nothing Jesus did was without purpose. Could it be that all of us who make up His Church fall personality-wise, emotionally, and spiritually into the category of one or the other of those twelve disciples?

This is a scary thought! Who would want to be the next Judas? No one in his or her right mind would desire this, and yet many of us love money so much and follow Jesus for what we think we can personally gain from him by way of some material benefit.

In fact this false gospel is blared forth from many a pulpit today. Jesus gave Judas charge of their money bag. Judas for his part dipped into it for his own purposes. What does this say about Judas? He loved himself. He had no love for Jesus or his fellow disciples. He lived only for Himself. Judas wanted what he wanted, and so he died spiritually. He then died physically as well because his love for himself and money, trumped his faithfulness to Jesus.

Jesus said,

*Give, and it will be given to you: good measure, pressed down, shaken together, and running over will be put into your bosom. For with the same measure that you use, it will be measured back to you. (Luke 6:38)*

Notice, Jesus said "*Give and it will be given to you.*" In other words, sow and you will reap. Does this statement Jesus made however, refer exclusively to money, as the broadly trumpeted neogospel seems to suggest? Jesus was actually teaching us a vitally important principle when He stated the famous words of Luke 6:38. If we go back just one verse we will find out more accurately what He was trying to get across to us.

*Judge not, and you shall not be judged. Condemn not, and you shall not be condemned. Forgive, and you will be forgiven. Give, and it will be given to you. A good measure . . . (Luke 6:37–38).*

Jesus was teaching us a lifestyle principle of how we are to treat others. In doing as He commands, we will find ourselves being abundantly blessed in whichever area we choose to obey. God is faithful and rewards those who obey Him. If we do not judge others we will not receive the pain of being judged. If we choose not to condemn, we in turn will not be condemned; if we forgive we will be forgiven, and whatever we give we will also receive in abundance. The love Jesus has poured on us we should freely share with others. Jesus said,

*So now I am giving you a new commandment: Love each other. Just as I have loved you, you should love each other. Your love for one another will prove to the world that you are my disciples." (John 13:34-35)*

Jesus trained and equipped twelve men to go out and do what He was doing. This is the pattern we should follow; *we must do what He did.*

In the meantime we might each want to take an inward look. Which of the twelve do you and I feel we personally resemble most? Peter denied Jesus, and Thomas doubted. James and John wanted the best seats in Heaven. Despite all of their shortcomings and faults the Lord loved them, and eleven remained faithful to Him because they loved Him too. Importantly, we should let the Lord reveal to us the true condition of our hearts for His love and mercy for us is guaranteed. So will we be as faithful to the Lord as the eleven were, or would we betray the Him for the lure of money, position or opportunity?

Jesus said,

*So don't be afraid, little flock.* **For it gives your Father great happiness to give you the Kingdom. "Sell what you have and give to those in need. This will store up treasure for you in heaven!** *And the purses of heaven have no holes in them. Your treasure will be safe—no thief can steal it and no moth can destroy it.* **Wherever your treasure is, there your heart and thoughts will also be.** *(Luke 12:32–34)*

If we really start storing up treasure in heaven, we will live in the wisdom, light and power that God has given us, and we will do what Jesus did because of our love for Him.

> *. . . And these signs will accompany those who believe: In my name they will drive out demons; they will speak in new tongues; they will pick up snakes with their hands; and when they drink deadly poison, it will not hurt them at all; they will place their hands on sick people, and they will get well. (Mark 16:17–18)*

If we would believe and go as the disciples did, permitting the glorious Head of the Church, Jesus Christ to control us as His body, we will find ourselves acting more like Him. Our mouths will begin preaching the Word, our hands will reach out to touch and bring healing to the sick, our feet will go wherever the Head tells us to, and demons will flee. The blind will see, the lame will walk, and the dead will be raised to the glory of God.

When this happens the Church will look more like the radiant Bride Jesus is returning for. We will become less and less like the woman in everyday clothes sitting idly by, with her leg in a brace, and doing absolutely nothing for the cause of Christ. Instead we will begin to live like Peter, John, and the other disciples. Paul didn't even give a thought to the poisonous snake that attached itself to his hand as he picked up wood to make a fire. He simply shook it off into the flames and that was the end of the serpent. Paul absolutely believed the Word of the Master and acted upon it.

The Lord exhorted the church, *"Be dressed ready for service and keep your lamps burning . . ." (Luke 12:35).* It is time we get dressed and ready for service. It's time our lamps are ablaze with the Gospel of Salvation. It's time to make certain that we have extra oil—*the anointing of the Holy Spirit that comes through submission to Him.* We have been entrusted with much and it is time to also give back much. Jesus said,

*. . . From everyone who has been given much, much will be demanded; and from the one who has been entrusted with much, much more will be asked. (Luke 12:48)*

The responsibility is great! The Master is soon returning and we must *wake up!*

# Chapter 6

# UNDERSTANDING

T here was now a big burlap bag filled to the brim with brown beans sitting on the floor of a small room! I wondered what this could mean, for this was what I was next shown by the Lord.

Jesus gently brought understanding to me. As we know, seed in the Bible refers to the Word. I wondered however, why the Lord was using brown beans to represent it. I figured that the color white would far better represent the purity of God's Word.

As I was prayerfully thinking on this, the Lord said, "I used beans because it sounds like the Hebrew word 'bin' which means 'understanding.'" "Brown beans," the Lord went on to explain, "Signifies an impure word." The word being preached in many churches today is one that has been mixed and mingled with the thoughts and intents of men. This impure gospel is being circulated, clouding the understanding of thousands of people.

The true Gospel is the good news that God wants us to share. It is His desire that we truly know and understand His great grace and love for us made manifest in Jesus Christ His Son, and His amazing sacrifice on the cross of Calvary.

*For God so loved the world that he gave his one and only Son, that whoever believes in him shall not perish but have eternal life. (John 3:16)*

The Bible tells us:

*In the past God spoke to our forefathers through the prophets at many times and in various ways, **but in these last days he has spoken to us by his Son, whom he appointed heir of all things, and through whom he made the universe. The Son is the radiance of God's glory and the exact representation of his being, sustaining all things by his powerful word. After he had provided purification for sins, he sat down at the right hand of the Majesty in heaven.** (Hebrews 1:1–3)*

God now wants us to have a clear understanding of who He is. To give us this understanding, He sent His Son Jesus, the exact image and personification of the Almighty. Yahweh God also gave us the Scriptures to teach us about Himself. Yet many sincere people do not know Him at all!

One might ask, if these dear people are religious and the answer would be, yes they are! Are they churchgoers? Absolutely! Do they really know God, the Lord Jesus, and the Holy Spirit? This time the answer has to be "No." Most of these precious people know *of* God and *about Him* but they *do not know Him* because they don't have a relationship with Him.

We must ask why this is so. Traditions, man-made rules, rituals, and false teaching have blinded them keeping them from the Truth. Dear friends, traditions and the rules of men have very little to do with the Gospel of Jesus Christ. So the Lord used brown beans to symbolize the modified Gospel that so many are hearing.

According to some who interpret dreams and visions, the color brown is used in association with fleshly desires, selfish ambition, and striving. Men and women have come up with their own versions of the Scriptures by mixing it with their thoughts and ideas, and in doing so they have created a "brown bean gospel" leading multitudes astray. Those who do this, do it at their own spiritual peril.

The Lord was very direct when he declared to the religious leaders of His day,

> *Woe to you, teachers of the law and Pharisees, you hypocrites! You travel over land and sea to win a single convert, and when he becomes one, you make him twice as much a son of hell as you are. (Matthew 23:15)*

The words of Jesus make it quite clear that any soul that is lost through the preaching of a different Gospel, will be held to the charge of the ones who taught it. Do these strong words from the Lord mean He is lacking in love? Actually it is His great love that causes Him to show us the Truth. Eternity is a very long time to spend repenting. No amount of money, fame, popularity, or anything else is worth the cost of eternal separation from the God of the Bible. Paul said,

> *But even if we or an angel from heaven should preach a gospel other than the one we preached to you, let him be eternally condemned! (Galatians 1:8)*

This is what Jeremiah had to say about teachers who twisted God's Word.

> *How can you say, **"We are wise because we have the law of the LORD,"** when your teachers have **twisted it so badly?** These wise teachers will be shamed by exile for their sin, **for they have rejected the word of the LORD. Are they so wise after all?** (Jeremiah 8:8–9)*

Jesus said,

*If you hold to my teaching, you are really my disciples. Then you will know the truth, and the truth will set you free. (John 8:31–32)*

Every faithful leader who fearlessly speaks the truth of God's Holy Word and so leads many to Jesus Christ have much to rejoice in! The Prophet Daniel said,

*Those **who are wise** will shine like the brightness of the heavens, **and those who lead many to righteousness, like the stars forever and ever.** (Daniel 12:3)*

Attendees of many large and prominent denominational churches may know that Jesus is the Son of God, but most never accept Him as Lord and Savior of their lives. This is because no one ever teaches them to do so. They give mental assent to Him as some distant deity, but have no personal relationship with Him.

No invitation is extended at the close of their services, and so they never have the opportunity to ask Jesus into their hearts. They don't know how to live for the Lord or walk in His light. Even though they might have spent all their lives in a church, they see Him as being somewhere off beyond the azure blue, and hope that perhaps through accomplishing enough good works or living a better life than someone else, they might be able to make it into heaven—a works-oriented gospel. This greatly grieves the heart of the Lord because He desires a close and loving relationship with each one of us.

In the words of Messiah there is only one way to the Father. He said,

*I am the way and the truth and the life. No one comes to the Father except through me. If you really knew me, you would know my Father as well. (John 14:6–7)*

"Hey, I'm a good person. Yes, I'd say I'm going to heaven." "I go to Church." We hear these statements all the time, but the "good works gospel" will not hold water with God. There is only one way to God and His name is Jesus. Jesus is the "Way, the Truth and the Life.

Listen to the Lord's answer to Phillip his disciple. *Philip said, "Lord, show us the Father and that will be enough for us." (John 14:8)* The Lord's answer was lengthy but it could not have shed more light.

*Jesus answered:* **"Don't you know me, Philip, even after I have been among you such a long time? Anyone who has seen me has seen the Father. How can you say, 'Show us the Father'? Don't you believe that I am in the Father, and that the Father is in me?** *The words I say to you are not just my own. Rather, it is the Father, living in me, who is doing his work. Believe me when I say that I am in the Father and the Father is in me; or at least believe on the evidence of the miracles themselves.* **I tell you the truth, anyone who has faith in me will do what I have been doing.** *He will do even greater things than these, because I am going to the Father.* **And I will do whatever you ask in my name, so that the Son may bring glory to the Father. You may ask me for anything in my name, and I will do it. "If you love me, you will obey what I command. And I will ask the Father, and he will give you another Counselor to be with you forever the Spirit of truth. The world cannot accept him, because it neither sees him nor knows him. But you know him, for he lives with you and will be in you.** *I will not leave you as orphans; I will come to you. Before long, the world will not see me anymore, but you will see me. Because I live, you also will live. On that day you will realize that I am in my Father, and you are in me, and I am in you.* **Whoever has my commands and obeys them, he is the one who loves me. He who loves me will be loved by**

**my Father, and I too will love him and show myself to him."** *(John 14:9–21)*

It is clear from the words of the Lord Jesus Christ, that it is not good works or exaggerated beliefs about oneself that counts, *but faith—total belief in Jesus as God, and love for Him.* Implicit faith in Jesus and love for Him produces the same works that He did, and even greater as He promised. Because of the love relationship that exists between Jesus and such a believer He will do greater works through this individual. The Lord promised to give us another Counselor—the Holy Spirit of truth, who would keep us close to Him.

John the Baptist referred to Jesus as *"The true light that gives light to every man . . ." (John 1:9).* Light brings understanding; obviously you cannot see in darkness and you cannot comprehend what you cannot see. The Bible informs us *"The entrance of Your words gives light; It gives understanding to the simple (Psalm 119:130).* God's Word brings light to our understanding, and once we understand the great love of the Lord for us, it becomes easy to obey, like Paul and the apostles did.

The pursuit of money, worldly knowledge, and the wisdom of men go directly opposite to the great treasures embedded in the Holy Scriptures. Satan prompts the tendency towards worldly attractions to prevent the light of the Word from entering the hearts and minds of people. Whatever a person is consumed with eventually becomes his or her god. This is Satan's goal because he hates Jesus and us. No wonder Jesus said,

*No servant can serve two masters. Either he will hate the one and love the other, or he will be devoted to the one and despise the other.* ***You cannot serve both God and Money.*** *(Luke 16:13)*

Money, knowledge and education among scores of other things are blessings the Lord bestows upon His faithful children. However when the overwhelming focus and desire of an individual becomes centered on worldly abundance, and this in turn is coupled with a false gospel that feeds this avaricious mindset, it replaces and opposes God's Word. The Lord's wisdom and instructions become blurred and the spiritual condition of the person becomes very grim. Paul warns us of this very thing, and we must be reminded that we are very much in the last days.

*But mark this: There will be terrible times in the last days.* ***People will be lovers of themselves, lovers of money, boastful, proud,*** *abusive, disobedient to their parents, ungrateful, unholy, without love, unforgiving, slanderous, without self-control, brutal, not lovers of the good, treacherous, rash,* ***conceited, lovers of pleasure rather than lovers of God—having a form of godliness but denying its power. Have nothing to do with them.*** *(2 Timothy 3:1–5)*

The Apostle Paul asks,

*Where is the wise man? Where is the scholar? Where is the philosopher of this age?* ***Has not God made foolish the wisdom of the world? For since in the wisdom of God the world through its wisdom did not know him, God was pleased through the foolishness of what was preached to save those who believe.*** *Jews demand miraculous signs and Greeks look for wisdom,* ***but we preach Christ crucified:*** *a stumbling block to Jews and foolishness to Gentiles,* ***but to those whom God has called, both Jews and Greeks, Christ the power of God and the wisdom of God. For the foolishness of God is wiser than man's wisdom, and the weakness of God is stronger than man's strength.*** *(1 Corinthians 1:20–25)*

First Corinthians 1:20–25 quite accurately addresses the foolishness of the pseudo gospel which the Lord symbolized through a bag of brown beans. By contrast the wisdom of God is made quite clear through Paul's words to the Romans.

*The word is near you; it is in your mouth and in your heart," that is, the word of faith we are proclaiming: That if you confess with your mouth, "Jesus is Lord," and believe in your heart that God raised him from the dead, you will be saved. For it is with your heart that you believe and are justified, and it is with your mouth that you confess and are saved. (Romans 10:8–10)*

This is the true Gospel—the heart of it. Jesus is the Word, and dear friends, you couldn't get much closer to God than when you confess Jesus Christ as Lord and believe in your heart that God raised Him from the dead. Actually once you do this the Lord is so close to you that He is in your heart and in your mouth, His radiant personality now permeates every atom and molecule of your being. God loves you so very much and desires you to know how close He really is to you. If you would just open your heart to Him, He will hold you in His arms and never let you go as long as you desire to stay in the blessed warmth of His loving embrace.

The truth of God's amazing love for us, expressed through the great victory achieved by Jesus through His death, burial, and resurrection, has progressively become clouded in the eyes of many within the professing Church, and great numbers of people continue to believe a lie. Some hold onto statues and crucifixes, expecting the symbols to work like a charm. Others may not go that route but treat the great sacrifice of the Lord with little concern. Having received wrong teaching and being dulled in spirit, they don't understand the immense love that Jesus has for them.

Dear friends God loves you and He wants you to know Him and love Him in return. It is that simple! This is relationship! God wants to be your Father—your Daddy God. Will you permit Him to do that by receiving His love and becoming His child?

If you are reading this book and realize that you are in a church that has never taught you to accept Jesus Christ as your Lord and Savior, just go back four paragraphs to *Romans 10:9–10* and do what Paul instructs. "*Confess with your mouth **Jesus is Lord,** and **believe in your heart** that God raised Him from the dead and **you will be saved.**"*

If you prayed that prayer, now permit the Lord to lead you to a church where this *truth* is taught. Follow the Lord's guidance to a Church that believes the Bible, and teaches you to personally study the Scriptures, because it alone will bring light and wisdom to your every step.

Jesus baptizes with the Holy Spirit. Receive the Baptism of the Holy Spirit by asking the Lord for it and then believing that He has done just that. You will receive your prayer language, accept it and use it as the Lord directs. Now begin your awesome journey with God by studying your Bible daily, and asking the Holy Spirit to give you revelation knowledge. Pray in the Spirit and walk in obedience to the Scriptures.

You will not automatically become perfect or sinless, but you will have the peace that comes from being in a close relationship with your Heavenly Father.

Through the power of the Holy Spirit in you, you have become a new creation.

*Therefore, if anyone is in Christ, he is a new creation; the old has gone, the new has come! All this is from God, who reconciled us to himself through Christ and gave us the ministry of reconciliation (2 Corinthians 5:17–18)*

As you study the Scriptures you will begin to understand the changes you'll need to make in your life as you learn to submit to God. Remember to be steadfast and unwavering in your faith, be intensely loyal to Jesus because you love Him. You will be able to do this through the power of the Holy Spirit and you will now understand with clarity what the Lord meant when He said,

*Watch out that no one deceives you. For many will come in my name, claiming, 'I am the Christ,' and will deceive many. (Matthew 24:4–5)*

Your sense of discernment will increase because the Holy Spirit, who now lives in you, provides supernatural wisdom and understanding. You will begin to recognize that you are growing in wisdom and discernment. Your thinking will change. Jesus warned us about a large number of people who will desert the faith, but you will not be among them. The Lord described this falling away as follows.

*Many will turn away from the faith and will betray and hate each other, and many false prophets will appear and deceive many people. Because of the increase of wickedness the love of most will grow cold,* **but he who stands firm to the end will be saved.** *(Matthew 24:10–13)*

The Lord concern for His Church is quite obvious because of His many warnings to us. He gave us a clear heads-up regarding the coming apostasy within the Church. Jesus said that false teachers and religious compromisers within the professing Church would continue to increase and deceive many. We see confirmation of this all the time. This is why we so desperately need the presence of the Holy Spirit in our lives. It is the Holy Spirit alone who gives us the ability to discern the spirits; it is He alone who gives us understanding. It is also the Holy Spirit who helps us to understand the Bible.

The brown-bean gospel is being propagated and kept alive because young children are not being taught the truth by their parents. Many parents have forgotten this command of the LORD.

*Love the LORD your God with all your heart and with all your soul and with all your strength. These commandments that I give you today are to be upon your hearts. **Impress them on your children. Talk about them when you sit at home and when you walk along the road, when you lie down and when you get up.** (Deuteronomy 6:5–7)*

Parents in so-called Christian homes seldom sit down with their children to teach them to love the LORD with all their hearts, souls and strength. The Word is not impressed upon the children. Instead, they are kept busy with all types of secular activities, television, and every electronic gaming device available. Consequently, children today are growing up with little or no faith or connection with their Savior, and they get their worldview from the world.

It is deplorable that the Bible is not the standard in every Christian home! Shouldn't it be given the greatest place of honor and respect in our homes? It is after all, God's own Word given by Him for our good!

As Jesus warned, a large part of Christendom continues to slip steadily into apostasy as each generation becomes more deeply deprived of the Holy Scriptures than the preceding one. As a result of this great deprivation, each consecutive generation continues to receive and accept in greater measure the wisdom that comes from the world. The Lord cautioned,

*Enter through the narrow gate. For wide is the gate and broad is the road that leads to destruction, and many enter through it. But small is the gate and narrow the road that leads to life, and only a few find it. (Matthew 7:13–14)*

All thanks to God however for the remnant that has entered the small gate and taken the narrow road that leads to life, holding fast to the Word, the Light—the Lord Jesus Christ.

As mentioned before, along with the increase of false leadership, the preaching of the tainted gospel continues to abound. In the final analysis, it is only through enduring faith in Jesus, submission to the Holy Spirit, unbending love for God, and a steadfast commitment to the absolute authority of His Word that we will be protected from falling into great deception.

Apparently this trend began quite early on and it is obvious that the devil never fails to use anyone who will submit to him. Listen to what Paul said to the church in Galatia.

> *I am astonished that you are so quickly deserting the one who called you by the grace of Christ and are turning to a different gospel which is really no gospel at all. Evidently some people are throwing you into confusion and are trying to pervert the gospel of Christ. **But even if we or an angel from heaven should preach a gospel other than the one we preached to you**, let him be eternally condemned! As we have already said, so now I say again: If anybody is preaching to you a gospel other than what you accepted, let him be eternally condemned! (Galatians 1:6–9)*

With this in mind, those who are in positions of church leadership should wake up and take heed to the Lord's strong warnings.

> *Things that cause people to sin are bound to come, but **woe to that person through whom they come.** It would be better for him to be thrown into the sea with a millstone tied around his neck than for him to cause one of these little ones to sin. **So watch yourselves.** (Luke 17:1–3)*

The strong warning words from the Lord should wake up every pastor, teacher, educator, parent, and anyone who has authority over the flock, and over children.

To spiritually lead someone astray by either deliberately, carelessly or pridefully exposing them to a changed and contaminated gospel is to bring upon oneself the fiercest wrath of the Lord Jesus Christ. *"Woe to that man" (Matthew 18:7)*, Jesus said. By implication physical death by drowning in the bottom of the sea would be preferable for such a person, than finding out what the Lord meant by *"Woe."*

The Messiah did not purchase His Church cheaply. He loves it dearly, and paid a great price for it. How dare anyone mess with His Holy Word—the truth!

One could only wonder how often the thoughts of the Eternal God travels back to that terrible day in the Garden of Gethsemane when His precious Son stared into that cup of inconceivable horror. It brimmed with every form of sin; pride, greed, depravity, disease, sickness, spiritual and physical decay, dishonor, lies, rage, malice, hatred, envy, murder, violence, homosexuality, child abuse, pornography, robbery, arrogance, insolence, faithlessness, love of self, boastfulness, witchcraft, idolatry, and every other type of evil one could ever conceive of.

The Lord Jesus knew He had to drink that terrible cup to the dregs, He knew He had to become sin if we were to be afforded salvation from the horrors of hell. As the agony of His spotless soul increased, Jesus pled,

> *Father, if you are willing, take this cup from me; yet not my will, but yours be done." An angel from heaven appeared to him and strengthened him. And being in anguish, he prayed more earnestly, and his sweat was like drops of blood falling to the ground. (Luke 22:42–44)*

Huge drops of blood spilled off His holy brow, as the Savior determinedly drank fully that detestable cup; the cup imposed upon the human race by Satan the arch deceiver. In the Garden of Gethsemane, Jesus humbly paid the price for the terrible choice that Adam and Eve made in yet another garden so long ago. The Lord also paid with His life for the disastrous choice that all the rest of us make each time we say, *"Not Your will but mine be done."*

Jesus, the holy and sinless One, became sin so that we might be set free. Bearing the whole weight of our guilt and shame, He went silently as a sheep to the slaughter, carrying the heavy cross upon His lacerated and bleeding back. Were the Father, the Holy Spirit and all Heaven agonized as they watched wicked and evil men, for whom Jesus was pouring out His precious life, drive cruel nails into His hands and feet? We can only imagine. What indescribable pain did the Father endure, when all alone upon the Cross of Calvary the parched voice of His only beloved Son cried out? *"My God, my God, why have you forsaken me?" (Matthew 27:46)*

*"Eloi, Eloi, lama sabachthani?"* the Lord cried in His dying breath. No, salvation did not come cheaply! It cost the Creator His very life to reverse the curse and purchase our redemption. Friends, *God does not take lightly the perversion of the Gospel.*

The great and loving gift of salvation from Jesus remains unwrapped by too many churchgoers who continue in darkness, never knowing if what they are hearing from the pulpits is true or not. They do not know or understand that they are responsible to study the Scriptures for themselves, and so they remain blindly dependent on whatever is told to them in their churches. The Lord says, much of what they receive is impure, a brown-bean gospel and so their understanding remains clouded, while all the time the pure Gospel is found in the Bible.

> *For if you confess with your mouth that Jesus is Lord and believe in your heart that God raised him from the dead, you will be saved. For it is by believing in your heart that you are made right with God, and it is by confessing with your mouth that you are saved. . . .Anyone who calls on the name of the Lord will be saved. (Romans 10:9–13)*

This dear friends, is the Gospel in its purest form, but let's listen to something very interesting that Paul said,

> *But how can they call on him to save them unless they believe in him? And how can they believe in him if they have never heard about him? **And how can they hear about him unless someone tells them? And how will anyone go and tell them without being sent?** That is what the Scriptures mean when they say, **"How beautiful are the feet of those who bring good news!** (Romans 10:14-15)*

The distinct qualification according to this Scripture for a preacher of the Gospel is that *he or she must be sent by the Lord.* The question then arises, has everyone who is preaching today actually been sent by the Lord, or are there some in the field who have never really been sent by Him? Are some of those who are preaching doing it for some reason other than obedience to the Great Commission? If this is the case then it is logical to conclude that these would also be the ones who are leading many astray by preaching a tarnished and contaminated gospel.

Jesus warned,

> ***Watch out for false prophets, they come to you in sheep's clothing, but inwardly they are ferocious wolves. By their fruit you will recognize them.*** *Do people pick grapes from thorn bushes or figs from thistles? Likewise every good tree bears good fruit, but a bad tree bears bad fruit. A good tree cannot bear bad fruit and a bad tree cannot bear good fruit. Every tree that does not bear good fruit is cut down and thrown into the fire. Thus, by their fruit you will recognize them.* (Matthew 7:15–20)

How lovingly the Lord speaks of those who truly preach His Word! *"How beautiful are the feet of those who bring good news!" (Romans 10:15)*

The Bible speaks of Jesus washing the feet of the ones He personally trained, commissioned, and sent to take the Gospel to the entire world. Could it just be that in addition to teaching humility and care for each other to the disciples, that the Messiah was also laying His loving, cleansing touch and eternal blessing upon them, by placing His hands on their feet and so preparing them to go and preach the pure and holy Gospel to all the world? These disciples would be bloodied, beaten, and put to death for the purity of the Gospel they preached.

> *After washing their feet, he put on his robe again and sat down and asked, "Do you **understand** what I was doing? You call me 'Teacher' and 'Lord,' and you are right, because it is true. **And since I, the Lord and Teacher, have washed your feet, you ought to wash each other's feet. I have given you an example to follow. Do as I have done to you.** How true it is that a servant is not greater than the master. **Nor are messengers more important than the one who sends them. You know these things—now do them! That is the path of blessing.** (John 13:12–17)*

While washing each other's feet speaks of humility and love for one another, clean feet symbolizes a purified walk. An amazing dialogue ensued between Jesus and Peter as the Lord attempted to wash Peter's feet. Understandably Peter could not conceive of his Lord and Master washing his feet. Let's take a look at how this conversation unfolded.

> *When he [Jesus] came to Simon Peter, Peter said to him, "Lord, why are you going to wash my feet?" Jesus replied, "You don't **understand** now why I am doing it; someday you will." "No," Peter protested, "you will*

never wash my feet!" *Jesus replied, "But if I don't wash you, you won't belong to me."* Simon Peter exclaimed, "Then wash my hands and head as well, Lord, not just my feet!" Jesus replied, *"A person who has bathed all over does not need to wash, except for the feet, to be entirely clean. And you are clean, but that isn't true of everyone here."* For Jesus knew who would betray him. That is what he meant when he said, *"Not all of you are clean. (John 13:6–11)*

Jesus said, *"A person who has bathed all over does not need to wash, **except for the feet, to be entirely clean.*** What does a person's feet represent, except for his or her walk? *As it is written, "How beautiful are the feet of those who bring good news!" (Romans 10:15)*

The Lord said *"Not all of you are clean"* because He knew the one who would betray Him. Judas betrayed Jesus for a measly thirty pieces of silver. He asked the Pharisees, *"What are you willing to give me if I hand him over to you?" So they counted out for him thirty silver coins. From then on Judas watched for an opportunity to hand him [Jesus] over"* (Matthew 26:15–16). Judas' walk was as spiritually unclean as his physical feet were. His feet were certainly not beautiful in the eyes of the Lord.

What do modern-day preachers receive in exchange for preaching a tainted, brown-bean gospel? Not unlike Judas, the answer is all too often, money, fame, and power. This is the very antithesis of the humble heart Jesus modeled. It is also the very opposite of the clean walk symbolized by the washed feet of His disciples. The Lord has had many betrayers, and this speaks for itself because so many preach a gospel that is impure and mixed with falsehood—for the very same thing that motivated Judas. Unfortunately, at this moment the numbers of pulpits that are filled with men and women who daringly declare a corrupt word is on the rise. The Lord warned us of this great falling away. *And many false prophets will appear and will lead many people astray. Sin* will be rampant everywhere, **and the love of many will grow cold** *(Matthew 24:11–12).*

Obviously some preachers start off doing what is right and end up going wrong. Within the professing Church there are at least four categories of those who preach.

1. First and rightly so, are those who have yielded to the distinct call of the Lord. With much prayer they continue to submit to the Holy Spirit teaching the flock the pure unadulterated Word of God. They rightly divide the Word of Truth and prepare God's people for the Kingdom of Heaven. Paul says it this way: *"to prepare God's people for works of service, so that the body of Christ may be built up until we all reach unity in the faith and in the knowledge of the Son of God and become mature, attaining to the whole measure of the fullness of Christ"* *(Ephesians 4:12–13).*

2. Next would be those who teach God's Word, but do it only partially because of unwillingness to recognize and yield to the Holy Spirit who guides us into all Truth. Paul warned, *"Do not put out the Spirit's fire; do not treat prophecies with contempt"* *(1 Thessalonians 5:19).* Paul warns that to reject the Holy Spirit's supernatural manifestations of tongues, prophesy, or other gifts would cause the loss of His Presence.

3. Then there are others who have bound themselves to the traditions of men. Jesus said,

*"And so, by your own tradition, you nullify the direct commandment of God. You hypocrites! Isaiah was prophesying about you when he said, 'These people honor me with their lips, but their hearts are far away.* ***Their worship is a farce, for they replace God's commands with their own man-made teachings"*** *(Matthew 15:6–9).*

4. Finally there are those false teachers who are wolves in sheep's clothing as Jesus referred

them. Not unlike the Pharisees these people are full of greed and self-indulgence, having a form of Godliness but denying the power thereof. They deny the doctrine of Jesus Christ and the authority of God's Holy Word. They add to the Word messages from false religions deliberately altering the Scriptures; they take the name of LORD out of His own Word and insert the names of false deities in its place. Paul severely warned, *"For such men are false apostles, deceitful workmen, masquerading as apostles of Christ. And no wonder, for Satan himself masquerades as an angel of light. It is not surprising then, if his servants masquerade as servants of righteousness. Their end will be what their actions deserve"* (2 Corinthians 11:13–15).

Wake up friends; can you tell a true shepherd from the wolf in sheep's clothing? The coming of the Lord's is very near. The Lord loves you so much, are you ready?

Be extremely careful to make sure the Gospel you are hearing in your church does agree with the Holy Bible. If this is not the case, ask the Lord to show you where He wants you to be and make haste, flee from where you are to the church to which the Lord leads you. Now continue to heed Paul's admonition,

*Examine yourselves, to see whether you are in the faith; test yourselves. Do you not realize that Christ Jesus is in you . . . unless, of course, you fail the test!* (2 Corinthians 13:5)

Wake up friend, get ready, the time is at hand!

# Chapter 7

# THE BIBLE AND THE CLAW

―∞∞∞―

This time a Bible with a dazzling white cover appeared before me. It lay open on a plain wooden table. The setting was an empty room with bare walls. In this room standing right next to the wooden table was a huge device that looked like a giant boom from an excavator. The mechanical contraption was fitted with a claw-like device. I could see that this iron claw had within its grasp some pages from the mid-section of the white Bible which lay on the table. The claw held up these few pages, but it was difficult to say with accuracy how many Books might have been in the grip of this thing. It could have been anywhere from about 1 Chronicles through Matthew. The rest of the Bible from Genesis to 1 Chronicles and again from Mark through the Book of Revelation rested untouched on the table.

I didn't quite understand what this meant and like each time previously the Lord Jesus enlightened me. Very simply He said, "The huge mechanical arm represents the section of the professing church that specializes in using only small parts of the Word of God." The Lord said, "They twist and manipulate even these little bits of Scripture to suit their own ends, and so they are very far from the Truth." "As you have noticed from the claw," He continued, "they left out the beginning and the end of the Bible; The Alpha and the Omega, the First and Last, which are two of my other names. They purposely twist the reason I came to earth and the truths of God's saving grace that come only through Me, Jesus. When they leave out the beginning of the Bible, they get rid of dealing with the sin factor, and when they leave the end out, they side-step the consequences of sin. This then automatically makes my sacrifice on the cross of no value. This again is why they deny that I actually died on the cross and that I rose up from the dead. To those who do not know the Word, these false teachers appear to know the Scriptures and to be following Me, but in reality they are not."

The explanation Jesus gave me regarding the mechanical claw and its operations is not much different from things He said while He was on earth. As we can see the Lord made some serious charges against the religious leaders of His day. "Jesus said,

*Woe to you, experts in the Law, because **you have taken away the key to knowledge. You yourselves have not entered, and you have hindered those who are entering.** (Luke 11:52)*

This is a very grave charge, considering that it came from the Lord Himself. Despite the Lord's strong condemnation of the experts of the Law in His day, this again seems to be a prevalent problem in the church today. Once again many of the current leaders are deliberately taking away the key to knowledge—the key being the Holy Spirit. Even though the Bible is explicit and the Words of Jesus are plain to read, these luminaries remove themselves from submission to God's Holy Spirit. Obviously they do not have a saving relationship with Jesus and through their false teachings they hinder those who are attempting to enter in. How great is this sin!

The Apostle Paul in his letter to the Romans said,

*Well then, what shall we say about these things? Just this: The Gentiles have been made right with God by faith, even though they were not seeking him. But the Jews, who tried so hard to get right with God by*

*keeping the law, never succeeded. Why not? Because they were trying to get right with God by keeping the law and being good instead of by depending on faith. They stumbled over the great rock in their path. God warned them of this in the Scriptures when he said,* **"I am placing a stone in Jerusalem that causes people to stumble, and a rock that makes them fall. But anyone who believes in him will not be disappointed.** *(Romans 9:30–33)*

Jesus Christ is the stone over which Israel stumbled; He is also the stone over which all those who choose their own ways of wisdom and traditions will stumble as well. Jesus Christ *is* the Rock that causes the prideful to fall.

Jesus said of Satan, the ultimate prideful one, *"I saw Satan fall like lightning from heaven" (Luke 10:18–19).* Just as the religious leaders of Israel fell when they disbelieved God's Word and rejected the Living Word, so will those of the twenty-first-century church who tamper with God's holy Word.

Are not these false teachers the "tares" Jesus warned about? He said they would enter in, rise to leadership and corrupt the church.

*But there were also false prophets among the people,* ***just as there will be false teachers among you. They will secretly introduce destructive heresies, even denying the sovereign Lord who bought them- bringing swift destruction on themselves.*** *Many will follow their shameful ways and will bring the way of truth into disrepute. In their greed these teachers will exploit you with stories they have made up. Their condemnation has long been hanging over them, and their destruction has not been sleeping. (2 Peter 2:1–3)*

Jesus said,

*. . . The kingdom of heaven is like a man who sowed good seed in his field; **but while men slept, his enemy came and sowed tares among the wheat and went his way.** (Matthew 13:24–25)*

The phrase, *"While men slept"* should sound a warning alarm to the church. *Sleeping in the Kingdom of God would be the same as being ignorant of His Word.* It is the lazy and complacent, the spiritually sluggish who provide the perfect entry-way for the enemy to slip in and plant tares—men and women, who mix the Truth with falsehood while giving the appearance of being wheat. Paul warns, *"So then, let us not be like others, who are asleep, but let us be alert and self-controlled." (1 Thessalonians 5:6).*

Many of these false teachers lead assemblies with congregations that number in the thousands. This also means that many thousands of people from these assemblies have no real understanding of the Truth of God's Word. They have no standard against which to measure the messages they hear. They lack discernment because they do not know the Scriptures and so are gullible. They simply receive the corrupted gospel that is preached to them. Of course, many of them are in these churches because they agree with the premise of the false teacher. Jesus once said to the Sadducees, *"You are in error because you do not know the Scriptures or the power of God" (Matthew 22:29).*

The Bible is clear; we have a responsibility to watch what we receive to see if it lines up with the Scriptures. The Holy Spirit made a point to compliment the Bereans for their diligence.

*Now the Bereans were of more noble character than the Thessalonians, for they received the message with great eagerness and examined the Scriptures every day to see if what Paul said was true. (Acts 17:11)*

Contrary to the glowing appraisal of the Bereans, Jesus had this to say of the Pharisees, who were leading people astray,

*Every plant which My heavenly Father has not planted will be uprooted. Let them alone. They are blind leaders of the blind. And if the blind leads the blind, both will fall into a ditch. (Matthew 15:13–14)*

If this was true for the Pharisees it would also be true for all present-day false teachers and their followers, unless they correct the error of their ways. God's love is great and He invites whosoever will to turn and come to Him.

Within this giant religious organization referred to as the Church, are the works of many that are not of righteousness, faith, and justice. It is common to hear preachers deny the justice of God while attributing the "love only" theory to Him. This great deception alone leads multitudes to continue in a lifestyle of sin with no need for repentance. Those who blindly follow these twisted and incorrect renditions of the Scripture continue in their sins, because they choose to believe that a loving God will not bring punishment upon them for their rebellion against Him. This is a blatant contradiction of God's holy Word. They choose to see Almighty God as being weak and indulgent and in doing so, they substitute for themselves a god of their own making. This is not the righteous and holy God of the Bible.

Listen to what John said:

*I saw heaven standing open and there before me was a white horse, whose rider is called Faithful and True. **With justice he judges and makes war.** His eyes are like blazing fire, and on his head are many crowns. (Revelation 19:11–12)*

It might do us all good to wake up and take a second look at the Lord Jesus who returns to judge with justice and make war. This time He will not be the humble Savior who walked the planet two thousand years ago. He will not appear in humility and lowliness riding on a donkey, but as the Righteous Judge, upon a white horse. His title will be the Word of God and from His mouth will appear a sharp sword. His eyes will be like blazing fire and upon His head will be many crowns. He will appear as *King of kings and Lord of lords (Revelation 19:16)*.

The writer of the Hebrew letter clearly defines the judgments of the Lord for those who continue in sin. It is obvious from this Scripture that God is not the benignly lenient and permissive being, who looks the other way when people deliberately violate His Word. Let's read this Scripture very carefully.

> ***If we deliberately keep on sinning after we have received the knowledge of the truth, no sacrifice for sins is left,*** *but only a fearful expectation of judgment and of raging fire that will consume the enemies of God. Anyone who rejected the law of Moses died without mercy on the testimony of two or three witnesses.* ***How much more severely do you think a man deserves to be punished who has trampled the Son of God under foot, who has treated as an unholy thing the blood of the covenant that sanctified him, and who has insulted the Spirit of grace?*** *For we know him who said, "It is mine to avenge; I will repay," and again,* ***"The Lord will judge his people." It is a dreadful thing to fall into the hands of the living God.*** *(Hebrews 10:26–31)*

Churches that openly ordain homosexuals into ministry, wink at fornication and adultery, turn a blind eye to abortion, treating these sins as non-issues and acts that require no accountability of any sort, are playing a very dangerous game. Pastors of these same Churches seldom or never extend an altar call inviting the lost to come to Jesus. Theologians of this mindset have gone so far as to deny the deity of the Lord Jesus Christ, the Virgin Birth, and the Resurrection. It is not uncommon at all to hear lukewarm Christians from such congregations blaspheming the Holy name of the Lord by using it as a swear or cuss word. They still refer to themselves as Christians of course.

The Apostle Peter stated,

*But there are those false prophets among the people, just as there will be false teachers among you.* ***They will secretly introduce destructive heresies, even denying the sovereign LORD who bought them. Bringing swift destruction on themselves. Many will follow their shameful ways and will bring the Way of Truth into disrepute. In their greed these teachers will exploit you with stories they have made up.*** *Their condemnation has long been hanging over them, and their destruction has not been sleeping. (2 Peter 2:1–3)*

Just as Satan has always done, he still continues to use false prophets and teachers to deceive many from within the church. The devil's greatest ambition is to hurt the Lord Jesus who loved and gave His life for us.

Going back to the scene where I saw the white Bible upon the table: it was very significant that the beginning of the Bible and the end of it lay untouched by the claw. Jesus Christ is the Beginning and the End. He is the Alpha and the Omega as John the Apostle called Him. Little wonder, the claw—a tool of the enemy, would have no desire to touch the Beginning and the End of God's Word.

Everyone who teaches that God's love nullifies His justice should carefully read the Words of the Lord Jesus Himself.

*He* [Jesus] *said to me:* ***"It is done. I am the Alpha and the Omega, the Beginning and the End.*** *To him who is thirsty I will give to drink without cost from the spring of the water of life. He who overcomes will inherit all this, and I will be his God and he will be my son.* ***But the***

**cowardly, the unbelieving, the vile, the murderers, the sexually immoral, those who practice magic arts, the idolaters and all liars-their place will be in the fiery lake of burning sulfur. This is the second death.** *(Revelation 21:6–8)*

As we can see from this Scripture, the presumption of an all-loving God, who excuses sin, is a great falsehood.

As mentioned earlier, all those symbolized by the claw who teach heresy as truth, are leading multitudes into error of the gravest sort. This claw not only signifies the ones who deny Jesus Christ as the only way of salvation, but it is also emblematic of all who deny the existence of hell and eternal judgment for everyone who refuses a saving relationship with the Lord. All who discredit the atoning Blood of Jesus Christ on the cross, the Rapture and the Second Coming of the Lord, and those who contradict the very identity of God the Father, are included in this picture. Certainly such preachers would not desire to touch the Beginning and the End of God's holy Word, the Alpha and the Omega, the Aleph and the Tav—Jesus Christ, because they would have too much to contend with.

Yet the Lord, in His great and awesome love has something to say to all these misguided and deceived people, and it would be in their own best interests to pay careful attention.

*I am God, and there is none like me.* **I make known the end from the beginning, from ancient times, what is still to come.** *I say:* **My purpose will stand, and I will do all that I please.** *From the east I summon a bird of prey; from a far-off land, a man to fulfill my purpose. What I have said, that will I bring about; what I have planned, that will I do.* **Listen to me, you stubborn-hearted, you who are far from righteousness. I am bringing my righteousness near, it is not far away; and my salvation will not be delayed.** *(Isaiah 46:9–13)*

If you are a member of a church such as we have described, you are reading this book, and you feel concerned for your eternal security, then you are thirsty and the Lord invites you to come to Him and receive the Water of Life without cost. If you do, you will overcome the sin in your life and inherit all the blessings of the Lord. Along with all others who have come to Him in spirit and truth, you will receive His special promise to be your God, and you will be His son or daughter.

The ones who deny Christ are those who have not overcome sin because they have chosen to justify the things they do. The Bible alerts us that perilous times are ahead for those choose the lifestyles and mind-sets listed by Timothy in this next Scripture.

> **There will be terrible times in the last days. People will be lovers of themselves,** *lovers of money, boastful, proud, abusive, disobedient to their parents, ungrateful, unholy, without love, unforgiving, slanderous, without self-control, brutal, not lovers of the good, treacherous, rash, conceited,* **lovers of pleasure rather than lovers of God-having a form of godliness but denying its power. Have nothing to do with them.** *(2 Timothy 3:1–5)*

The Bible declares that all liars will have their place in the fiery lake of burning sulfur, so we might then ask who the greatest liars would be. The answer of course is, the ones who profess to be followers of Jesus Christ and yet deny His Word, and teach others to do so as well.

If the Truth of this Book offends anyone, let it be said, that while this is not the purpose, *it is also not intended to cause someone living the kind of lifestyle mentioned above to feel good, but to jolt that person into the reality of Truth before it is too late.* It is my prayer that many will have their eyes opened and turn to the Lord in repentance and humility and be saved. Jesus loves so us greatly and is so eager to save!

*To him who is thirsty I will give to drink without cost from the spring of the water of life. He who overcomes will inherit all this, and I will be his God and he will be my son. (Revelation 21:6–7)*

It does not matter that the massive body symbolized by the giant claw, identifies itself as the Church; it will not be recognized by Jesus Christ as His Bride as long as it is not in obedience to Him.

If you are reading this book and have come this far, and you realize that you have been feeling uncomfortable in the church you presently attend because of the actions and words of the leadership regarding Jesus Christ or the Bible, it is time for you to sit up and do something about it.

If your church does not believe the Bible as the absolute inerrant Word of God, and if they deny the Truth of any part of it, RUN! and don't stop running until, with God's help, you find a church that loves, honors and obeys Jesus Christ as Lord and Savior, a church that believes the Bible as God's Holy Word and submits to the Holy Spirit.

If you are feeling spiritually starved in your church and you recognize that some or all of the things we discussed are true of your particular leadership, know that the Holy Spirit is speaking to you.

The Holy Spirit is God, and He is trying to draw you towards a living and vibrant body of believers that is being shepherded by a Bible-believing Pastor. Remember your eternal destination depends upon your decision to believe and obey the Lord Jesus or to deny Him. If you hear His call and choose to ignore it, you will receive the same judgment as all those who remain and adhere to the teachings of the false church referred to above. Having belonged to that organization will not get you into Heaven. In fact you will miss Heaven because you chose to identify with the error they taught. So please listen to the voice of the Holy Spirit and do as He leads.

There will be no acceptable excuse on the day of the Lord. All those who have allowed sin to rule and overtake them, and have sought refuge in places that twisted the precious Word of God, will have done so at their own peril, as will the teachers of any gospel different to the one Jesus and the Apostles taught. The Lord said, He will say to people such as these "I don't *know you or where you come from. Away from me, all you evildoers!" (Luke 13:27)*

Ministers who have feared the dissatisfaction and disapproval of their flock above that of the Lord's and have spoken lies and words of deception, thereby lulling the hearers into a sense of false security so that they never turn from their sins, have no real love, loyalty, or fear for the Lord Jesus, the Beginning and the End. These men and women will not be guiltless of the blood of the ones they misguided and led astray. Paul said,

*Therefore I declare to you today that I am innocent of the blood of all men. For I have not hesitated to proclaim to you the whole will of God. (Acts 20:26-27)*

Paul was sincerely able to say this of himself. Take a prayerful look at what several Biblical writers had to say on this subject. The acts of twisting, manipulating, changing, adding to, and taking away from God's Word have deadly consequences.

Jude said of these false teachers:

*Dear friends, although I was very eager to write to you about the salvation we share, I felt I had to write and urge you to contend for the faith that was once for all entrusted to the saints. For certain men whose condemnation was written about long ago have secretly slipped in among you. They are godless men, who change the grace of our God into a license for immorality and deny Jesus Christ our only Sovereign and Lord. (Jude 3–4)*

Paul said,

*But even if we or an angel from heaven should preach a gospel other than the one we preached to you, let him be eternally condemned. As we have already said, so now I say again: if anybody is preaching to you a gospel other than what you accepted, let him be eternally condemned. (Galatians 1:8–9)*

John said,

*But the cowardly, the unbelieving, the vile, the murderers, the sexually immoral, those who practice magic arts, the idolaters and all liars-their place will be in the fiery lake of burning sulfur. This is the second death." (Rev 21:8)*

Paul said,

*Do you not know that the wicked will not inherit the Kingdom of God? Do not be deceived. Neither the sexually immoral nor idolaters nor adulterers nor male prostitutes nor homosexual offenders, nor thieves not the greedy nor drunkards nor slanderers nor swindlers, will inherit the Kingdom of God. (1 Corinthians 6:9–10)*

If you are a pastor, be careful that you do not cause any person with the sinful issues mentioned in the verses above to think that their spiritual condition is okay; please tell them the truth and lead them to repentance and forgiveness; and obey the Lord Jesus Christ.

Regardless of what we hear in our churches, each of us has a responsibility to study God's Word for ourselves so as to find out if what we are being taught is true. Paul said:

*Be diligent to present yourself approved to God, a worker who does not need to be ashamed, rightly dividing the word of truth. (2 Timothy 2:15)*

Jesus said:

**As for the person who hears my words but does not keep them,** *I do not judge him. For I did not come to judge the world, but to save it.* **There is a judge for the one who rejects me and does not accept my words; that very word which I spoke will condemn him at the last day.** *For I did not speak of my own accord, but the Father who sent me commanded me what to say and how to say it. I know that his command leads to eternal life.* **So whatever I say is just what the Father has told me to say.** *(John 12:47–50)*

*Dear friends, do not let anyone deceive you.* Eternity is too long a time in which to finally discover that you were misled. Hell would also be the wrong place in which to wake up to the fact that God's Word was right all along and you never obeyed it.

*Wake up, beloved, the time is at hand.* Keep your eyes and ears open in your church. Be very careful to note if Jesus is being glorified as God's only Son and Savior. Is Jesus received as Immanuel—God with us? Are the Virgin Birth, the death, burial, resurrection, and ascension of Jesus Christ believed and taught as absolute truth? Is salvation through Jesus Christ *alone* preached in your church, or are you being taught that there are many ways to heaven? Is anyone or anything added to or taken away from this eternal truth? Is the Bible believed to be the absolute, inerrant Word of God and His final instruction to us? Be careful and observant and do not hesitate to leave the church you are in, if any of these thing are not so.

At the risk of redundancy let me reiterate, leave immediately and go to a church where Jesus is honored as Lord and

Savior and the Son of the Living God. Receive Him into your heart, begin to study your Bible daily, obey the Scriptures and trust the Holy Spirit to lead you into all truth as you study. *Tell others about Jesus, and be sure that when the Lord comes to take His Church home your name will be in the Lamb's Book of Life.*

The time is at hand and the Lord could come today! Wake up and be blessed.

# Chapter 8

# THE ARM OF THE LORD

⸺◦⸰⸰◦⸺

I was next permitted to see the mighty arm of the Lord Jesus Christ. He appeared huge in stature, and He was great and awesome. It was impossible to miss the extreme strength of His mighty right arm. As I watched closely to see what was going to happen, the Lord reached out His powerful hand toward the massive boom with the claw-like structure that I had previously seen holding up the mid-section pages from the Bible. Jesus grasped a large circular controlling device which was attached to this boom and shut it off with unmistakable and total finality.

It wasn't difficult to see that the Lord was greatly displeased with this huge mechanized contraption and everything that it represented. "Enough is enough!" His action seemed to say. Obviously the time had come for Jesus Christ to take control, and with one turn of the knob, the power of this monster was permanently shut down by the Lord. This could only mean one thing; every so-called church organization represented by this perfunctory giant had come to its end. Jesus made me understand that He had shut them down and no man could ever revive them again. My mind immediately went to the Church at Ephesus and the warning words He had spoken to them.

*Remember the height from which you have fallen!*
***Repent and do the things you did at first, if you***

**do not repent, I will come to you and remove your Lampstand from its place.** *(Revelation 2:5)*

The church of Jesus Christ is required by the Messiah to be a light to the world. However, when a light-giver loses its light, it becomes of no use. A quick Google search will reveal the massive numbers of church closings on a yearly basis. To the world this might appear to be caused by various and diverse reasons, but from what Jesus showed me it became frighteningly clear that it is really He who is shutting them down. The question is, why?

The Lord answered this mental inquiry of mine by leading me to the words He commanded Jeremiah to speak to the shepherds of Israel.

**Woe to the shepherds who are destroying and scattering the sheep of my pasture!"** *declares the* **LORD.** *Therefore this is what the LORD, the God of Israel, says to the shepherds who tend my people: "Because you have scattered my flock and driven them away and have not bestowed care on them, I will bestow punishment on you for the evil you have done," declares the LORD."***I myself will gather the remnant of my flock out of all the countries where I have driven them and will bring them back to their pasture, where they will be fruitful and increase in number. I will place shepherds over them who will tend them, and they will no longer be afraid or terrified, nor will any be missing,** *declares the LORD.* *(Jeremiah 23:1–4)*

Just as it was necessary for the shepherds of Israel to be obedient and faithful servants of God, it also takes men and women *of obedience and integrity* to shepherd the Church of Jesus Christ.

Pastors who love the Lord, who honor Him and teach His Word truthfully, and are good and faithful servants of the Lord, are a blessing from God and we should never forget to give thanks and praise to God for them. However, it is becoming increasingly hard to miss the parallel between the evil shepherds Jeremiah addressed, and the increasing number of false teachers today.

Many times leaders of both large and small churches today do not know where to turn for answers to the problems of their congregants. These leaders do not have answers because they really don't know God. They simply do not believe His Holy Word. Consequently the emptiness and void within the hurting masses begin to explode in frustration, bitterness, and hopelessness. As a result many of these people give up and drift off into New Age ideas and heresies; they blindly dabble about in the occult, witchcraft, yoga, and the like, trying to find answers to their misery.

They look to the stars and celestial bodies for help; they go to palm-readers or worship the earth and are spiritually no better off than those who have totally and openly rejected the Lord by calling themselves atheists. At least the professed atheists declare themselves not to believe in God, but these unfortunate people are in a state of complete confusion. Many people consider themselves to be Christians while messing around with the occult.

The Lord told Jeremiah that the leaders of Judah would be destroyed, and the people sent into exile for these same sins. Unless the Lord is unjust and He certainly is not, this is exactly what will happen and is actually happening to the false teachers of this postmodern era as well. Any person being shepherded by men such as these, is either knowingly or unknowingly living in a state of spiritual exile. When someone chooses to believe false doctrine he or she becomes instantly guilty of rejecting the Son of God whose title is *the Word of God.* "*He* [Jesus] *is dressed in a robe dipped in blood, **and his name is the Word of God**" (Revelation 19:13).* Because they have rejected parts of the Bible, great numbers of professing evangelicals do not even believe that Jesus Christ is *the* only way to salvation. No matter that Jesus Himself declared, *"I* *am the way and the truth and the life. No one comes to the Father except through me" (John 14:6–7).*

God's great love and compassion for the damaged and hurting sheep of Israel of whom Jeremiah spoke is quite apparent. The fact that He would gather them from all the places to where they had been exiled and bring them back home is proof of this. While Jeremiah was primarily referring to the Jewish people, his warning certainly has its application for today. Jeremiah said the Lord would bring the hurting ones back to a pasture where they would be fruitful and increase in number. No doubt this would also be true for the lost and hurting sheep within these false churches. While the false teachers will not go unpunished, the Lord Jesus will gather those who will be saved from the different denominations and churches that have led them astray and bring them into gatherings where faithful shepherds teach the pure, unadulterated and wholesome Word of God. These great men and women who boldly proclaim the Truth, while binding up the broken-hearted and setting the captives free in the name of the Lord Jesus, will find their churches being filled with hungry sheep who are ready to receive the Bread of Life.

The Word of the Lord that came through Jeremiah carries a strong and chilling warning to the false teachers of today as it did in the day of Jeremiah,

*Weep and wail, you shepherds, roll in the dust, you leaders of the flock. For your time to be slaughtered has come; you will fall and be shattered like fine pottery. The shepherds will have nowhere to flee, the leaders of the flock no place to escape. Hear the cry of the shepherds, the wailing of the leaders of the flock, for the LORD is destroying their pasture. The peaceful meadows will be laid waste because of the fierce anger of the LORD. Like a lion He will leave His lair, and their land will become desolate because of the sword of the oppressor, and because of the LORD'S fierce anger. (Jeremiah 25:34–37)*

The Bible is more than clear. *"Jesus Christ is the same yesterday and today and forever" (Hebrews 13:8, NIV).* All those who have taken liberties with God's Word, while choosing to teach false doctrines should repent and turn away from their sins while there still is time. God is merciful and forgiving, but they will not be held guiltless by the Son of God if they do not repent.

Every faithful believer should remember this one thing. Faithfulness comes with a price. Just as Jesus and His disciples were constantly persecuted by the religious leaders and Pharisees, those who are faithful today can also expect to be continuously attacked and opposed. All who persevere in teaching the Truth in loving obedience to the Lord Jesus and His Word will suffer opposition and persecution for the sake of their faith. We see it happening right now, and it is vitally important for all faithful believers to continue steadfastly in prayer and petition before our Heavenly Father.

As we know, the author and instigator of all harassment directed towards the Church of Jesus Christ is the devil himself, and so we will see this persecution continue to happen. The faithful will be lied about, ridiculed, and harassed until Jesus comes back in all His power and glory to take His radiant church home. The Lord warned. *"All men will hate you because of me, but he who stands firm to the end will be saved" (Matthew 10:21–22).*

Dear friends, it is the urgent responsibility of every true believer to pray faithfully and continually for each other. We must pray specifically and daily, interceding for our brothers and sisters in Christ and those in leadership over us. We *must* pray for the Church.

Jesus spoke candidly to everyone who would follow Him,

**A student is not greater than his teacher, nor a servant above his** *master. It is enough for a student to be like his teacher, and a servant like his master.* **If the head of the house has been called Beelzebub, how much more the members of his household!**

*So do not be afraid of them. There is nothing con-cealed that will not be disclosed, or hidden that will not be made known. What I tell you in the dark, speak in the daylight; what was whispered in your ear, proclaim from the roofs. Do not be afraid of those who kill the body but cannot kill the soul. Rather be afraid of the one who can destroy both soul and body in hell. (Matthew 10:24–28)*

The Lord gave this awesome promise to everyone who remains faithful in service to Him.

*All authority in heaven and on earth has been given to me. Therefore go and make disciples of all nations, baptizing them in the name of the Father and of the Son and of the Holy Spirit, and teaching them to obey everything I have commanded you. And surely I am with you always, to the very end of the age. (Matt 28:18–20)*

How comforting it is to know that Jesus is *"surely"* with us as we faithfully spread the Gospel. The key to having His constant presence in our lives is faithfulness to the Lord and obedience to His teaching and commission.

As for the unfaithful church, the fingerprints of Satan are all over this organization. The prints of the enemy are well camouflaged, just as the leaders of the apostate churches are. While carnality, hypocrisy, and every other ungodly thing is present, these organizations still continue to pose as the Church of Jesus Christ, but the polarization of the Church is becoming more obvious daily. Jesus warned,

*Watch out for false prophets. They come to you in sheep's clothing, but inwardly they are ferocious wolves. By their fruit you will recognize them. (Matthew 7:15–16)*

*"By their fruit"* Jesus said, *"you will know them."* It certainly is their fruit that's exposing them. Their fruit is the changed and distorted word they disseminate, combined with their corresponding lifestyles. Their fruit comes from the *tree of the knowledge of good and evil.*

What did Satan do as he worked on Eve to partake of the forbidden fruit? He altered God's Word by adding to it. The deceiver continues to make one appeal after another to the carnality of men and women. He whets the appetites of self-indulgent people with dainty morsels of untruth, in his diabolical quest to keep as many as possible out of the Church Jesus built. The Lord shed His precious Blood for all, and His love is great, but it is only those who humbly believe His Word and receive His precious gift of salvation that belong to Him. No wonder Jesus made this amazing statement:

> **Not everyone who says to me, 'Lord, Lord,' will enter the kingdom of heaven, but only he who does the will of my Father who is in heaven.** *Many will say to me on that day, 'Lord, Lord, did we not prophesy in your name, and in your name drive out demons and perform many miracles?' Then I will tell them plainly, 'I never knew you. Away from me, you evildoers!' (Matt 7:21–23)*

"Being tolerant" is a popular term thrown around by the elites. Unfortunately it has become the phrase of the day, even in the church. It is just another approach to the mushy "love and respect" lingo that embraces the actions of those who are in complete violation and rebellion to the Word of God. The Bible tells us, *"You who love the LORD, hate evil!" (Psalm 97:10).* To agree with or embrace things and behaviors that are diametrically opposed to Scriptures in the name of tolerance, does not place a person on the same side as Jesus Christ.

Those who do not have a personal relationship with the Savior, choose to believe the lie of tolerance and live their lives from this viewpoint. It is impossible to condone lifestyles that God specifically forbids in His Word and still be in agreement with Him. Amos asks the million-dollar question, *"Can two walk together, unless they are agreed?" (Amos 3:3)*

The Bible declares,

*Let those who love the LORD hate evil, for He guards the lives of the faithful ones and delivers them from the hand of the wicked. (Psalm 97:10)*

We are told, *"Hate what is evil, cling to what is good" (Romans 12:9)*. We are to hate the sin, *not the sinner.* All who claim to love the Lord will be tested by how much we hate evil and love good. The Scriptures are clear and the choice is ours. Every true believer in Christ who is filled with the Holy Spirit will automatically hate the things Jesus hates and love the things He loves. The Bible says concerning Jesus,

*You have loved righteousness and hated wickedness; therefore God, your God, has set you above your companions by anointing you with the oil of joy. (Hebrews 1:9–10)*

Anyone who takes a stand against the God's Word in any way, chooses to agree with the devil. Jesus said to the Pharisees,

*If God were your Father, you would love me, for I came from God and now am here. I have not come on my own; but he sent me. **Why is my language not clear to you? Because you are unable to hear what I say. You belong to your father, the devil, and you want to carry out your father's desire. He was a murderer from the beginning, not holding to the truth, for there is no truth in him. When he lies, he speaks his native language, for he is a liar and the father of lies. Yet because I tell the truth, you do not*** *believe me! Can any of you prove me guilty of sin? If I am telling the truth, why don't you believe me? **He who belongs to God hears what God says. The reason you do not hear is that you do not belong to God.** (John 8:42–47)*

The great counterfeit church, represented by the huge mechanical arm-like structure that I saw, is also the one that will not hear what God says. It is this huge machine, comprised of all the false churches that the Mighty Hand of Jesus moved against in my vision. I saw the Lord cutting off power to this the huge apostate body. The Messiah said, *"Every tree that does not bear good fruit is cut down and thrown into the fire" (Matthew 7:19).* As we know contaminated seed can only bring forth one thing: bad fruit. Those who know God's Word will find it possible to identify the false church from the true one. Jesus said very plainly, *"By their fruit your will recognize them" (Matthew 7:20).*

Churches that have fallen away from the Truth through theological apostasy and rebellion against the teachings of the Lord Jesus and His apostles will appear to thrive for awhile. As the Lord warned, there will be many false teachers. Countless professing believers will accept the so-called new revelations taught by them. The emergent church exemplifies this. The blending of New Age doctrines and other false religions with Christianity is deplorable, but it is the order of the day in these so-called churches. The Lord predicted,

*At that time many will turn away from the faith and will betray and hate each other, **and many false prophets will appear and deceive many people.** Because of the increase of wickedness the love of most will grow cold. **But he who stands firm to the end will be saved.** (Matthew 24:10-12)*

Despite all the subtle maneuvers of the devil, and the one important fact that these modern-day false prophets have forgotten, *the Church belongs to Jesus and the faithful Church built by Jesus Christ will stand, because Jesus said, "upon this rock I will build my church; and the gates of hell shall not prevail against it" (Matthew 16:18).* The rock Jesus referred to was Peter's confession and the subsequent confessions of everyone who truly believes and lives by the truth of this profound God given revelation, *"Thou art the Christ, the Son of the living God" (Matthew 16:16).*

What a glorious day the faithful remnant church has to look forward to—the day when Jesus Christ comes to receive His Bride. The Bible tells us,

> *For the Lord himself will come down from heaven, with a loud command, with the voice of the archangel and with the trumpet call of God, and the dead in Christ will rise first. After that, we who are still alive and are left will be caught up together with them in the clouds to meet the Lord in the air. And so we will be with the Lord forever. (1 Thessalonians 4:16–17)*

The prayer, purpose, and heart-cry of this book are to plead with "whosoever will" to come to the Lord. Be alert; choose Jesus Christ and His Holy Word above the words, ideas and enticements of any man or organization. Please be careful that anything you engage in is absolutely and completely Biblically sound. In order to do this, study the Bible prayerfully. The Holy Spirit of God will lead you into all Truth.

We should keep in mind the fact that the time of the coming of the Lord is very near at hand. The Apostle warned us:

> *Now, brothers, about times and dates we do not need to write you, for you know very well that the day of the Lord will come like a thief in the night. While people are saying "Peace, and safety" destruction will come on them suddenly, as labor pains on a pregnant woman and they will not escape. (1 Thessalonians 5:2–3)*

If the day of the Lord was near two thousand years ago, how much closer is it now?

Dear reader if you find yourselves in a church that has deviated from the Gospel that was taught by Jesus and the Apostles, then you are not fellowshipping in *the Church Jesus built. So please do not remain there any longer.* Pray sincerely and humbly, ask the Lord, and the Holy Spirit will lead you to the safety of a faithful gathering of believers. The Lord Jesus Himself will meet you there and you will feel the warmth and peace of His arms as He wraps them around you in a loving welcome.

As you find refuge in the Lord's Church, the *"oil of gladness"* will be upon you, and you will be able to rejoice with the ransomed. Paul says,

> *But you brothers, are not in darkness so that this day should surprise you like a thief. You are all sons of the light and sons of the day. We do not belong to the night or to the darkness. So then, let us not be like others, who are asleep, but let us be alert, and self-controlled. For those who sleep, sleep at night, and those who get drunk, get drunk at night. But since we belong to the day, let us be self-controlled, putting on faith and love as a breastplate, and the hope of Salvation as a helmet.* **For God did not appoint us to suffer wrath but to receive Salvation through our Lord Jesus Christ.** *He died for us so that, whether we are awake or asleep we may live together with Him.* **Therefore encourage one another and build each other up, just as in fact you are doing.** *(1 Thessalonians 5: 4–11)*

The Lord Jesus is coming back soon to rule and reign as *Lord* and *King*. Prayerfully, you and I will be among those who come back with Jesus, having been caught up to be with Him at an earlier date in the Rapture.

The Apostle John described the return of the Lord to the earth this way:

*I saw heaven standing open and there before me was a white horse, whose rider is called Faithful and True. With justice he judges and makes war. His eyes are like blazing fire, and on his head are many crowns. He has a name written on him that no one knows but he himself. He is dressed in a robe dipped in blood, and his name is the Word of God. The armies of heaven were following him, riding on white horses and dressed in fine linen, white and clean. Out of his mouth comes a sharp sword with which to strike down the nations. "He will rule them with an iron scepter." He treads the wine-press of the fury of the wrath of God Almighty. On his robe and on his thigh he has this name written: KING OF KINGS AND LORD OF LORDS. (Revelation 19:11–16)*

One of these days we will all meet the Lord regardless of what we do or do not believe. Dear reader, if you have chosen to trust Jesus Christ as your Lord and Savior, you will be riding one of those white horses along with Him as He comes back to rule and reign upon the earth. But if you for any reason have chosen to reject His salvation or believe and participate in a false doctrine, you will certainly not enjoy the day of His return.

Ask yourself *now* while you still have time, "Have I really accepted Jesus Christ as the Lord of my life?" If for some reason you are not sure, you can correct that right now. *Stop now* and pray this simple prayer.

Lord Jesus, I believe that you died on the cross for me. I recognize that I have sinned against you and I ask you to please forgive me of all my sins. Please come into my heart and be the Lord of my life. I will love you and serve you forever.

If you have previously given your life to Jesus, but somehow slipped away from Him, or if you have knowingly or unknowingly engaged yourself in false doctrine—anything that does not agree with the Bible, then *stop* and pray. Ask forgiveness of the Lord and ask Him to help you get back into close intimacy with Him.

If you prayed the simple prayer above, and meant it with all your heart, or if you repented and recommitted your life to Jesus, *start rejoicing!* The Bible tells us the angels in Heaven are rejoicing over you. You have just changed your eternal destination and your name is written in the *Lamb's Book of Life*. Remember a white horse is reserved for you. You are now *awake;* keep your eyes fastened on Jesus, the Author and finisher of our faith.

Open your Bible and begin to prayerfully read the Gospel of John. Ask the Lord to lead you to a faithful Church, and start trying to *wake up* everyone you can think of who does not know Jesus Christ as Savior and Lord.

Let the Bride of Christ rejoice and shout for joy, Maranatha! *Lord Jesus, come soon* for the time is at hand!

# Chapter 9

# WOOD, HAY AND STUBBLE

⸺∞⸺

T he Lord now showed me a vast area of land which was covered by dry wood chips. All these chips appeared to be about the same size and shape. Each chip in my estimate was about an inch long and approximately three quarters of an inch wide.

This scene seemed to suggest that some sort of shredder had gone through, chopping all the trees in the area into these equal-sized chips. The wood chips were very dry and parched and lay one upon the other, several layers deep.

Standing few and far between in this desolate place, were some small, weak and sickly looking plants, the stalks of which were very slender. These plants were wilting, their leaves were yellowing and the branches and upper parts of their stalks drooped, but these thirsty little plants had somehow escaped the shredding machine and managed to remain alive. From the heavens above, a great beam of light shone down upon these drooping plants, and it was apparent that this light alone was the sustainer of their lives.

I gazed at this bleak picture trying to understand it, then suddenly the scene changed and I was shown another great area of land. This time it was covered with hay. Once more a few droopy little plants stood here and there in the midst of this hay covered area. They too were struggling to survive, and just as before the Heavenly light beamed down upon them keeping them alive.

While I was attempting to take all this in, yet another change of scene occurred, and this time the wilting plants stood in another large area that was blanketed with broken stubble type hay. Again the light from above shined down upon them to keep them alive.

This Scripture now came to mind. *"In Him was life, and the life was the light of men" (John 1:4).* With that the Lord proceeded to give me understanding of what I had seen. He said, "The great area of wood chips, hay, stubble and the wilting plants interpret the effects of the work of many so called shepherds upon the spiritual lives of the multitudes they influence. Through the teachings of these men and women, great numbers of people erroneously believe that they are spiritually healthy, when in fact they are dead in their sins.

The souls of these people, wood, hay, and stubble, will be required by God at the hands of the ones that caused them to become so. In various and diverse ways these leaders kept their flock from the true Light, the Giver of Life—Jesus Christ. The huge cold, heartless machine, the Excavator Arm fitted with a claw that I had previously seen, was the illustration the Lord used to show me how these leaders had systematically turned countless numbers of precious souls into spiritual wood, hay, and stubble.

> *For men will be lovers of themselves, lovers of money, boasters, proud, blasphemers, disobedient to parents, unthankful, unholy, unloving, unforgiving, slanderers, without self-control, brutal, despisers of good, traitors, headstrong, haughty, lovers of pleasure rather than lovers of God,* **having a form of godliness but denying its power.** *(2 Timothy 3:2–5)*

In many seeker-friendly, megachurches people never hear the true Gospel. They certainty do not hear the Gospel that

Jesus and the apostles taught. Many smaller churches, having received counsel from leaders of the large institutions, have bought into these false doctrines, thereby creating the same problem within their own churches as well. The congregants of these churches seldom hear the word *heaven* or *hell*. If they do hear the word *heaven*, they are left to believe that there are many ways to get there. According to these leaders, there is no judgment by God, so sin remains unconfessed and unforgiven and each man's lifestyle, whatever it may be, becomes totally acceptable.

The scene I saw portrayed the numerous many who consider themselves to be thriving spiritually, but instead are simply traveling through years of mechanical religious maneuvers and meaningless traditions that never teach them the truth of the Gospel of Jesus Christ.

Regrettably, the wood chips, hay, and stubble represented deceived people who had believed a false gospel of one kind or another, and considered it to be acceptable worship to the Lord. Obviously they knew nothing of repentance and relationship with Jesus Christ. The saving power of His precious blood obviously received no place in their churches or their lives. *They have never been taught! They are never told and so they never accept Jesus as Lord of their lives, or live as He taught His disciples to do.*

Even as I write, the gears of false doctrines are effectively grinding their treacherous wheels, shredding countless more souls into spiritually dried-out wood chips, hay, and stubble. The years of this systematized deadening of human souls was apparent through the depth of the layers of wood chips, hay, and stubble. They all looked exactly alike and their spiritual conditions were identical. Though the techniques employed by the leaders of the different churches down through the ages may have changed it was obvious their work had produced the same results; large numbers of souls oblivious to a living, vital relationship with Jesus Christ.

Would the Lord say to these false teachers "Woe to you" as He said to the Pharisees who were the false teachers of His day?

Paul said:

*For no other foundation can anyone lay than that which is [already] laid, which is Jesus Christ (the Messiah, the Anointed one).* But if anyone builds upon the Foundation, whether it be with gold, silver, precious stones, wood, hay, straw, The work of each [one] will become [plainly, openly] known (shown for what it is); for the day [of Christ] will disclose and declare it, because it will be revealed with fire, and the fire will test and critically appraise the character and worth of the work each person has done. If the work which any person has built on this Foundation [any product of his efforts whatever] survives [this test], he will get his reward. But if any person's work is burned up [under the test], he will suffer the loss [of it all, losing his reward], though he himself will be saved, but only as [one who has passed] through fire. (1 Corinthians 3:11–15, AMP)

A teacher who builds on the Foundation already laid— Jesus Christ, will have his or her work scrutinized on the day of the Lord. If the work survives, reward is to be expected. If the work is burned up he or she would suffer loss of reward but be saved although only as one who has passed through fire. *So then what happens to those preachers who build on any other foundation than Jesus Christ?* "Woe to you!" Jesus said to the Scribes and Pharisees. What exactly does "woe" mean? My guess is, no wise person would want to find out!

What a dismaying picture! Except for the few droopy plants, in all three of these vast areas covered with wood, hay, and stubble, there was no life, no love, no feeling of any sort. It is difficult not to think of the many thousands of people, so preconditioned and hardened in their beliefs that they will not even consider the thought that *Life* might be waiting for them just outside what they have always chosen to believe. Sadly, hundreds upon hundreds of such people continue to turn a deaf ear to the faithful disciples of Jesus Christ who invite them to receive Him as Lord and Savior. *Because they believe that they are okay based on what they have been taught, they shut their ears and refuse to listen.*

Apostasy reared its ugly head not too long after Jesus empowered His Church through the Holy Spirit on the Day of Pentecost. We must not forget that the Messiah warned, *"Wide is the gate and broad is the road that leads to the destruction, and many enter through it" (Matthew 7:13).*

The Lord made me understand that I was being shown the terrible consequences that come through the work of people attempting to lead churches while rejecting the Presence and the Person of the Holy Spirit. Paul says,

> *He has made us competent as ministers of a new covenant-not of the letter but of the Spirit; for the letter kills, but the Spirit gives life. (2 Corinthians 3:6)*

Those who reject the Holy Spirit end up functioning under their own standards of righteousness, and so their works are without Life. This speaks of both the legalistic mind-sets as well as the ultra liberal postmodern methods of leading without the Holy Spirit. The Word of God tells us:

> *But when the kindness and love of God our Savior appeared, he saved us, not because of righteous things we had done, but because of his mercy. **He saved us through the washing of rebirth and renewal by the Holy Spirit, whom he poured out on us generously through Jesus Christ our Savior, so that, having been justified by his grace, we might become heirs having the hope of eternal life.** (Titus 3:4–7)*

This Scripture is very clear. It tells we are saved because of God's mercy, and this, only through the washing of rebirth and renewal by the Holy Spirit through Jesus Christ. Yet one of the biggest lies believed by the misled many is salvation through works. Many believe they will make it to Heaven because of acts of good work that they attribute to themselves. The seeker-friendly proponents do a good job of keeping the questions of sin and repentance out of their vocabulary, and so those who attend their services don't worry too much about such topics, either.

Others entrenched in the Emergent/New Age philosophies, deny the even atonement. They deny the need for what Jesus did on the cross. When asked, "Do you believe that you will go to Heaven when you die?" "Yes, I will go to Heaven, I go to church, I am a good person. Everyone is part of the body of Christ." Sadly, the illusion they live with is one that does not agree with the Bible, which tells us,

> *Since they did not know the Righteousness that comes from God and sought to establish their own righteousness they did not submit to God's Righteousness. (Romans 10:3)*

Because these false teachers do not discuss sinful lifestyles, and behaviors that are specifically mentioned in the Scriptures as being an abomination to God, many people remain in their sin and think they are acceptable to God. Yes, the Word of the Lord specifically alerts us to God's personal view and stand.

> *Do you not know that you are the temple of God and that the Spirit of God dwells in you? If anyone defiles the temple of God, God will destroy him. For the temple of God is holy, which temple you are. (1 Corinthians 3:16–17)*

If you at any point and time gave your life to Jesus and then slipped back into sin, *repent*, turn back to God, ask forgiveness in Jesus' name and be set free. God loves you so very much and He is calling you to Himself. Ask Him to lead you to a church where the Word of God is taught in spirit and truth. Jesus said,

> **Yet a time is coming and has now come when the true worshipers will worship the Father in spirit and truth, for they are the kind of worshipers the Father seeks.** *God is spirit, and his worshipers must worship in spirit and in truth. (John 4:23–24)*

Unless deceptive doctrines are squelched in the lives of those who hear them, they will keep those who believe these lies from ever coming humbly to the Lord Jesus Christ for the grace of His great salvation and the *". . . washing of rebirth and renewal by the precious Holy Spirit . . ." (Titus 3:5).*
Jesus said:

> *. . . I tell you the truth: It is for your good that I am going away.* **Unless I go away, the Counselor will not come to you; but if I go, I will send him to you. When he comes, he will convict the world of guilt in regard to sin and righteousness and judgment:** *in regard to sin, because men do not believe in me; in regard to righteousness, because I am going to the Father, where you can see me no longer; and in regard to judgment, because the prince of this world now stands con-demned. "I have much more to say to you, more than you can now bear.* **But when he, the Spirit of truth, comes, he will guide you into all truth. He will not speak on his own; he will speak only what he hears, and he will tell you what is yet to come. He will bring glory to me by taking from what is mine and making it known to you.** *All that belongs to the Father is mine. That is why I said the Spirit will take from what is mine and make it known to you. (John 16:7–15)*

The little wilting plants I had seen standing amidst all the dead wood chips, were the ones whose hearts had not petrified; there was still the hope of eternal life for them through the Lord Jesus. Obviously they were being sustained by the light of the Holy Spirit for the day of their salvation. *"The entrance of Your Word brings Light it gives understanding to the simple" (Psalm 119:130).* These few, spiritually droopy people are those who will receive the Lord Jesus the Light, and His Holy Spirit, when someone brings the message of salvation to them.

Little wonder the giant claw I saw, that represented the false church, held onto only a small part of God's Word. How could anyone truly understand the truth of Scripture while rejecting the Author, the Holy Spirit? Paul gave young Timothy some very good advice to live by. Listen to what he had to say:

> *In fact, everyone who wants to live a godly life in Christ Jesus will be persecuted, while evil men and impostors will go from bad to worse, deceiving and being deceived.* **But as for you, continue in what you have learned and have become convinced of, because you know those from whom you learned it, and how from infancy you have known the holy Scriptures, which are able to make you wise for salvation through faith in Christ Jesus. All Scripture is God-breathed and is useful for teaching, rebuking, correcting and training in righteousness, so that the man of God may be thoroughly equipped for every good work.** *(2 Timothy 3:12–17)*

As we can see the true Church of Jesus Christ is coming under ever-increasing levels of persecution. The devil uses every tool available to him to attack the true Church. Many of these attacks come from within the professing church. The world, which is part and parcel of this false church, hates us, and as we can see we have a multitude of restrictions being placed upon our freedom of religious expression. The name of Jesus is the foremost subject of attack, and they do everything to keep us from sharing the Gospel.

As we look at this situation, the overwhelming cry of our hearts should be:

Oh! God, we who are called by Your name, intercede for those who have rejected Your Holy Spirit. We beg Your forgiveness, Lord, for this great transgression. We repent to You, precious Holy Spirit; You so very graciously left Your home in Heaven and came into this dark world of pain and despair to lead, guide, strengthen, and renew all who submit to Your gentle voice. Great foolishness within our hearts keeps us from recognizing the tremendous price You paid for our redemption, Lord Jesus.

How deep a blindness has caused Your awesome blessings to be trodden under the feet of prideful people? Save us, O Lord, from continually grieving You. Save us we pray LORD from putting out the fire of Your gentle Holy Spirit in our lives.

O God, the sin of the entire human race is very great against You. Lord, we repent and plead Your forgiveness. Please heal us and revive us, O God! Revive all those who will hear Your voice and obey, we pray. Cause us to glorify Your awesome name, in spirit and in truth. Cause us to worship, adore, and magnify Your holy name, for You alone are holy, You alone are worthy!

Create in us clean hearts O God, and consume us with the desire to serve You in spirit and truth. Remove from us the hearts of mediocrity and flood our spirits with love and longing for You.

Father, create in us an insatiable hunger for Your Word. Teach us to walk in Your light and in humble submission as Jesus did. For You alone are holy and righteous. You alone are God, and we praise Your holy name forever.

Returning for an instant to the people represented by the droopy wilting plants, let those of us who love the Lord pray that they will become strong, healthy, and vibrant believers in the Lord Jesus Christ. As we pray for their spiritual revival and health, we should also pray that they will rise up and move from their present unhealthy environment. Obviously if they remain where they presently are, they will receive no nourishment, and sooner or later they will starve to death.

If you are reading this book and see yourself as one of those wilting plants, pull yourself up while the light of Jesus still shines on you. Start prayerfully studying the Bible and move as God leads you to a place where the Holy Spirit is yearned for, and a river of living waters flow. Go where the Presence of the Lord is sought, and the people simply can't get enough of Jesus.

> *On the last and greatest day of the Feast, Jesus stood and said in a loud voice, "If anyone is thirsty, **let him come to me and drink. Whoever believes in me, as the Scripture has said, streams of living water will flow from within him."** By this he meant the Spirit, whom those who believed in him were later to receive. (John 7:37–39)*

Sheep need a shepherd, and where Jesus is greatly desired and sought after, the Spirit of God is present. The Bible tells us,

> *Blessed is the man who does not walk in the counsel of the wicked, or stand in the way of sinners or sit in the seat of mockers. **But his delight is in the law of the LORD, and on his law he meditates day and night. He is like a tree planted by streams of water which yields its fruit in season and whose leaf does not wither. Whatever he does prospers.** (Psalm 1:1–3)*

Believers who continually seek the presence of the Holy Spirit and the life-giving Word are as trees planted by the water. Only strong, healthy trees can produce fruit. The wilting plants I saw could bear no fruit because they had been so severely deprived of the spiritual food and water of God's Word. God in His great love, desires all those called by His name to be strong and healthy fruit bearers.

The Bible warns,

*Not so the wicked! They are like chaff, that the wind blows away. Therefore the wicked will not stand in the judgment,* **nor sinners in the assembly of the Righteous. For the LORD watches over the way of the Righteous, but the way of the wicked will perish.** *(Psalm 1:4–6)*

It doesn't take much wind to blow hay and stubble away. The reason why so many who call themselves Christians also dabble about with tarot cards, palm reading, fortune telling, horoscopes, and other things of the occult is because they do not see anything wrong with doing what God strictly forbids. The winds of false doctrine blow many away from God.

Many of us were at one time or another in some denomination where very little time was spent in the Bible, and only a small part of it was taught. Many times the Word was distorted and the Holy Spirit was rejected. If you were ever in a place like that, you too were once one of those little wilted plants. Except for the reviving light of the Gospel that Jesus Christ the Light of the world shines down on us in His great love, we might also have been turned into wood chips, hay, or stubble.

I thank God with all my heart that He revived me enough to see that I needed to get up and run to a place that was amply irrigated by the life-giving River of God. I believe that all who have experienced a similar move are rejoicing that they are free as well, and are also praying hard for others who are still stuck among the dead and dying.

If you are feeling ill and suffocated in your church, then you are missing the life-giving oxygen of God's holy breath that comes through His Word.

*All Scripture is God-breathed and is useful for teaching, rebuking, correcting and training in righteousness, so that the man of God may be thoroughly equipped for every good work. (2 Timothy 3:16–17)*

It is the light of Jesus shining on you that is causing you to want to get up and to move you to a place of abundant life. Let the Lord lead you to where the Holy Spirit will revive and strengthen you. Wake up, shake off the chains of tradition, and false man-made religion and listen to the loving voice of Jesus saying to you *"Follow me . . ." (Matthew 9:9)*

Isaiah the Prophet voiced the call of the LORD this way:

**Come, all you who are thirsty, come to the waters; and you who have no money come, buy wine and milk without money and without cost.** *Why spend money on what is not bread, and your labor on what does not satisfy.* **Listen, listen to me and eat what is good and your soul will delight in the richest of fare. Give ear and come to me; hear me, that your soul may live. I will make an everlasting covenant with you, my faithful love promised to David.** *(Isaiah 55:1–3)*

Wake up, friends. Listen, move, and live in Jesus. He loves you so much.

The time is incredibly short and the giant mechanical tree shredders should wake up too, humble themselves and turn in repentance to the Lord. Jesus Himself will gladly receive you, but He will deal with those who do not do so.

So come out, be separate from them, walk into His loving arms, and live.

The time is at hand.

# Chapter 10

# THE LION OF JUDAH

~∞∞∞~

I mmediately after I had seen the area of wood, hay, and stubble, the Lord showed me a chariot descending from the sky and heading towards the earth.

The front end of the chariot looked like the face of a lion and it was being driven by none other than the Lord Jesus. The words of the Apostle John passed quickly through my mind. *"See, the Lion of the tribe of Judah, the Root of David, has triumphed. He is able to open the scroll and its seven seals (Revelation 5:5).*

I saw Jesus Christ the Lord, the Lion of the tribe of Judah, descending in this amazing chariot. He headed straight towards a vast area that was covered with multiple rows of short, gray gravestones. These gravestones were standing in sticky, orange-colored mud. Every stone was about three or four feet tall, and they all looked exactly alike.

The chariot advanced at a very high rate of speed, slamming powerfully into the gravestones, crushing and destroying every one of them as it raced through. What remained after this was nothing but a heap of rubble and rising dust from the broken concrete gravestones. It was hard to imagine what this meant. But the Lord led me to the Book of Jeremiah. Jeremiah said,

*Look! He advances like the clouds, his chariots come like a whirlwind, his horses are swifter than eagles. Woe to us! We are ruined! (Jeremiah 4:13)*

I watched in amazement, as the Lord revealed to me what all this meant. The gravestones again were symbolic of the so-called churches that neither love nor serve Him, the Lord said. They were shown to be stuck in sticky mud because they remain obstinately stuck in their own thinking and ways. These churches are those that do not change or submit their hearts in obedience to Him or His Word. They were represented by gravestones because they were dead in their sins. They had rejected Jesus Christ as Lord and Savior. They had rejected His Word, His way, and the guidance of His Holy Spirit.

God's Word shows us that those who trust in Jesus, the precious cornerstone, will also become *living stones* that are built into God's spiritual house. Listen to Peter as he quotes Isaiah. He said:

**As you come to him, the living Stone-rejected by men but chosen by God and precious to him- you also, like living stones, are being built into a spiritual house to be a holy priesthood, offering spiritual sacrifices acceptable to God through Jesus Christ.** *For in Scripture it says: "See, I lay a stone in Zion, a chosen and precious cornerstone, and the one who trusts in him will never be put to shame." Now to you who believe, this stone is precious. But to those who do not believe, "The stone the builders rejected has become the capstone," and, "A stone that causes men to stumble and a rock that makes them fall. They stumble because they disobey the message-which is also what they were destined for. (1 Peter 2:4–8)*

This beautiful Scriptural picture is given by God to show us how close we actually become with Him when we trust and obey the Lord Jesus!

When a house is built, every stone used in its construction becomes an integral part of the structure and remains permanently attached. Each stone functions perfectly in its unique position as an important building block. This is how each believer fits into the construction of God's spiritual house.

Jesus once asked His disciples,

> Who do people say the Son of Man is?" They replied, "Some say John the Baptist; others say Elijah; and still others, Jeremiah or one of the prophets." "But what about you?" he asked. "Who do you say I am?" Simon Peter answered, "You are the Christ, the Son of the living God. (Matthew 16:13–16)

You could visualize the Son of God looking deeply into the eyes of each of His disciples, longing to hear the words that finally came from Peter's lips. *"You are the Christ, the Son of the Living God."* Praise God! Peter got it! He had actually believed!

Jesus replied:

> **"Blessed are you, Simon son of Jonah, for this was not revealed to you by man, but by my Father in heaven.** And I tell you that you are Peter, and on this rock I will build my church, and the gates of Hades will not overcome it. I will give you the keys of the kingdom of heaven; whatever you bind on earth will be bound in heaven, and whatever you loose on earth will be loosed in heaven. (Matthew 16:17–19)

Isn't this the very same confession the Church of Jesus Christ still continues to be built upon?

> . . . if you confess with your mouth, "Jesus is Lord," and believe in your heart that God raised him from the dead, you will be saved. For it is with your heart that

*you believe and are justified, and it is with your mouth
that you confess and are saved. (Romans 10:9–10)*

Just as Peter did by his confession, anyone who confesses and believes in his or her heart that Jesus is Lord and that God raised Him from the dead, is saved and becomes a *"living stone"* in the church Jesus Christ built. After this glorious event, the believer must remain steadfastly loyal, true and connected to Jesus, just as a natural stone remains connected to a physical building.

The true Church, the Bride of Christ, consists of all those who believe in their hearts that God raised Jesus from the dead. They also fearlessly declare before all men as Peter and the rest of the Apostles did, that Jesus is the Christ the Son of the Living God. Jesus said,

*Whoever acknowledges me before men, I will also
acknowledge him before my Father in heaven.
(Matthew 10:32)*

Any person who does not believe or confess Jesus as the Christ, the Son of God, and the Lord of their own lives will never be part of His Bride. Listen to the words of Jesus. *"But whoever disowns me before men, I will disown him before my Father in heaven." (Matthew 10–33)*

The Lord's unfailing question to every individual upon the face of the earth remains the same. *"Who do you say that I AM?"* The eternal outcome for each person is of course determined by his or her response to that very personal question from the Lord. Just as He yearned to hear Peter's answer, the Savior also yearns to hear that same answer from the mouth of every human being, keeping in mind that,

*Salvation is found in no one else, for there is no other
name under heaven given to men by which we must be
saved. (Acts 4:12–13)*

We must remember that it is *not* the Lord's desire that anyone should be lost. Peter said,

*The Lord . . . is longsuffering toward us, not willing that any should perish but that all should come to repentance. (2 Peter 3:8–10)*

Jesus gave the keys of the kingdom of Heaven to Peter and all the other faithful disciples, and He has also given them to every faithful child of God. Peter used the keys on the day of Pentecost to open a floodgate of salvation. Three thousand souls were added to the Church that very day. This is what we are all called to do. Everyone who has been saved must, in turn, boldly proclaim salvation through Jesus to the lost. This is the explicit purpose of the Church of Jesus Christ.

Peter preached the Gospel, and three thousand people who were on their way to eternal damnation, changed course. Instead of following the blind leaders of their day, they turned and followed Jesus and were saved. Jesus said of the Pharisees: *"Can the blind lead the blind? Will they not both fall into the ditch?" (Luke 6:39–40)*

Today thousands remain in a continuing state of spiritual blindness because they follow ungodly leaders and know only what these false teachers teach them. They must hear the truth from faithful believers in the Lord. They must commit their lives to Jesus, be saved, and then be properly discipled.

Currently, churches are built under the leading of one man or another, and multitudes of people follow them because of their style or personal charisma, but not all these leaders are true disciples of Jesus Christ. The Apostle Peter said:

**But there were also false prophets among the people, just as there will be false teachers among you. They will secretly introduce destructive heresies, even denying the sovereign Lord who bought them-bringing swift destruction on themselves. Many will follow their shameful ways and will bring**

**the way of truth into disrepute.** *In their greed these teachers will exploit you with stories they have made up. Their condemnation has long been hanging over them, and their destruction has not been sleeping. For if God did not spare angels when they sinned, but sent them to hell, putting them into gloomy dungeons to be held for judgment; if he did not spare the ancient world when he brought the flood on its ungodly people, but protected Noah, a preacher of righteousness, and seven others; if he condemned the cities of Sodom and Gomorrah by burning them to ashes, and made them an example of what is going to happen to the ungodly; and if he rescued Lot, a righteous man, who was distressed by the filthy lives of lawless men (for that righteous man, living among them day after day, was tormented in his righteous soul by the lawless deeds he saw and heard)-* **if this is so, then the Lord knows how to rescue godly men from trials and to hold the unrighteous for the day of judgment, while continuing their punishment. This is especially true of those who follow the corrupt desire of the sinful nature and despise authority. Bold and arrogant, these men are not afraid to slander celestial beings; yet even angels, although they are stronger and more powerful, do not bring slanderous accusations against such beings in the presence of the Lord. But these men blaspheme in matters they do not understand.** *They are like brute beasts, creatures of instinct, born only to be caught and destroyed, and like beasts they too will perish. They will be paid back with harm for the harm they have done. Their idea of pleasure is to carouse in broad daylight. They are blots and blemishes, reveling in their pleasures while they feast with you. With eyes full of adultery, they never stop sinning; they seduce the unstable; they are experts in greed-an accursed brood! They have left the straightway and wandered off*

*to follow the way of Balaam son of Beor, who loved the*
*wages of wickedness. (2 Peter 2:1–15)*

Churches led by leaders, such as Peter described, are the ones that the Lord portrayed as gravestones that He himself will destroy. Every true and faithful pastor is very precious to the Lord Jesus Christ and is greatly loved and protected by Him.

Peter was speaking under the direct inspiration of the Holy Spirit, and he did not water down the word given to him by the Lord. He described these false leaders in the strongest of terms and spelled out their sins. Listen to Peter:

*These men are springs without water, and mists driven*
*by a storm. Blackest darkness is reserved for them. For*
*they mouth empty boastful words, and, by appealing to*
*the lustful desires of sinful human nature, they entice*
*people who are just escaping from those who live in*
*error. They promise them freedom, while they them-*
*selves are slaves of depravity for a man is a slave to*
*whatever has mastered him. (2 Peter 2:17–19)*

Peter's scathing words were inspired by the Holy Spirit, and he spoke them to all who depart from the truth and lead others astray. His words leave us very little doubt about how God feels regarding teachers of false doctrines who lead many astray.

There is a very important thing Peter said that we should not miss. He was specific about how in the past the Lord saved the righteous before He destroyed the ungodly. Peter reminds us of Noah, the preacher of righteousness, and righteous Lot who were saved by the Lord from the destruction that came upon the rebellious. In like manner, every person who has a sincere heart towards God, and faith in His Son Jesus Christ will be rescued by the Lord, and be brought out from whichever apostate organization he or she may be in, before Judgment falls.

Even as I write, there is a great shifting among the believers. People are moving around, searching for a church in which the Gospel of Truth is being preached. Jesus said,

*My sheep listen to my voice; I know them, and they follow me. I give them eternal life, and they shall never perish; no one can snatch them out of my hand. **My Father, who has given them to me, is greater than all; no one can snatch them out of my Father's hand.** I and the Father are one. (John 10:27–30)*

Just as Noah and Lot were faithful to God under very difficult circumstances, true sheep of Jesus listen to His voice. God's children will disturbed and vexed in spirit by erroneous teachings, and they will be able to tell if the place they are in is dead to Christ or alive in Him by asking themselves a few questions:

1. Am I being taught that the Bible is the absolute, inerrant Word of God?
2. Is the truth of the Virgin Birth, the death, burial, resurrection, and ascension of Jesus Christ being upheld?
3. In clearest terms, am I being taught of the existence of the Father, Son, and Holy Spirit?
4. Am I being taught that there is salvation in no other name than the name of Jesus Christ of Nazareth, the Son of the Living God?
5. Am I being taught that salvation comes only by accepting Jesus as my personal Savior and Lord?
6. Can I be sure that what I am being taught is biblically accurate, or is something being added, taken away, slanted, or twisted to support any manmade doctrine?
7. What about sin and repentance? Am I being told that I must repent of my sins so as to receive forgiveness, or is this an unmentioned issue?
8. How about Hell and Satan? Am I being told they are real, or are these facts being denied?

9. Am I being encouraged to eagerly watch for the return of Jesus Christ for the Church—the Rapture, and to occupy and serve Him faithfully until He comes?

If the honest answer to any or all of these questions is "No," then be sure Jesus, the Good Shepherd, is calling to you dear one, to come out from where you are. Listen to His voice and obey. All those who resist His call will end up being among the gray gravestones that He will take out of the way. Remember, Jesus referred to the religious leaders of His day, as sepulchers. He said,

*Woe to you, teachers of the Law and Pharisees, you hypocrites! You are like whitewashed tombs, which look beautiful on the outside but on the inside are full of dead men's bones and everything unclean.* In the same way, *on the outside you appear to people as righteous but on the inside you are full of hypocrisy and wickedness . . . You snakes!* You brood of vipers! How will you escape being condemned to hell? (Matthew 23:27–33)

Jesus weeps over you as He wept over Jerusalem the city He so loved, when He declared these words:

O Jerusalem, Jerusalem, you who kill the prophets and stone those sent to you, *how often I have longed to gather your children together, as a hen gathers her chicks under her wings, but you were not willing.* Look, your house is left to you desolate. For I tell you, you will not see me again until you say, 'Blessed is he who comes in the name of the Lord.' (Matthew 23:37–39)

However, the hardness of the hearts of the leaders in that city and their lack of repentance exacted the punishment He predicted. Destruction surely came to them and not one stone of the Temple was left upon another, exactly fulfilling the Words of the Savior. This horrific event came to pass just about forty years after He left the earth and the desolation lasted until May14, 1948 when Israel became a nation again. We must not forget that Jesus Christ is *"the same yesterday, today and forever" (Hebrews13:8).* His Word is immutable.

The Lord warned us to keep an eye open for professional religionists. These men will seek to be popular, prominent, and noticed by others, seeking their own honor as the Pharisees did. Jesus warned,

> *Beware of the teachers of the Law. They like to walk around in flowing robes and love to be greeted in market places and have the most important seats in the Synagogues and the places of honor at banquets. They devour widows' houses and for a show make lengthy prayers.* ***Such men will be punished most severely.*** *(Luke 20:46–47)*

Any believer, who in the name of tolerance or anything else chooses to go along with unscriptural teachings, no matter how slight, is taking a stand against Jesus Christ and participating with the false prophets and teachers. Jesus said: *"He who is not with me is against me, and he who does not gather with me scatters." (Matthew 12:30)*

Paul had no hesitancy in declaring,

> *As we have already said, so now I say again: If anybody is preaching to you a gospel other than what you accepted, let him be eternally condemned! (Galatians 1:9)*

Paul was so zealous for the Truth, that he even confronted Peter stating *"I opposed him to his face." (Galatians 2:11, NIV).* Paul did this because Peter who had been eating with the Gentile believers chose to draw back from doing so because he was afraid of the "circumcision group" when they arrived. Paul saw this behavior as being hypocritical and not in line with the Gospel. By his action Peter was forcing the Gentile believers to follow the Jewish custom of circumcision as a requisite for salvation, thereby adding to the truth that salvation comes through faith in Jesus Christ alone and His sacrifice on the cross. This account is found in Galatians 2:11–21. Peter, being a true servant of the Lord obviously accepted Paul's rebuke in humility and repentance and later on referred to Paul as *"Our dear brother Paul" (2 Peter 3:15)*.

Jesus firmly addressed the unfaithful, hypocritical leaders of His day.

> *You nullify the word of God for the sake of your tradition. You hypocrites! Isaiah was right when he prophesied about you. These people honor me with their lips, but their heart is far from me. They worship me in vain; their teachings are but rules taught by men.'"* *(Matthew 15:6–7)*

The Lord's warnings and chastisements are strong, but they come from the depths of His love for us. If we don't sincerely welcome the anointed Son of God into our assemblies through the Holy Spirit, and humbly permit Him to cleanse out all our pride, deceit, immoral and secular thinking, the liberalization and desecration of His Holy Word, along with everything else that is displeasing to Him, then Jesus will do that cleansing Himself, and when He does many are going to feel pain.

It was this same Jesus who cleansed the Temple at Jerusalem, knocking over the moneychangers tables as He drove them out with a whip that He had deliberately made for the occasion. They certainly felt pain. *"It is written," he said to them, "'My house will be called a house of prayer, but you are making it a 'den of robbers'" (Matthew 21:13)*.

We had better wake up! Paul says:

> **Do you not know that your body is a temple of the Holy Spirit, who is in you, whom you have received from God?** *You are not your own; you were bought*

*at a price. Therefore honor God with your body. (1 Corinthians 6:19–20)*

Each one of us is a temple of the Holy Spirit, and we are called to be houses of prayer, not dens of robbers. When the priest sprinkled the blood of the sacrifice on the mercy seat of the Ark of the Covenant, the manifest presence of the Holy Spirit, the Shekinah Glory of God would descend over the mercy seat, lighting up the Holy of Holies. This same Shekinah Glory of God, seen as tongues of fire, descended upon the apostles and those who were gathered with them when the Holy Spirit came upon them on the day of Pentecost. It is this same Holy Spirit who comes to dwell within each believer when he or she is saved by the Blood of Jesus Christ.

This great and holy blessing from God has been given to each one of us, and as temples of the Holy Spirit we must be holy even as He is holy. Your heart and mine have become the mercy seat in the temples of our bodies, because the precious Blood of the Lamb of God has touched, cleansed, and made them pure like the gold of the original mercy seat. When God looks at the heart of one who is saved, He sees the holy Blood of Jesus, His Son, and His glorious presence manifests in the form of the Holy Spirit. Beloved, how greatly we should love Him! Our adoration and gratitude to the Everlasting, and Eternal God should be overflowing, as we submit to His holy presence, recognizing what He has done for us.

Jesus said,

**You are the light of the world. A city on a hill cannot be hidden.** [The light is the Glory of God the Holy Spirit within us.] **Neither do people light a lamp and put it under a bowl.** *Instead they put it on its stand, and it gives light to everyone in the house.* **In the same way, let your light shine before men, that they may see your good deeds and praise your Father in heaven.** *(Matthew 5:14–16)*

No wonder Jesus was angered! What Israel did in the Temple at Jerusalem, is what many believers do in the temples of their bodies! We permit ourselves to become dens of robbers when we steal the time allotted to us by the Holy Spirit of God, for worship and the furtherance of the Gospel, and use it on selfish and worldly pursuits. We also become dens of robbers when we take no time to spend with the Lord in prayer or to be holy and separate unto Him.

In the days of the Old Testament, Amos the prophet addressed God's people in both Samaria and Judah. His words could seriously apply to our modern churches.

> *Woe to you who are complacent in Zion, and to you who feel secure on Mount Samaria, you notable men of the foremost nation, to whom the people of Israel come! . . . You lie on beds inlaid with ivory and lounge on your couches. You dine on choice lambs and fattened calves. You strum away on your harps like David and improvise on musical instruments. You drink wine by the bowlful and use the finest lotions, but you do not grieve over the ruin of Joseph. **Therefore you will be among the first to go into exile; your feasting and lounging will end.** (Amos 6:1–7)*

The abundant prosperity of Judah and Samaria had caused them to become exceedingly complacent. They had arrived at the conclusion that material success was a sign that they were living under God's great favor. They didn't think God's judgment would ever come to them. As we mentioned previously, a great part of the Church in America has arrived at this same place of complacency, and just as the people addressed by Amos did not grieve over the sins of their nation, few in the Church grieve over the sins, error, and immorality within the Church and the nation.

This is a wake-up call to all faithful believers. Jesus wept over Jerusalem, and all those faithful to Him should be weeping too, and praying over those in the church who are grievously out of step with God, for He cares for them and desires them to return to Him.

Being one with Jesus is to also feel His pain for those who are lost and going into eternal destruction. We must weep; we must pray; we must be of one accord with the Savior. We must intercede even as He and the Holy Spirit do. We must fast and repent and call on the name of the Lord on behalf of those who have gone down a wrong path, so that even a few will turn and listen to the voice of Jesus, come out and be healed, saved, and set free.

Just as the iron and clay on the feet of the statue in King Nebuchadnezzar's dream could not mix or hold together, neither will God Word and His ways mix with the ways of the world or the doctrines of the worldly church; both of which are of the same system.

Daniel described what Nebuchadnezzar saw in his dream as follows:

> *While you were watching, a rock was cut out, but not by human hands. It struck the statue on its feet of iron and clay and smashed them.* **Then the iron, the clay, the bronze, the silver and the gold were broken to pieces at the same time and became like chaff on a threshing floor in the summer. The wind swept them away without leaving a trace.** *But the rock that struck the statue became a huge mountain and filled the whole earth. (Daniel 2:34–35)*

All the works of men will ultimately amount to nothing. The Word of God is clear. *"Unless the LORD builds the house, its builders labor in vain" (Psalm 127:1).*

This false kingdom will fall. All those who have a form of godliness, but deny God's power, will suddenly be struck on their ungodly feet by the Mighty Rock—Jesus Christ the Lion of the Tribe of Judah, because their walk has not been pure. They will be smashed and the chaff will be blown away by the holy wind—the *Ruach*, the breath of God.

There came a time in the past when God said; *"My Spirit will not contend with man forever . . ." (Genesis 6:3)*

Such a time seems to be fast arriving for the false church along with all those who are against Him. The Book of Jude tells us,

> **See, the Lord is coming with thousands upon thousands of his holy ones to judge everyone, and to convict all the ungodly of all the ungodly acts they have done in the ungodly way, and of all the harsh words ungodly sinners have spoken against him."** *These men are grumblers and faultfinders; they follow their own evil desires; they boast about themselves and flatter others for their own advantage. But, dear friends, remember what the apostles of our Lord Jesus Christ foretold. They said to you,* **"In the last times there will be scoffers who will follow their own ungodly desires."** *These are the men who divide you, who follow mere natural instincts and do not have the* **Spirit.** *(Jude 14–19)*

The words of Jude truly describe today's leaders who dare to theorize that God's righteous judgments declare Him to be a despot, a tyrant. Therefore they claim God's salvation to be all inclusive, regardless of what man continues to does. They dare to say that Jesus merely came to create a peaceful new way of life on earth.

Jude encourages all faithful believers in the midst of all this chaos with the following words.

> *But you, dear friends,* **build yourselves up in your most holy faith and pray in the Holy Spirit.** *Keep yourselves in God's love as you wait for the mercy of our Lord Jesus Christ to bring you to eternal life.* **Be merciful to those who doubt; snatch others from the fire and save them; to others show mercy,**

**mixed with fear-hating even the clothing stained by corrupted flesh.** *(Jude 20–23)*

Truly the Lord is calling all true believers to build themselves up in the faith. We are to be praying and keeping ourselves in God's love, as we wait for the coming of the Lord. We must remember to be merciful to those weak in the faith and snatch as many as we can from the fire, so to speak. We are to be merciful, but we are to hate evil. To those who will be faithful, the Holy Spirit will be a beautiful, gentle breeze. He will bless, purify, and draw the hurting and broken in spirit to the Great Physician—Jesus Christ, the Lion of the tribe of Judah, who will heal and restore. But as for those who continue in their sins and lead others astray, the story won't be quite as pretty.

A story the Lord once told the chief priests and elders of the law, gives us a good idea of how He feels about those who do not faithfully carry out what He entrusted them to do. Jesus said:

**A man planted a vineyard, rented it to some farmers and went away for a long time.** *At harvest time he sent a servant to the tenant so they would give him some of the fruit of the vineyard. But the tenants beat him and sent him away empty handed. He sent another servant, but that one also they beat and treated shamefully and sent away empty-handed. He then sent still a third and they wounded him and threw him out. Then the owner of the vineyard said, 'What shall I do?" I will send my son whom I love; perhaps they will respect him.' But when the tenants saw him they talked the matter over. 'This is the Heir, they said, let's kill him and the inheritance will be ours.' So they threw him out of the vineyard and killed him. "What then will the owner of the vineyard do to them? He will come and kill those tenants and give the vineyard to others." When the people heard this they said, "May this never be!" Jesus looked directly at them and asked, 'Then what is the meaning of that*

*which is written: **"The stone the builders rejected
has become the capstone? Everyone who falls on
that stone will be broken to pieces, by he on whom
it falls will be crushed.** (Luke 20:9–18)*

Jesus told this story to emphasize the response he
received from the teachers of the Law and the chief priests.
Their hearts were filled with jealousy, great anger, and hatred
towards Him. Jesus was trying to get them to correct themselves, but they did not want to hear the truth. The response
of some leaders today is about the same, when their actions
are confronted. It is not uncommon to hear some of these
people on a talk show tearing down God's Word, picking bits
and pieces of it while twisting and denying other parts of it, to
defend their own ungodly actions. These same people don't
hesitate to support unbiblical ways of life.

Anyone who twists or denies God's Word, directly denies
and rejects Jesus Christ because He is the Living Word.

*In the beginning was the Word, and the Word was with
God, and the Word was God. He was with God in the
beginning. (John 1:1–2)*

When Jesus spoke of the capstone, referring to Himself,
He said all who fall on it would be broken to pieces. These
people would be broken of pride, self-will, anger, fear, doubt,
or whatever else has kept them from Him. However, the ones
upon which the Stone—the judgment of God—falls, will be
crushed, just as the grave stones—the sepulchers that I was
shown, were crushed by the powerful chariot of the Lord.

The Church, the Ecclesia, the "called out," is a people called
out of the world and into the Word which is God's Righteous
Kingdom. We are called to be special and separate unto God.
The Bible tells us,

***But you are a chosen people, a royal priesthood,
a holy nation, a people belonging to God, that you***

*may declare the praises of him who called you
out of darkness into his wonderful light. Once you
were not a people, but now you are the people of God;
once you had not received mercy, **but now you have
received mercy.** (1 Peter 2:9-10)*

The Jewish nation, to whom Jesus came, was expected
by God to have a similar relationship with Him.

*Now therefore, if you will indeed obey My voice and
keep My covenant, then you shall be a special treasure
to Me above all people; for all the earth is Mine. **And
you shall be to Me a kingdom of priests and a holy
nation.**' These are the words which you shall speak to
the children of Israel. (Exodus 19:5–6)*

Israel was to be holy—separate unto God. They were to
obey His voice and keep his commands. Likewise the Church
is to hear the voice of the Lord Jesus Christ, the Shepherd of
our souls, and obey Him.

*"**If you love me, you will obey what I command.**
And I will ask the Father, and he will give you another
Counselor to be with you forever-the Spirit of truth.
The world cannot accept him, because it neither sees
him nor knows him. **But you know him, for he lives
with you and will be in you. I will not leave you as
orphans; I will come to you.** (John 14:15-18)*

We have a command that warns us:

*Do not be yoked together with unbelievers. For what
do righteousness and wickedness have in common?
Or what fellowship can light have with darkness? What
harmony is there between Christ and Belial? What
does a believer have in common with an unbeliever?
What agreement is there between the temple of God*

*and idols? **For we are the temple of the living God. As God has said: "I will live with them and walk among them, and I will be their God, and they will be my people." "Therefore come out from them and be separate, says the Lord. Touch no unclean thing, and I will receive you." "I will be a Father to you, and you will be my sons and daughters, says the Lord Almighty.** (2 Corinthians 6:14–18)*

All true believers are called to come out from among those who do not believe or obey the Truth. There can be no harmony or compromise with darkness. Please be wise and obey the Lord. He always knows what's best for us, so let us obey Him and be blessed.

The time really is at hand, and those who are called by His name must take a stand for Jesus. It is time to *wake up* and come out from among those who compromise the Word of God. John the apostle heard a voice from heaven say,

**Come out of her, my people, so that you will not share in her sins,** *so that you will not receive any of her plagues; for her sins are piled up to heaven, and God has remembered her crimes. (Revelation 18:4-5)*

The Lord Jesus, the Lion of Judah will surely arrive with power and majesty, and we should all ask ourselves whether it will be a joyful or fearful time for us.

Dear friends, please make sure your choice is the right one, The Lord's love for us is so great and He wants us all to be with Him forever, so let His return be a time of great rejoicing for you and your loved ones.

Wake up, Church; please wake up!

# Chapter 11

# THE RADIANT BIBLE

———∞∞∞———

I now saw the Lord Jesus Christ clothed in a radiant white robe, and He was holding a beautiful golden object in the palm of His right hand. I gazed at the Lord in awe and He suddenly smiled and reached out His hand, offering me what He was holding.

Amazed, I heard myself say, "What is it Lord?"

As I spoke brilliant light flashed from the object that Jesus held in hand. Now I could clearly see that this radiant thing was a Bible. Beautiful as the purest of gold, with crystal beams of light reflecting and refracting from it, this Bible lay nestled in the palm of the awesome Son of God.

The Lord now moved His hand directing the light from the dazzling Bible onto some slabs of stone that were lying on the ground. He then shone this light on some droopy, unhealthy looking plants that were standing around.

As the vision faded, the amazing beauty of the glory of the Lord's presence played over and over on the screen of my mind and I slid to my knees in prayer, seeking the Lord for understanding. I began studying Bible verses as He led me to them. It was hard not to delve into the precious pages of the Book which the Lord had so magnificently displayed. Then Jesus led me to Habakkuk's Prayer:

*LORD, I have heard of your fame; I stand in awe of your deeds, O LORD. Renew them in our day, in our time make them known; in wrath remember mercy. God came from Teman, the Holy one from Mount Paran. His glory covered the heavens and his praise filled the earth. His splendor was like the sunrise;* **rays flashed from his hand, where his power was hidden.** *(Habakkuk 3:2–4)*

I didn't know this Scripture very well, until Jesus led me there. Now the power of this beautiful passage began to take shape in my spirit. I went back and read it again. Habakkuk said, *"His splendor was like the sunrise; rays flashed from His Hand where His Power was hidden."* The meaning of what I had just seen now began to unfold, and what Jesus was trying to get across to me came into focus. As Habakkuk had described, I too saw glorious rays of light that flashed from the Bible that Jesus held in His hand. It became plain; God's power *is* hidden in His glorious Word.

Jesus now explained that the reason He had reached out and offered the beautiful, shining Bible to me was because I was a Blood-bought believer and part of His Church. When He offered the power of His Word to me, He was in effect extending it to every Blood-bought believer, His sanctified body—the Church.

> He was saying to us, "Do you realize what My Word really is? Can you comprehend its Power? Take it and use it. It is your right and privilege to do so because I have given it to you for this very purpose."

*"LORD, I have heard of your fame; I stand in awe of your deeds, O LORD. Renew them in our day, in our time make them known; in wrath remember mercy"* (Habakkuk 3:2). Habakkuk was obviously crying out for a fresh manifestation of God's power and presence among his people. *"Renew them in our day"* he pled.

God's people in Habakkuk's day urgently needed the out-pouring of His great grace and His Spirit just as we do today! We so desperately need a true spiritual awakening! This can only come by a Church that is willing to humble itself in the presence of the Holy Spirit, and cry out to Him to bring us God's mercy and power afresh! We so desperately need renewal and revival today! We need it more than anything else!

God is ready to give it to us, but He is waiting for our response. I believe Jesus was trying to get me to see that He is inviting us to a much higher level of relationship with Him. He is saying,

> "Seek Me earnestly in My Word; obey Me with all your hearts, and make yourselves available to Me. Spend time with Me. When you do this My power and glory will shine forth on your behalf through the presence of the Holy Spirit and you will see amazing things begin to happen. Signs and wonders will explode in your midst."

*You will seek me and find me when you seek me with all your heart. I will be found by you, declares the LORD, "and will bring you back from captivity . . . (Jeremiah 29:13-14)*

Jeremiah's people were in physical captivity, but the church today is in spiritual captivity. One form of captivity comes from constantly seeking God's hand but not His face. We desperately seek His acts of benevolence; once we receive it, we walk away rejoicing but forgetting to seek His face or honor Him. We His children miss the joy of fellowship with Him. How wonderful it would be to seek Him with all our hearts, to know Him, to serve Him, to daily pour out our love to Him in truth, deep adoration, and awe.

Ten lepers came to Jesus one day for healing. Only *one* returned to thank Him, to adore Him, to seek His face, and this one was a Samaritan, the outsider. Listen to the sad remarks of Lord:

*Jesus asked, **"Were not all ten cleansed? Where are the other nine? Was no one found to return and give praise to God except this foreigner?"** Then he said to him, "Rise and go; your faith has made you well." (Luke 17:17–19)*

Nine-tenths of those who were blessed with healing, walked away and never returned to give thanks or to fellowship with the Lord who healed them. Do we resemble these nine men?

This takes us right back to the Garden of Eden where Adam and Eve experienced this true close-up intimacy with the Lord until the fateful day of disobedience. One day they listened to the voice of the serpent and submitted to the treachery of a reptile, bringing upon all men the leprous condition of sin and separation from the living God. Have you noticed that the disease of leprosy in Biblical times called for the separation of those smitten with the disease from those who were clean? Even currently, lepers live in leper colonies, separate from others. So it happened with Adam and Eve, the minute they became unclean with sin, they immediately plunged into a state of separation from the one true, perfectly holy God, who then mercifully condescended to take upon Himself the leprous condition of sin so as to cleanse us, and buy back the relationship that we once had with Him.

Not much different from the nine Jewish lepers who were healed by Jesus, we the Church, now cleansed from the leprosy of sin by the enormous price Jesus paid, walk away to show ourselves to the priests—yes we go to church, but forget to come back, to really give thanks and praise to the God who healed us at tremendous expense to Himself. We forget to adore Him, to spend time with Him, to yearn for His presence, until we hit the next catastrophe in our lives. How could we be so cold, so thankless, and so unloving towards the One who gave His very life to purchase us from the claws of the devil? Church it is time to wake up! It is time to re-think our daily routines. It is time to come back to Him in love and adoration, in worship and thanks that overflow from the depths of our innermost beings. He deserves all our deepest love, passionate praise, devotion and loyalty.

If we truly seek the face of God in His Word, we will also experience the return of true intimacy and a deep and loving relationship with Him. It is only at this place of devotion that we will get back the communion of Eden. Our dependence upon God will increase to amazing levels, and so we will instinctively give Him the opportunity to radiate the power of His glorious Word in us and through us, for our good at all times. At this place, we will begin to live, breathe, speak, and shine forth His Word in our daily lives. *"Deep calls to deep . . . By day the LORD directs his love, at night his song is with me—a prayer to the God of my life (Psalm 42:7–8).*

In Psalm 119:130 we read, *"The entrance of Your words gives light; It gives understanding to the simple."*

Even the simplest of us will gain great understanding of the Word through the light of the presence of the Holy Spirit—the Author. By developing a strong relationship with the Lord in His Word, we who believe in Jesus Christ will gain supernatural understanding of what to do in every circumstance. The wisdom that comes through revelation knowledge from God's Word by the precious Holy Spirit, is our strength. Solomon's describes perfectly what our heart-cry should be.

*My son, **if you accept my words and store up my commands within you, turning your ear to wisdom and applying your heart to understanding, and if you call out for insight and cry aloud for understanding, and if you look for it as for silver and search for it as for hidden treasure, then you will understand the fear of the LORD and find the knowledge of God. For the LORD gives wisdom, and from his mouth come knowledge and understanding.** (Proverbs 2:1–6)*

In doing as Solomon advises, we could enjoy intimate relationship with the Lord, and by knowing and applying His

Word to every life situation, we could constantly walk in His light. *"Your word is a lamp to my feet and a light for my path" (Psalm 119:105).* God's abiding presence continually lights up our way, laying bare the snares and pitfalls the enemy so skillfully places before us daily, and the power of His Word now truly becomes both our sword and shield.

> *Friendship with the LORD is reserved for those who fear him. With them he shares the secrets of his covenant.* ***My eyes are always looking to the LORD for help, for he alone can rescue me from the traps of my enemies.*** *(Psalm 25:14–15)*

The Gospel of John holds the key to life. Its revelation powerfully emphasizes the very core of our faith.

> *In the beginning was the Word, and the Word was with God, and the Word was God.* ***He was with God in the beginning*** *. . .* ***In him was life, and that life was the light of men.*** *(John 1:1–4)*

We should never forget that to ignore the written Word of God is to also ignore the person of Jesus Christ. It is impossible to separate Him from His Word because *He is* what He says: He is the Word, He is Truth and He is the Life. Apart from Him there can be no truth or life. The writer of the Hebrew letter states,

> *Therefore holy brothers, who share in the heavenly calling,* ***fix your thoughts on Jesus, the apostle and high priest whom we confess.*** *He was faithful to the one who appointed him, just as Moses was faithful in all God's house. Jesus has been found worthy of greater honor than Moses, just as the builder of a house has greater honor than the house itself. For every house is built by someone, but God is the builder of everything. Moses was faithful as a servant in all God's house*

*testifying to what would be said in the future.* **But Christ is faithful as a son over God's house. And we are his house, if we hold on to our courage and the hope of which we boast.** *(Hebrews 3:1–6)*

We become qualified to be part of His House when we fix our thoughts on Jesus and hold fast to our courage and hope, through a vibrant relationship with Him. This now brings us to the "living stones" we are called to be.

*As you come to him, the living Stone-rejected by men but chosen by God and precious to him-* **you also, like living stones, are being built into a spiritual house to be a holy priesthood, offering spiritual sacrifices acceptable to God through Jesus Christ.** *(1 Peter 2:4–5)*

This is the kind of relationship the disciples—the first church—had with the Lord. Somewhere along the line it was diminished and in some cases even lost in the throes of religion versus relationship. Through His beautiful gesture of extending to us the radiant Bible, Jesus invites us all back into that glorious love and intimacy with Him.

If we do not choose to accept the Lord's invitation to receive, to study and fix our minds steadfastly upon Him through the Word and the guidance of the Holy Spirit, we will continue to live at a lower level of intimacy with Him than is available to us. This intimacy is the strength and glory of His abiding presence. If we receive His invitation to dine on the manna of His Word, we will continue to overcome the constant flow of evil messages that the enemy throws at us through the world. Communications that are in direct opposition to God's Word will not flood our thoughts and minds and we will not act, walk, talk, and live by the same standards of the world.

When Jesus lovingly extended the beautiful, radiant Bible to me, He made it quite clear that it is exclusively through the power and light of His Word that true understanding comes.

It is available to anyone who will receive the offer, for it is the key that enables all who believe to live victoriously and abundantly.

The Lord continuously offers His Word to everyone who is called by His name; He invites Christians to unclutter their lives and minds from the things of the world and to receive the awesome blessings that are so freely available through God's holy Word.

The world vehemently rejects the Scriptures, and they consequently reap what they sow. Our first parents were the initial examples of this great mistake. Not long after, God reached out to Cain with His Word to keep him from falling into grave sin, but Cain rejected the offer and destroyed himself.

Abel, on the other hand, received and obeyed the Word of the Lord. The Bible tells us,

*By faith Abel offered God a better sacrifice than Cain did. By faith he was commended as a righteous man, when God spoke well of his offerings. And by faith he still speaks, even though he is dead. (Hebrews 11:4)*

Abel obviously knew God's Word and chose to respond correctly to what God required of him. By offering a blood sacrifice Abel clearly declared his need for a Savior. Cain's offering was not accepted by God because he acted without faith and contrary to the command of the Lord. Cain acted upon the dictates of his own will. His offering was bloodless, and in making this type of offering Cain was rejecting his need for a blood covering of his sins. Consequently, he was rejecting the future Savior, the Lamb of God, who would finally pay the price for his sins and the sins of all men.

*And without faith it is impossible to please God, because any one who comes to him must believe that he exists and that he rewards those who earnestly seek him. (Hebrews 11:6)*

186

Cain was without faith, and so it was impossible for him to please God. His rebellion to the LORD came because he rejected God's Word.

Faith is accepting God's Word and trusting Him to do exactly as His Word promises. *"So then Faith comes by hearing and hearing by the word of God" (Romans 10:17).* Faith that comes from knowing and abiding in God's Word causes us to act upon it, and we steadfastly choose to believe that God will surely do as He has promised, even if we do not see immediate results. *"Now faith is being sure of what we hope for and certain of what we do not see" (Hebrews 11:1).*

God said to Cain,

*Why are you angry? Why is you face downcast?* ***If you do what is right will you not be accepted?*** *But if you do not do what is right, sin is crouching at your door; it desires to have you, but you must master it. (Genesis 4:6–7)*

God's question, *"if you do what is right will you not be accepted?"* indicates that Cain clearly knew what was right but chose not to do it. God specifically reminded Cain of what he could and should do to make things right, but again Cain chose to reject the Word of salvation with finality. Even though God lovingly reached out to Cain with His Word as He does to all of us, Cain rejected it, and this sin led him to kill his righteous brother. We are warned,

***Do not be like Cain, who belonged to the evil one and murdered his brother.*** *And why did he murder him? Because his own actions were evil and his broth-er's were righteous. (1 John 3:12)*

The Lord's act of reaching out with the glorious Bible in the palm of His hand was a picture of what God has been doing from the beginning of time. Adam and Eve rejected God's Word and the consequences are still being felt today. Cain rejected God's Word and lost his soul and so it has been with countless others who have said "no" to Jesus Christ. Judas rejected the Living Word and lost his soul along with every blessing he could have had.

The Lord continuously tries to save us from the deadly pitfalls that we become victim to through lack of knowledge of His Word. David prayed: *"Direct my footsteps according to your word; let no sin rule over me" (Psalm 119:133).*

If we choose to walk in ignorance of the Scriptures we act in ways that are both detrimental to ourselves and displeasing to God. Human nature prompts us to act upon the emotions of the moment, and many times we too like Cain commit murder against our brothers and sisters through anger and feelings of hate, malicious talk, gossip, and slander. Jesus warned us:

*You have heard that it was said to the people long ago, 'Do not murder, and anyone who murders will be subject to judgment.'* **But I tell you that anyone who is angry with his brother will be subject to judgment.** *(Matthew 5:21–22)*

The Scriptures advice us,

**For though we live in the world, we do not wage war as the world does. The weapons we fight with are not the weapons of the world. On the contrary, they have divine power to demolish strongholds.** *We demolish arguments and every pretension that sets itself up against the knowledge of God,* **and we take captive every thought to make it obedient to Christ.** *(2 Corinthians 10:3–6)*

Like Cain, every one of us can trace all our problems to either ignorance of God's Word or willful disobedience to it. *"My people are destroyed from lack of knowledge" (Hosea 4:6).*

Once we mess up by walking in our own ways, we want God to immediately fix our problems. When things don't turn out exactly as we would like them to, we proceed to walk around with downcast faces, we complain, pout, and are angry that God has not answered our disgruntled prayers. While we indulge in our little pity-parties, Jesus continues to lovingly reach out to us with a smiling invitation; He offers us the Radiant Bible that reflects and refracts the light of His answer, and His power for our victory. These blessings however, are only to be found etched upon the pages of His Holy Word, and we will find them if we search for them.

> *How precious to me are your thoughts, O God! How vast is the sum of them! Were I to count them, they would outnumber the grains of sand. When I awake, I am still with you. (Psalm 139:17–18)*

We should understand that God is not primarily interested in fixing the problems we bring upon ourselves through ignorance of His Word and disobedience to it. He is interested in fixing *us.* He wants us to live in obedience to Him, because it is the only right way. Apart from a lifestyle of prayer and study of the Scriptures, we can have no victory over Satan and the snares he sets for us. The Bible tells us, "*. . . seek first his kingdom and his righteousness, and all these things will be given to you as well" (Matthew 6:33).*

Too many broken and hurting people run from church to church seeking someone to lay hands on them and pray that they would be set free from some immediate problem, *but they have no plans to change their ways.* It certainly doesn't make sense to continue doing the same thing in the same way and expect different results. Even if God was to immediately fix every problem of those who do not know the Word, they will soon find themselves back in the same mess or worse once again. The Bible tells us, *"Wisdom is supreme; therefore get wisdom. Though it cost all you have get understanding" (Proverbs 4:7).*

Often God extends His grace to supernaturally help someone, but His love extends far beyond the immediate problem and calls out for their attention, because He desires them to make His way their lifestyle.

*If you abide in Me, and My words abide in you, you will ask what you desire, and it shall be done for you. By this My Father is glorified, that you bear much fruit; so you will be My disciples. (John 15:7–8)*

A Christian who lives like the world commits spiritual adultery. Change must happen if we are to walk victoriously in the Lord. The Bible tells us,

*For those whom He foreknew [of whom He was aware and loved beforehand], He also destined from the beginning [foreordaining them] to be molded into the image of His Son [and share inwardly His likeness], that He might become the firstborn among many brethren. (Romans 8:29, AMP)*

God knew us and loved us before the foundation of the earth. His significant purpose is to mold us into the image of His Son. Those who understand this go from glory to glory, but the ones who do not, continue to grumble and complain their way many times around the same mountain, just as the children of Israel did. Israel's God was right there with them, and all His power and light was available to them, but many times they did not submit to Him or benefit from His power because they would not receive it. As a result many of them died in the desert of their own obstinacy.

This certainly was not the will of the Lord for the Israelites any more than it is for His Church. We must keep in mind that the keys that unlock the great treasures of God's Word *are also only found within His Word.*

Believers, who do not to study the Bible, run around looking for someone to give them a "word." They are looking for someone to prophesy something good to them, not entirely unlike a fortune-teller. Usually these people are so desperate to hear something appealing that they are ready to receive anything from anyone. They have no idea if what they just heard was from God or Satan because they have nothing to measure it by. Since they do not know the Scriptures they also don't know if what they heard lines up with God's Word or not. The Bible clearly warns,

*Dear friends, do not believe every spirit, but test the spirits to see whether they are from God, because many false prophets have gone out into the world. (1 John 4:1)*

Not all things that sound good necessarily come from God. The Bible tells us, *"Satan himself masquerades as an angel of light" (2 Corinthians 11:14).* It isn't what sounds good that comes from God, but that which is good.

As we spend time in earnest prayer and study, seeking to know God, the Holy Spirit will manifest His great love for us, and our desire to know and understand the Word will become a thirst that is unquenchable. The Psalmist wrote,

*As the deer pants for streams of water, so my soul pants for you, O God. My soul thirsts for God, for the living God. When can I go and meet with God? (Psalm 42:1–2)*

The Holy Spirit helps us to see ourselves as He sees us. The mirror of God's Word, reveals the real you and me and spurs within us the desire to change and conform to the image of Christ. As our thirst for time with Him increases we also become more eager and willing to let go of everything in our lives that displeases Him. The yearning to submit completely to the Lord now becomes dominant and we will not be satisfied until we change to become more and more like Jesus. James tells us,

*. . . The man who looks intently into the perfect law that gives freedom, and continues to do this, not forgetting what he has heard, but doing it—he will be blessed in what he does. (James 1:25)*

It won't be too long down this road of total submission to the Lord, before we will find ourselves pleading as David did.

*Search me, O GOD, and know my heart; test me and know my anxious thoughts. See it there is any offensive way in me, and lead me in the way everlasting (Psalm 139:23–24)*

To return to the vision I saw of Jesus shining the light of His Word first on slabs of stone, and then on a few unhealthy plants, the Lord proceeded to reveal what all this meant. He said the sickly plants were representative of people who were being offered the opportunity to turn to God's Word, receive nourishment from it, and become healthy and live. Of course they had the freedom to refuse to do so. The slabs of stone, on the other hand, represented those who had continually chosen to reject the Word and had reached a level of such hardness of heart that they had actually petrified. Regardless of how much light was shone on them at this point, they would never receive it. The Bible warns, *"So as the Holy Spirit says: 'Today if you hear his voice do not harden your hearts . . .'"* (Hebrews 3:7).

We should be determinedly willingness to humbly ask God to show us what displeases Him in our lives and be ready to change it.

*For the word of God is full of living power. It is sharper than the sharpest knife, cutting deep into our innermost thoughts and desires. It exposes us for what we really are. (Hebrews 4:12)*

The Word of God shows us our sins and weaknesses and gives us the strength to change and overcome. How careful we should be not to let our hearts become hardened. Paul urges us to not only think of ourselves, but also to encourage other believers as well. This is one way of keeping our hearts soft.

*See to it, brothers, that none of you has a sinful, unbelieving heart that turns away from the living God. **But encourage one another daily, as long as it is called today, so that none of you may be hardened by sin's deceitfulness.** We have come to share in Christ if we hold firmly till the end the confidence we had at first. **As has just been said: "Today, if you hear his voice, do not harden your hearts as you did in the rebellion.** (Hebrews 3:12–15)*

Unbelieving Israel hardened their hearts, and so many of them never entered the Promised Land; sadly, they died in the wilderness instead. This pictures the danger of being callous towards God's holy Word. Israel's goal was to enter the Promised Land, and only those who believed achieved it. Our Promised Land is the Kingdom of Heaven, and again it is only those who believe who will make it. Let's make sure we do not miss it.

God has given us the responsibility to know and apply His Word to our lives so that we remain spiritually healthy, vibrant, and pleasing to Him. He has also given us the mandate to share the Word with others, so we must share the Gospel with the spiritually sick, and dying.

I wondered why Jesus continued to shine the light of His Word on the slabs of stone. I knew these slabs represented those without any hope of restoration. As I prayed for understanding Jesus made me see that He was saying to us: Take My Word and keep sharing it with all people. *Do not attempt to judge the living from the dead.* God alone reserves that right. The Bible tells us,

*There is a judge for the one who rejects me and does not accept my words; **that very word which I spoke will condemn him at the last day.** For I did not speak of my own accord, but the Father who sent me commanded me what to say and how to say it. **I know that his command leads to eternal life. So whatever I say is just what the Father has told me to say.** (John 12:48–50)*

The many Word-starved people within the Church are in this condition not because they haven't had the opportunity to study the Bible, but because they have chosen not to. These are the ones, the weak droopy plants represented. They had reached the perilous position of near-death spiritually, by putting the world and the things of it first in their lives. As we mentioned before, the group represented by the slabs of stone had continuously rejected the saving grace of the Lord Jesus Christ until their time ran out. Their hearts had hardened to the point where they had actually perished spiritually even though their bodies still walk this earth, until finally they pass into a Godless eternity.

Webster's New World dictionary defines the term "petrify" as follows: "To replace the normal cells of organic matter with silica or other mineral deposits; re-form as a stony substance. To make rigid, inflexible, or inert; to harden or deaden."

Sadly this description fits the condition of those who constantly refuse to hear the Gospel or respond to it because they have no desire to turn form their evil ways. The Apostle Paul spent a whole day speaking to some Jews in Rome who would not believe. He said,

*The Holy Spirit spoke the truth to your forefathers when He said through Isaiah the Prophet: "Go to this people and say, 'You will be ever hearing but never understanding; you will be ever seeing but never perceiving. **For this people's heart has become calloused; they hardly hear with their ears, and they have closed***

**their eyes.** *Otherwise they might see with their eyes, hear with their ears, understand with their hearts and turn, and I would heal them. (Acts 28:25–27)*

Although the people Paul was speaking to had hard, rigid, and inflexible hearts, Paul still continued to shine the light of the Gospel upon them. He did not presume to make a judgment upon their final condition by withholding the Word from them. We also must do as Paul did and continue to shine the light, not making a judgment that is reserved for God alone.

*Let us not become weary in doing good, for at the proper time we will reap a harvest if we do not give up. Therefore, as we have opportunity, **let us do good to all people, especially to those who belong to the family of believers.** (Galatians 6:9)*

Our obedience to Jesus Christ can bring marvelous results. We have no idea whom the Lord can touch and whom He can change, so we must leave judgment to Him and serve diligently as the Apostles did. God promised miracles for Israel and He can do it for anyone. Of Israel the Lord said,

*I will give them an undivided heart and put a new spirit in them; I will remove from them their heart of stone and give them a heart of flesh. Then they will follow my decrees and be careful to keep my laws. They will be my people, and I will be their God. (Ezekiel 11:19–20)*

So the Lord expects all faithful believers to obey Him by sharing His Word. *"Let the redeemed of the LORD say so"* *(Psalm 107:2)*. Jesus extended an urgent message to us by offering that radiant Bible to me. He was saying to the Church,

"Wake up, the hour is late, Work with Me, Share My Word with the lost and dying. Revive the weak and desperately sick among you by shining the light of My Word upon them. Remember also to take it to those who appear dead in spirit, and those in deep, deep darkness. Give everyone the opportunity to be exposed to the light and power of My glorious Word."

When the Lord Jesus spoke to John the Apostle regarding the Seven Churches in Asia, He was no longer the meek and gentle Savior who walked this earth preaching the Gospel, healing the sick, receiving insults, being rejected by men, and humbly making His way to the cross to pay for all our sins. The powerful Lord we see in the Book of Revelation is the One the Church will be accountable to for how faithful we have been to His teaching and commission. Listen to John's description of the ascended Lord.

*On the Lord's Day I was in the Spirit, and I heard behind me a loud voice like a trumpet, which said: "Write on a scroll what you see and send it to the seven churches: to Ephesus, Smyrna, Pergamum, Thyatira, Sardis, Philadelphia and Laodicea." **I turned around to see the voice that was speaking to me. And when I turned I saw seven golden lampstands, and among the lampstands was someone "like a son of man," dressed in a robe reaching down to his feet and with a golden sash around his chest. His head and hair were white like wool, as white as snow, and his eyes were like blazing fire. His feet were like bronze glowing in a furnace, and his voice was like the sound of rushing waters. In his right hand he held seven stars, and out of his mouth came a sharp double-edged sword. His face was like the sun shining in all its brilliance. When I saw him, I fell at his feet as though dead.** Then he placed his* *right hand on me and said: "Do not be afraid. I am the First and the Last. I am the Living one; I was dead, and behold I am alive forever and ever! And I hold the keys of death and Hades. "Write, therefore, what you have seen, what is now and what will take place later. The mystery of the seven stars that you saw in my right hand and of the seven golden lampstands is this: The seven stars are the angels of the seven churches, and the seven lampstands are the seven churches. (Revelation 1:10–20)*

Jesus instructed John to write what he had seen as He explained the mystery of the seven stars and seven lamp-stands. The angels of the seven churches were in His hand, so they were obviously subject to His great power. We wonder if these angels were the pastors of the churches or angels on assignment. If these were indeed pastors, they would have been in complete obedience to Jesus because He held them in His hand. However, if they were assigned angels, then conceivably, they would have been keeping very accurate records for Him regarding the things that took place within each congregation. So it might be interesting for us to take a look at our local congregations and note the defining characteristics within them that seem to compare or identify with any one of the Seven Churches of Asia. We might just be surprised by what we find. These seven churches were the lampstands or light-givers to the world at that time, and this is exactly what we the Church are supposed to be right now—light-givers.

When Jesus addressed the churches in Asia we see that He first commended the good in each of them, and then pointed out their weaknesses, warning them of coming consequences if they would not repent and turn from their sins. For the sake of time and space we will just focus on the warnings the Lord gave to some of them. Let's keep in mind that Jesus said, *"I am the light of the world. Whoever follows me will never walk in darkness, but will have the light of life" (John 8:12).*

The Lord had this to say to the churches.

1. **Ephesus**: *"I hold this against you:* **You have forsaken your first love.** *Remember the height from which you have fallen.* **Repent and do the things you did at first.** *If you do not repent, I will come to you and remove your Lampstand from its place . . . He who has an ear let him hear what the Spirit says to the churches"* (Revelation 2:4–7)

Jesus warned the Ephesians about their lack of love for Him. He warned that He would remove their Lampstand if they did not repent and return to their first love. This is a warning we should take very seriously as we look at our own level of love for the Lord. Our love level could be measured by the extent of our desire to obey Jesus by spending time with Him in His Word and sharing it with the lost.

2. **Smyrna**: *"Do not be afraid of what you are to suffer. I tell you the devil will put some of you in prison to test you and you will suffer much persecution for ten days.* **Be faithful even to the point of death**, *and I will give you the Crown of Life.* **He who has an ear let him hear."** *(Revelation 2:10-11)*

Be faithfulness even unto death! Are we as faithful as the Church at Smyrna? If not we should be. Are we being taught this? Are we personally and collectively in such deep covenant with Jesus Christ that we would be willing to die for our faith in Him? We had better examine ourselves in case we ever have to face such a situation.

3. **Pergamum**: *"I have a few things against you:* **You have people there who hold to the teaching of Balaam, who taught Balak to entice the Israelites to sin by eating food sacrificed to idols and by committing sexual immorality. Likewise you also have those who hold to the teaching of the Nicolaitans. Repent therefore!** *Otherwise, I will*

*soon come to you and will fight against them with the sword of my mouth. **He who has an ear let him hear what the Spirit says to the churches.***" *(Revelation 2:14–17)*

If there is false teaching in our churches do we agree with them, or do we agree with God's Word—the Bible?

4. **Thyatira:** *"Nevertheless, I have this against you: **You tolerate that woman Jezebel who calls herself a prophetess. By her teaching she misleads my servants into sexual immorality and the eating of foods sacrificed to idols.** I have given her time to repent of her immorality, but she is unwilling. So I will cast her on a bed of suffering, **and I will make those who commit adultery with her suffer intensely, unless they repent of her ways. I will strike her children dead.** Then all the churches will know that I Am he, who searches hearts and minds, and I will repay each of you according to your deeds . . . **He who has an ear let him hear what the Spirit says to the churches***" *(Revelation 2:20–29)*

According to Jesus, the sin that prevailed in the church at Thyatira was their tolerance of unrighteousness, and teachings that were not consistent with the Scriptures. Jezebel, a wicked queen mentioned in the Old Testament was known for idolatry and persecution of the righteous. Jezebel was spiritually and physically immoral. God hates spiritual and physical immorality. Jezebel was also conniving and controlling. We should carefully check the churches we attend. Is immorality accepted and tolerated? What about the so-called alternate lifestyles? Do the people with these types of lifestyles hear from the pulpit what God's Word has to say on the subject, or are they being led to think that God accepts what they are doing? What about the acceptance level of people of false faiths? Are they permitted to speak from the pulpit things that do not agree with the Bible? Are such people welcome to speak in your church? We must be exceedingly careful not to deviate even slightly from the written Word. Jesus told us we could know the spiritual state of a person by how they speak and act. Jesus said *". . . by their fruit you will recognize them"* *(Matthew 7:20).*

5. **Sardis** *"I know your deeds; you have a reputa-tion for being alive, but you are dead. Wake up! Strengthen what remains and is about to die, for I have not found your deeds complete in the sight of my God. Remember therefore, what you have received and heard; obey it, and repent.* *But if you do not wake up,* **I will come like a thief, and you will not know at what time I will come to you** *. . . He who overcomes will . . . be dressed in white. I will never blot his name out of the Book of life, but will acknowledge his name before my Father and his angels.* **He who has an ear, let him hear what the Spirit says to the churches"** *(Revelation 3:1–6)*

What a startling revelation! How very carefully pastors and leaders of the churches should seek the face of the Lord with reference to their own spiritual state and that of the flocks they shepherd. How easy it is to get carried away by appearance and reputation and miss the Lord's evaluation. We should be carefully seeking God's face regarding our own spiritual conditions. What a frightening thing it would be to think we are in good shape and then find ourselves left behind when the Lord Jesus returns for His Church. It is vitally important for us to be overcomers and to know that we will actually be dressed in white. How wonderful to know that the Lord will never blot our names out of the Book of Life. Jesus says, *"He who has an ear let him hear what the Spirit says to the churches."* Let us listen carefully to the Holy Spirit!

6. **Philadelphia** *"I know your deeds. See I have placed before you an open door that no one can shut. I know that you have little strength, but you have kept my word and not denied my name.* I will make those of the synagogue of Satan, who claim to be Jews though they are not, but are liars—I will make them come and fall down at your feet and acknowledge that I have loved you. *Since you have kept My command to endure patiently, I will also keep you from the hour of trial that is going to come upon the whole world to test those who live on the earth.* I am coming soon. Hold on to what you have so that no one will take you crown. Him who overcomes I will make a pillar in the temple of my God. Never will he leave it. I will write on him the name of my God and the name of the city of my God the New Jerusalem which is coming down out of heaven from my God. And I will write on him my new name. *He who has an ear to hear, let him hear what the Spirit says to the churches."* (Revelation 3:8–13)

This is the church we should all desire to be part of. This is the Bride, the faithful Bride who did not deny her Lord but kept His command and endured patiently as did the Church at Smyrna. Every one of us should go to the Lord and ask Him to reveal what we must let go of in our lives. We should let Jesus make us pure, holy and faithful to Him so that we will be kept from the hour of trial—the tribulation period. How glorious it will be to leave with Jesus in the Rapture; but our ears must be open to the Spirit of the Lord, *now.*

6. **Laodicea** *"To the angel of the church in Laodicea write: These are the words of the Amen, the faithful and true witness, the ruler of God's creation.* **I know your deeds, that you are neither cold nor hot. I wish you were either one or the other!**

*So, because you are lukewarm-neither hot nor cold-I am about to spit you out of my mouth. You say, 'I am rich; I have acquired wealth and do not need a thing.' But you do not realize that you are wretched, pitiful, poor, blind and naked. I counsel you to buy from me gold refined in the fire, so you can become rich; and white clothes to wear, so you can cover your shameful nakedness; and salve to put on your eyes, so you can see. Those whom I love I rebuke and discipline. So be earnest, and repent. Here I am! I stand at the door and knock. If anyone hears my voice and opens the door, I will come in and eat with him, and he with me. To him who overcomes, I will give the right to sit with me on my throne, just as I overcame and sat down with my Father on his throne. He who has an ear, let him hear what the Spirit says to the churches." (Rev 3:14–22)*

This obviously is the mindset we want to avoid at all costs! We should earnestly pray, be alert, and make sure that we are not lukewarm toward the things of the Lord. It would be terrible to think we are in good shape with the Lord and then have Jesus spit in disgust at the sound of our name. How awful it would be, to be spewed out of His Holy Mouth because we chose to live in a tepid, unfaithful state. To choose not to be loyal or faithful to Him is a great sin.

When Jesus said, *"Here I AM, I stand at the door and knock. If anyone hears my voice . . ."* He was speaking to a church who thought it was doing so well that it needed nothing. This church was rich financially, but wretched, poor, pitiful, blind, and naked in the sight of the Lord. Obviously the church at Laodicea was not true to the Lord. They did what they thought was good for themselves for the moment. In other words they lived for themselves.

Is this the kind of church you and I are today? We should all stop and ask: If this is me, Lord, please forgive me; open my eyes that I might see. I give my heart to you. Lord, cleanse me and set me free from myself and grant me grace that I might dine with You at Your table.

The Lord said over and over, to every church, *"He who has an ear to hear, let him hear what the Spirit says to the Churches."* It is extremely important that we heed His Words. Habakkuk said, *"The LORD is in his holy temple; let all the earth be silent before him."* (Habakkuk 2:20) It is time to get silent before Almighty God so that we can hear the voice of the Holy Spirit. Jesus is trying to get our attention as He says, *"He who has an ear to hear, let him hear what the Spirit says to the Churches."* It is also time for us to not only hear but **do** as God instructs. *"Do not merely listen to the word, and so deceive yourselves. Do what it says" (James 1:22).*

Those of us who see ourselves as the "faithful Church" have the same responsibility Ezekiel did. We must share the Word of God with all people.

*Son of man I have made you a watchman for the house of Israel; so hear the word I speak and give them warning from me. When I say to a wicked man 'You will surely die,' and you do not warn him or speak out to dissuade him from his evil ways in order to save his life, that wicked man will die for his sin, and I will hold you accountable for his blood. But if you warn the wicked man and he does not turn from his wickedness or evil ways, he will die for his sins; but you will have saved yourself. (Ezekiel 3:17–18)*

The time is at hand, and obviously no Christian will want to appear before God with the blood of his neighbor on his hands. It is time for all of us, who are called by His name, to rekindle the fire of our first love for Jesus by allowing Him at every available opportunity, to shine the light of His Word through us on the lost and dying.

The Lord's love for us is amazing and unending; it is time Jesus becomes our first love again, and our lives a passionate and worshipful relationship with Him.

The time is truly at hand and we must wake up!

# Chapter 12

# THE BIBLE AND THE CHAIN

———œœœ———

I was now shown a very simply furnished room. On a table in the center of this room was a beautiful gold Bible. Suddenly I saw a thick black chain begin to creep up from under the table and slip around the Bible. An ugly, black, scaly hand tugged hard at the two ends of the chain trying to bring them together in order to secure them with a padlock.

I did not like what I saw at all, but felt somewhat relieved as I realized that the task was impossible for this creature to accomplish in a one-handed attempt.

No matter how hard this ugly thing kept pulling on the ends of the chain, it could not succeed in getting the two ends together. As one end of the chain got fairly close, the other end would slip away, and so these futile attempts continued back and forth. I thought it was noteworthy however, that no matter how many times it failed, this beast did not stop trying to achieve its diabolical goal. It worked feverishly, never giving up its quest to chain up the Bible. It was plain to see that the intended purpose of chaining up God's Word, was to deprive people of reading, understanding, and believing it.

It did not take much to figure, that this hideous hand belonged to Satan. The fact that only one hand was employed, reveals two things. Firstly, Satan single-handedly attempts day and night to chain up the Bible to every person on earth. Second, his power to prevail over the Word of God is limited.

History has disclosed the devil's countless attempts to suppress and destroy the written Word of God, but history has also shown that the Bible has prevailed every time. Doubtless it will continue to do so forever. Jesus said,

*I tell you the truth, until heaven and earth disappear,* ***not the smallest letter, not the least stroke of a pen, will by any means disappear from the Law until everything is accomplished****. (Matthew 5:18)*

The Lord revealed to me that while the devil could not prevail in his attempts to chain up the Bible, there was something very disturbing about this scene that might not have caught the eye right away. It certainly did not catch my attention until the Lord pointed it out. God's holy Word lay untouched, unopened, and neglected on this bleak table and there wasn't anyone around while Satan continued to launch his relentless attack upon the Bible.

The Lord explained that this sad picture is exactly how the Bible is treated in many homes across the world. The life-giving Word is all is too often not read, studied, or lived by; instead it is neglected and forgotten upon a table or a shelf. This happens even in the homes of many who identify themselves as born-again Christians. The fact that Satan couldn't chain up God's Word indicated that people are yet free to pick up the Bible at any given time, open it, read it, live by its instructions, be blessed, and lead others to salvation. God Himself keeps Satan from eradicating the Holy Scriptures, and this for our best benefit. Paul made an interesting statement to Timothy. He said,

*Never forget that Jesus Christ was a man born into King David's family and that he was raised from the dead. This is the Good News I preach. And because I preach this Good News, I am suffering and have been chained like a criminal.* ***But the word of God cannot be chained.*** *I am willing to endure anything if it will*

206

*bring salvation and eternal glory in Christ Jesus to those God has chosen. (2 Timothy 2:8–10)*

Paul was willing to endure anything to bring salvation and eternal glory in Jesus Christ to those God had chosen. This should be our attitude as well but the Lord's final instruction to His Church, has not been followed by the vast majority of believers. Jesus commissioned,

*"Go into all the world and preach the good news to all creation. Whoever believes and is baptized will be saved, but whoever does not believe will be condemned. And these signs will accompany all those who believe: In my name they will drive out demons; they will speak with new tongues; they will pick up snakes with their hands; and when they drink deadly poison, it will not harm them at all; they will place their hands on sick people and they will get well." (Mark 16:15–16)*

How greatly it must grieve God to see His children blindly fall into one satanic trap after another simply because they neglect to study His Word. Too many believers have no knowledge of how to avoid the daily snares of the devil. Once having fallen in, they have no idea how to get out, when all the time God's Word shows the way and sheds the light. *"Your word is a lamp to my feet and a light to my path" (Psalm 119:105).*

The importance of knowing the Scriptures and obeying them cannot be stressed more clearly than how Moses put it:

*These are the commands, decrees and laws the LORD your God directed me to teach you to observe in the land that you are crossing the Jordan to possess,* **so that you, your children and their children after them may fear the LORD your God as long as you live by keeping all his decrees and commands that I give you, and so that you may enjoy long life.** *Hear, O Israel, and be* **careful to obey so that it may go** *well with you and that you may increase greatly in a land flowing with milk and honey, just as the LORD, the God of your fathers, promised you. Hear, O Israel: The LORD our God, the LORD is one. Love the LORD your God with all your heart and with all your soul and with all your strength. These commandments that I give you today are to be upon your hearts. Impress them on your children. Talk about them when you sit at home and when you walk along the road, when you lie down and when you get up. Tie them as symbols on your hands and bind them on your foreheads. Write them on the doorframes of your houses and on your gates.* (Deuteronomy 6:1–9)

The Lord commanded parents to keep the Word before their children, but every new fad that floods the market takes precedence over the Word of God. This is extremely dangerous! The Lord has graciously given us the reason for His command to know and obey His Word. *"So that you may enjoy long life . . . that it may go well with you and that you may increase greatly"* To know and obey God's word is to enjoy a long life, to have things go well for us, and that we as believers might multiply. This is clearly for our own good.

Many parents have failed to obey this vital command of the Lord and so children today struggle with rebellion, anger, and rage. Should we wonder why they kill each other in schools, speak foul and filthy language, engage in things that lead them into the occult, demonism, witchcraft, drugs, alcoholism, sex, and everything else that is a snare to their souls? Many lose out on enjoying long life, and too many die long before their appointed time.

Every crafty snare carefully engineered by the devil, is specifically to keep people from knowing and accepting Jesus Christ—*the "Way, the Truth, and the Life" (John 14:6)*.

Depending on which survey you look at, anywhere from sixty to eighty-five percent of young people fall away from church. Why is this? Much of it comes from not having a relationship with their parents that is built upon God's Word. Children grow up in homes where their "Christian" parents are too busy engaging them in every available activity of the world, and giving very little time if any, to studying the Scriptures. Children today can't help but notice their parent's major emphasis on worldly interests, while time with the Lord and the Word, take a backseat. The Bible tells us,

*All Scripture is God-breathed and is useful for teaching, rebuking, correcting and training in righteousness, so that the man of God may be thoroughly equipped for every good work. (2 Tim 3:16-17)*

Christians, who attempt to walk without the lamp of God's Holy Word, run the serious risk of straying down a wrong path. This truth is more than apparent in the lives of teens and the young- adult population today.

The importance of the Word of God in a believer's life cannot be stressed enough. Because we have not done as God commanded, but have neglected the Word and walked in our own ways, we have also walked in blindness and without its power. This in turn has brought much ridicule to the Gospel.

Unbelievers watch the lives of those who claim Jesus as Lord, looking for any opportunity to mock and decry the power of the Gospel. Light-bearers without light are of little help to a dark world. Jesus said,

**You are the light of the world. A city on a hill cannot be hidden.** *Neither do people light a lamp and put it under a bowl. Instead they put it on its stand, and it gives light to everyone in the house.* **In the same way, let your light shine before men, that they may see your good deeds and praise your Father in heaven.** *(Matthew 5:14–16)*

As the Church we should be ready, filled with the Word, and willing to obey the Lord's last and Great Commission to us. There are yet many that have never heard the Gospel. Great numbers of people yet don't even know that there is a way of salvation, and we should be doing everything in our power to get the Good News out to them.

Thank God for Christian television! Those who have made this wonderful method of sharing the Gospel with millions, have done so with much inconvenience and difficulty to themselves many times, and they should be highly commended and prayed for.

Be this as it may, the vast majority of believers don't do much more than warm church pews, desiring to be ministered to over and over again. It is time these dear people grow up in and through God's Word and prayer. It is also time they rise up to minister to the lost around them. One easy way to obey the Great Commission is to financially support the massive outreaches of Christian television. We should also remember to pray faithfully for these frontline soldiers of the Lord, because the enemy does not rest or give up on his deadly desire to quench the Word.

Everyone who has been purchased by the precious Blood of the Lamb should be a powerhouse filled with the knowledge of God's Word. The light of the Gospel should beam brightly through us, because the time is short. The freedom of Christians to share the Word in many countries around the world is greatly limited. Opposition to the freedom of Christians in the United States has grown big and continues to escalate. It has reached a point where it is almost considered a crime to mention the awesome name of Jesus or to carry a Bible into public schools or other places. Regardless, the Lord Jesus expects every believer to be a light to the world. He said,

*Whoever acknowledges me before men, I will also acknowledge him before my Father in heaven. But whoever disowns me before men, I will disown him before my Father in heaven. (Matthew 10:32–33)*

As we mentioned previously one major reason Christians are hesitant to share the Gospel, is because they feel inadequate for the task. This inadequacy comes from not studying or knowing God's Word sufficiently. One of the last things the Lord said to His disciples was,

> *. . . Peace be with you!* **As the Father sent me, I am sending you,** *and with that He breathed on them and said, "Receive the Holy Spirit. (John 20:21–22)*

When the Lord reached out the shining Bible to me as one belonging to the Church, it was obvious that He was reminding us all to wake up. Jesus was indicating that the hour is late, and that we must shine the light of His Word upon the lost and dying. Jesus was urging us to let His Word revive the droopy ones within the Church, and to keep shining it also upon those in deep, deep darkness, even if we think their hearts are as hard as stone."

As Satan vigorously struggles to keep the Word from us, we must not forget that the Word is the same powerful sword that Jesus Himself used against Satan. The Lord said to the devil, *"Man shall not live by bread alone, but by every Word that proceeds from the mouth of God" (Matthew 4:4).*

It is urgent that every Christian to begins to study and understand the Scriptures. It is God's precious gift to us; it is life. Even though the devil's power has been greatly impeded by the Lord, he continues to struggle desperately and tirelessly to destroy God's Word. This is because Satan knows how dangerous a weapon the Bible really is to his kingdom. So we must not hesitate to use it.

There are eleven hundred and eighty-nine chapters in the Bible. If we read just five chapters a day, perhaps two and a half chapters in the morning and two and a half in the evening, we will read the entire Bible through in four months. At this rate we could read it three times in a year. If every faithful believer determinedly keeps him or herself in God's Word on a daily basis, Satan will not be able to chain up the blessings of the Scriptures from us because we will know how to resist him through the authority and the power of God's holy Word.

If every believer not only reads but does what the Word teaches, we will be blessed with long lives and things will go well for us. What's more, there will be an increase of new believers around us, because we will be compelled by the Word to live and share the Gospel as the apostles did. The Word promises, *"Out of your belly will flow rivers of living water" (John 7:38).* Life usually gives birth to life!

There are many times that we feel an inner call to the Word. How we choose to answer that call parallels the responses of those who heard the Lord's invitation, *"Follow Me."* Some chose to do just that, and were immeasurably blessed, while others made excuses and missed the greatest blessing they could ever have received.

The Lord still invites us to His banqueting table, where He breaks the Bread of Life. If we accept and dine at His table, on the Word, we will receive the *"Authority to trample on snakes and scorpions, and to overcome all the power of the enemy" (Luke 10:19).* God's Word promises, *"Nothing will harm you" (Luke 10:19).*

Anyone who submits to God and resists Satan is counted as the pure and spotless Bride that Jesus is coming back for. The Lord had these words for the Church at Philadelphia,

> *. . . you have kept my word and not denied my name . . ."*
> *Since you have kept my command to endure patiently,*
> *I will also keep you from the hour of trial that is going*
> *to come upon the whole world to test those who live on*
> *the earth. (Revelation 3:8–10)*

This mighty promise from the Lord Jesus Christ is priceless! Every faithful believer has the assurance of the Lord, that he or she will not have to go through the tribulation period. What a tremendous blessing! However, we must keep in mind the Lord's warning as well.

**But take heed to yourselves, lest your hearts be weighed down with carousing, drunkenness, and cares of this life, and that Day come on you unexpectedly.** *For it will come as a snare on all those who dwell on the face of the whole earth.* **Watch therefore, and pray always that you may be counted worthy to escape all these things that will come to pass, and to stand before the Son of Man.** *(Luke 21:34–36)*

Some will be wise and accept the Lord's holy invitation; they will watch and pray while others decline it to their own detriment. The Lord grieves for them, just as He did for Jerusalem. Jesus wept as He said,

*O Jerusalem, Jerusalem . . ." How often I have longed to gather your children together as a hen gathers her chicks under her wings, but you were not willing. (Matthew 23:37)*

The Lord longs to gather all of us to the safety of His embrace, but remember, it is only the chicks that scurry to the safety of their mother's wings at the sound of her urgent call, that remain protected from the predator. So it is with us. Run to Jesus so you will not be left wide open to the one who comes "*. . . to steal and kill and destroy*" *(John 10:10).*

Dear Reader,

- Do you really know the voice of the Lord?
- Are you willing to obey His Word and submit to Him?
- Do you permit the devil to shut God's Word up to you by being negligent of it?
- Will you obey the Lord's call to His Word so that you will begin to look more like Him? If you do, you will be conformed to His image and you will be changed to resemble Him.
- Will you receive His loving invitation today?

When we receive God's Word—our daily bread, and begin to fellowship with Him, and when we determinedly submit to the sovereign Lord, the mighty power of His Word within us gives us strength to resist the devil, and he will flee from us. We must however, wake up while the Lord still calls.

*Come to me, all you who are weary and burdened, and I will give you rest. Take my yoke upon you and learn from me, for I am gentle and humble in heart, and you will find rest for your souls. For my yoke is easy and my burden is light. (Matthew 11:28–30)*

Wake up dear ones, and receive His loving invitation. The time surely is at hand!

# Chapter 13

# DOCTOR, DELIVER ME

A t this point I saw several amber-colored, see-through, balloon-like objects that were suspended in the air like the helium kind. They were not attached to anything but floated separately and individually near the ceiling of the room where I had previously seen the one-handed enemy attack on the golden Bible.

I was spiritually aware that the Bible was still on the table where I had first seen it and once again there was no one in the room, except for the ugly, black, scaly-handed creature that was still relentlessly trying to chain up the Bible.

Quite suddenly I was able to see into each of those amber colored balloons. Amazingly each balloon contained a little baby, full-term and ready to be delivered. I wondered what this could mean.

Then the Lord explained; this was a delivery room for souls of people who were ready to be born- again. They were waiting to be birthed into the Kingdom of the Lord. The instrument for the birthing procedure, the Bible, was on the table and ready for use. The safe delivery of each of these unborn babies could only be achieved through the life-giving Word of God. *Somehow, all the Dr. Believers were significantly absent.* With the notable absence of Christians who had been authorized by Jesus to share the Gospel, the ugly hand of the devil worked feverishly to chain up or silence the life-giving Word in its diabolical thrust to abort these little full-term babies.

It is noteworthy that Satan's greatest desire is to both physically and spiritually abort God's children. While most Christians would strongly oppose physical abortion as well they should, they don't even realize that much of the time Satan is using their very own sense of apathy and unconcerned life-styles to spiritually abort multitudes of babies. Jesus said, as He looked with compassion on the hurting, harassed masses,

> *The harvest is plentiful but the workers are few.* **Ask the Lord of the harvest, therefore, to send out workers into his harvest field.** *(Matthew 9:37–38)*

How hard can this be? Jesus says, at least pray and ask the Lord of the harvest to send out workers into the harvest field if you will not go yourself.

This snapshot in time, portrays with great accuracy the spiritual climate of today! Jesus trusted those of us who are saved to remain faithful on the job He started. But from what He showed me, it was apparent that no one had turned up to work. Every Dr. Christian was missing in action, and the babies hung precariously in the balance, in danger of losing their souls.

If a physical baby remains too long in the birth canal, it could suffer oxygen deprivation, causing major dysfunction like cerebral palsy. Doubtless, these spiritual babies would suffer much greater damage through deprivation of the eternal life-giving oxygen of the breath of God—the Scriptures. They would miss their chance of being born-again if they were not delivered into the Kingdom of God's dear Son.

The prophetic plea of the Messiah in this psalm, should be deeply felt by all of us.

> *O my people, hear my teaching; listen to the words of my mouth. I will open my mouth in parables, I will utter hidden things, things from of old—what we have*

*heard and known, what our fathers have told us. **We will not hide them from their children; we will tell the next generation the praiseworthy deeds of the LORD, his power, and the wonders he has done.** He decreed statutes for Jacob established the law in Israel, **which he commanded our forefathers to teach their children, so the next generation would know them, even the children yet to be born, and they in turn would tell their children. Then they would put their trust in God and would not forget his deeds but would keep his commands.** They would not be like their forefathers—a stubborn and rebellious generation, whose hearts were not loyal to God, whose spirits were not faithful to him. (Psalm 78:1–8)*

This Psalm should cause every Christian to share the praiseworthy deeds of the Lord with the young, the old, the children—the next generation of all those who will be saved! We should take every opportunity to do so.

Psalm 78 was primarily written to Israel to emphasize to them the importance of sharing with their children the wonders of what God had done for the nation of Israel. They did not do this, and each consecutive generation fell into the same sins of the previous one. They even plunged into worse sins than those of their fathers. This psalm is quoted in Matthew 13:35. Jesus taught by using parables. Those who believed the Lord, understood what He taught, but those who would not believe, could not understand what the Lord was teaching even though they were hearing the truth from the lips of the Messiah Himself.

This is something that Christians all over should take careful heed of. Are we really listening to the Word of the Lord? Do we understand it, obey it, and share it with the next generation of those waiting to be birthed into His Kingdom?

The scene I was shown made it exceedingly clear that we as believers in Jesus Christ have fallen into Israel's sin. Christians seldom share the Gospel thereby giving birth to the full-term babies who are ready and willing to receive the Word, believe it, and be saved. As mentioned earlier, we have become too deeply involved in our day-to-day living, not unlike the Israelites of David's day. Doesn't the Bible refer to this very attitude as being lukewarm? The prosperity of our times, the pleasures of the world, and the pursuit of them, have slowly but surely dulled the passion and faithfulness of many believers, plunging them into the self-focused, lukewarm mindset of the church at Laodicea.

Children of worldly Christians grow up tepid and disinterested in the things of the Lord because they have not been birthed into the Word by their parents. Instead they have been left to suffer the deadly consequences of being deprived of the life-giving oxygen of God's Holy Word.

Children of Christian parents attend public schools where the name of Jesus Christ cannot be mentioned. The Bible has no place, and God and prayer are taboo. The less children hear about God and His amazing love for them, the smaller the place they will have in their hearts for Him. Many parents don't read or study the Bible with their children. So one might ask, how these children, who grow up in such a tepid spiritual climate, could possibly take a strong stand for Jesus Christ in the face of the many atheistic teachers and professors who dominate the schools and universities they attend.

There will doubtless come a time of accounting for the many souls who were never delivered into eternal salvation, because too many "Dr. Believers" were busy ignoring the Word and the command of the Lord. These commissioned ones chose to remain "too busy," "too scared," or too disinterested to obey the Great Commission.

Our children are impressed to have great knowledge regarding athletes and celebrities of various sorts. They are made to feel that being involved in one kind of sport or another is about *the* most important thing in life. While there is nothing intrinsically wrong with interest in sports, the problem arises when it or anything else takes preeminence over God and His Holy Word. Children who grow up in such world-centered environments, end up as adults who have been extremely deprived of the Holy Word of God.

As the lack of oxygen to the physical body causes brain damage and even death, the deprivation of the pure oxygen of God's Word causes damage that could lead to spiritual death. While games, fun, and fads clog our day-to-day lives, many believers never stop to consider the warning words of Jesus Christ.

*Just as it was in the days of Noah, so also will it be in the days of the Son of Man. People were eating, drinking, marrying and being given in marriage up to the day Noah entered the ark. Then the flood came and destroyed them all. (Luke 17:26–27)*

Again, the Bible I saw under attack by Satan was pictured to be lying on a table *with no one there but the enemy,* who was working nonstop to shackle up the Word. While he can never be totally successful in accomplishing his goal, he has achieved a degree of success in the lives of many Christians. He has done this by flooding the lives of believers with so many worldly targets that they simply have no time left over for the treasures of the precious Word of God.

> **Teaching the Scriptures to our children is not a suggestion from the Lord; it is a command.**

The responsibility for obeying and diligently carrying out this command lies directly in the camp of parents. Those who neglect this command and de-emphasize the importance of knowledge and obedience to God's Word, become answerable to Him for their children's ignorance of His standard for living; Apathetic, and misguided children grow up into apathetic and misguided adults. How will such parents not be held guilty for such great unfaithfulness to the Lord?

We have no excuse for being ignorant of God's Word, and for not obeying it. What God decreed for Israel regarding knowledge of His Word is also His standard for us, seeing that it is for our good.

*He decreed statutes for Jacob, and established the law in Israel, **which he commanded our forefathers to teach their children, so the next generation would know them, even the children yet to be born and they in turn would tell their children. Then they would put their trust in GOD and would not forget his deeds but would keep his Commands.** (Psalm 78:5–7)*

The Lord Jesus plainly explained His position regarding knowledge and acceptance of His Word. He said:

**There is a judge for the one who rejects me and does not accept my words; that very word which I spoke will condemn him at the last day.** *For I did not speak of my own accord, but the Father who sent me commanded me what to say and how to say it.* **I know that his command leads to eternal life. So whatever I say is just what the Father has told me to say.** *(John 12:48–50)*

Pharisees in the time of Jesus were extremely prideful about their knowledge of the Word. They wore Scriptures in extra large phylacteries on their heads and arms, but this did not mean that they obeyed God's word. They did not obey the Scriptures but kept their own traditions.

Christians today have gone to the other extreme. Many don't even bother to read God's Word, and they too keep their own traditions. Just as the Pharisees thought themselves to be superior and bound for heaven because of their knowledge, many professing Christians think they are fine just because they once prayed the salvation prayer. They operate under a sense of false security just as the Pharisees did. They say "We are saved," although they take no time to study the Word, obey it, or teach it to their children. They live exactly as they please, justifying their every action. This kind of living bears no resemblance to the Church Jesus built.

Paul said to the church at Philippi,

*Your attitude should be the same as that of Christ Jesus: (Phil 2:5)*

He also said to them:

*Dearest friends, you were always so careful to follow my instructions when I was with you. **And now that I am away you must be even more careful to put into action God's saving work in your lives, obeying God with deep reverence and fear.** For God is working in you, giving you the desire to obey him and the power to do what pleases him. (Phil 2:12-13)*

The disciples spent every waking moment with Jesus and they left everything to follow Him. Consequently they became so much like Him that they were not only willing to obey His command to bring others into His Kingdom, but they were willing to lay down their lives to accomplish it.

Thank God for the faithfulness of these believers, or we would not have the Bible today, or the opportunity to be saved.

We should have the same attitude as Jesus and the disciples, but we have been sluggish and thoughtless. So except that the Holy Spirit intervenes directly on behalf of those who are ready to be born into His Kingdom, thousands will perish, having been deoxygenated in the spiritual placenta, pictured by the amber colored balloons that I was shown. This great sin would occur because many Christians don't care enough to deliver even one person from darkness into the light of the Gospel.

The Church must get up and do as the disciples did; but the Word of Truth must first dwell richly in the hearts of us all. As we the Church pray, study, and meditate on God's Word, plenty of opportunities to birth many full-term babies into the Kingdom of the Lord will arise.

The Lord made it clear to me that Satan's works hard to silence the Word to the Church through its leadership. Every believer who is full of God's Word and His Spirit is both vibrantly alive and a mighty threat to the devil. Therefore his strategy is to neutralize the minds of Christians through false teachers and a plethora of diversions that keep them from spending any time at all with the Lord in His Word. The devil tried desperately to silence the Living Word, the infant Jesus, but his pawn, Herod, failed miserably. The Bible tells us that instead, *"Jesus grew in wisdom and stature and in favor with God and men" (Luke 2:52).*

Knowledge of God's Word and obedience to it brings wisdom. Wisdom is God's Word applied accurately and consistently. Listen to Solomon the wisest man who ever lived! This was his advice:

*My son, if you accept my words and store up my commands within you, turning your ear to wisdom and applying your heart to understanding, and if you call out for insight and cry aloud for understanding, and if you look for it as for silver and search for it as for hidden treasure, then you will understand the fear of the LORD and find the knowledge of God. For the LORD gives wisdom, and from his mouth come knowledge and understanding. He holds victory in store for the upright, he is a shield to those whose walk is blameless, for he guards the course of the just and protects the way of his faithful ones. (Proverbs 2:1–8)*

If every Christian continued in the initial joy they experienced when they were first saved, by studying and obeying God's Word, they too would rise up and share the Gospel as the disciples did. Our level of zeal, commitment, and purpose would match or be very close to that of the first Church, and we would take the world or at least a large part of it for Jesus.

Think how you felt when you were first saved! You wanted to introduce every person you met to the Lord. Why? This is because you had just been in very close contact and communion with Jesus. You had fallen in love with Him, and His beautiful personality had totally captivated your heart and mind. You had just come to life in Him and an awesome relationship with the Lord had begun. However, relationships, even the best of them, are kept alive only through constant contact and communion. When less and less time is spent together in any relationship, love grows cold and eventually fades; it could even die. But the Bible tells us this about Jesus. *"If we are faithless, He will remain faithful for He cannot disown himself" (2 Timothy 2:13).* Jesus is always faithful, and it is imperative that we remain faithful to Him. Remember what the Lord said to the Ephesian church?

*Yet I hold this against you: You have forsaken your first love. Remember the heights from which you have fallen! Repent and do the things you did at first."* **If you do not repent, I will come to you and remove your lampstand from its place.** *(Revelation 2:4–5)*

When a lampstand goes so does its light and only darkness remains.

The parable of the four different kinds of soils or hearts, explains pretty much what we have been discussing. At the time of hearing the Gospel, the *wayside heart* remained totally outside the Kingdom of God because they would not receive it. The other three types belong to those who receive the Word joyfully. The *rocky-ground heart* starts off vigorously in its new life but falls away not long after, because it has no deep root system. It ends up scorched to death from the heat of the sun, or in other words, the persecution from the devil. As the heat of persecution turns up, so goes the faithfulness of the person with the rocky-ground heart.

*The thorny-ground heart is the category into which too many Christians fall.* The deceitfulness of riches and the cares of the world choke the Word making the person unfruitful. These folks do not bear any fruit or lead anyone to the Lord because they are so wrapped up in themselves.

It is only the fourth heart type, *the good-ground heart* that perseveres and brings forth fruit, thirty, sixty, or hundred fold. We should all prayerfully read Matthew 13:19–23 and then take a close look at our own lives. What are our priorities in life? What kind of ground is your heart and mine? A few prayerful minutes in these five verses from the Book of Matthew, could help us all make the eternal changes that are so vitally important for our own spiritual health and the work of the Kingdom.

Keeping up with the Jones's will not pay off in the world to come— unless the Jones's were busy serving the Lord. Let's remember what the Apostle Paul admonished, and do it. He said:

*Endure hardship with us like a good soldier of Christ Jesus. No one serving as a soldier gets involved in civilian affairs-he wants to please his commanding officer. Similarly, if anyone competes as an athlete, he does not receive the victor's crown unless he competes according to the rules. The hard-working farmer should be the first to receive a share of the crops. Reflect on what I am saying, for the Lord will give you insight into all this. Remember Jesus Christ, raised from the dead, descended from David. This is my gospel, for which I am suffering even to the point of being chained like a criminal. But God's word is not chained. Therefore I endure everything for the sake of the elect, which they too may obtain the salvation that is in Christ Jesus, with eternal glory. Here is a trustworthy saying: If we died with him, we will also live with him; if we endure, we will also reign with him. If we disown him, he will also disown us; if we are faithless, he will remain faithful, for he cannot disown himself. (2 Timothy 2:3-13)*

The staggering statistic of the Matthew13:19–23 parable is that only one-fourth of all the people Jesus discussed was faithful to Him and diligently bore fruit. It is only the good-ground-hearted people that receive the Word, endure persecution, resist the chains of the deceit of riches, and the cares of this world. These are the ones who produce fruit; thirty, sixty, and a hundred-fold. These are Christians who study the Word, live the Word, pray and submit to God, and resist Satan with the very Word he continually attempts to chain up. These, are the "Dr. Believers" who continually deliver the full-term babies waiting in their spiritual placentas, to be birthed into the Kingdom of the Lord Jesus Christ. *"You are from God, little children, and have overcome them; because greater is He who is in you than he who is in the world" (1 John 4:4).*

Jesus invited the Church to remain strongly connected to Him. He said:

> **Remain in me, and I will remain in you.** *No branch can bear fruit by itself; it must remain in the vine.* **Neither can you bear fruit unless you remain in me. "I am the vine; you are the branches. If a man remains in me and I in him, he will bear much fruit; apart from me you can do nothing.** *If anyone does not remain in me, he is like a branch that is thrown away and withers; such branches are picked up, thrown into the fire and burned.* **If you remain in me and my words remain in you, ask whatever you wish, and it will be given you. This is to my Father's glory, that you bear much fruit, showing yourselves to be my disciples.** *(John 15:4–8)*

By portraying babies in their spiritual placentas, Jesus was impressing upon me the all important fact that Christians need to be less focused upon themselves, their own wants and needs, and more focused on obeying God and the Great Commission. In the natural, when you give birth to a baby, your focus automatically becomes the baby, for it has many needs that only you as a parent can fulfill.

Jesus informs us that we need to quit worrying about ourselves. The Lord assures us that while we take care of the brand new babies that we birth into the kingdom, we can know with certainty that our Heavenly Father takes care of us. Listen to Jesus:

> *And why do you worry about clothes? See how the lilies of the field grow. They do not labor or spin. Yet I tell you that not even Solomon in all his splendor was dressed like one of these. If that is how God clothes the grass of the field, which is here today and tomorrow is thrown into the fire, will he not much more clothe you, O you of little faith?* **So do not worry, saying, 'What shall we eat?' or 'What shall we drink?' or 'What shall we wear?'** *For the pagans run after all these things,* **and your heavenly Father knows that you need them. But seek first his kingdom and his righteousness, and all these things will be given to you as well.** *Therefore do not worry about tomorrow, for tomorrow will worry about itself. Each day has enough trouble of its own. (Matthew 6:28–34)*

As we study the Bible we will find that those who lived in a close relationship with God were blessed beyond their wildest imagination. The Bible tells us, *"The LORD would speak to* **Moses, face to face,** *as a man speaks with a friend" (Exodus 33:11).* Abraham was called God's friend. Again,
King Jehoshaphat prayed:

> *O our God, did you not drive out the inhabitants of this land before your people Israel, and give it forever to the descendants of* **Abraham your friend?** *(2 Chronicles 20:7)*

What caused Abraham and many others to have such privileged positions with God? They all had one thing in common. They sought God, they talked with Him, they spent time with Him, and they loved and honored Him above all else. They worshipped Him and depended upon His leading in every area of their lives. Did they make mistakes? Sure they did, but their hearts were always loyal to God, and they desired Him above all else.

The disciples and first century believers are prime examples of this same devotion to the Lord. Notice what they did after Jesus ascended to Heaven, *"They all joined together constantly in prayer"*
*(Acts 1:14).*

Now look at the reward for this kind of faithfulness. The Bible tells us,

*When the day of Pentecost came, they were all together in one place. Suddenly a sound like the blowing of a violent wind came from Heaven and filled the whole house where they were sitting. They saw what seemed to be tongues of fire that separated and came to rest on each of them. All of them were filled with the Holy Spirit and began to speak in other tongues as the Spirit enabled them. (Acts 2:1–4)*

The Holy Spirit came upon them and the Church was empowered. About three thousand full-term babies were birthed that day by Dr. Peter as he boldly taught them, walking them through the Scriptures.

*With many other words he warned them; and he pleaded with them, "Save yourselves from this corrupt generation. Those who accepted his message were baptized, and about three thousand were added to their number that day. They devoted themselves to the apostles' teaching and to the fellowship, to the breaking of bread and to prayer. (Acts 2:40–43)*

It is noteworthy that the first thing these newly birthed babies did was to devote themselves to the apostles' teaching, to fellowship, to the breaking of bread, and to prayer. There is no doubt that if we too seek God with all our hearts as the disciples did, He will meet us as well and bless and empower us to do His Will.

We should not forget that it was these same disciples who were so fearful, that they all fled on the night Jesus was arrested. Peter even denied his Lord. Yet, after they obeyed the Lord's command and tarried in prayer and worship in Jerusalem, the Holy Spirit came upon them and these men became valiant soldiers for Jesus.

Dear brothers and sisters in Christ let us all wake up! Jesus said,

*Go into all the world and preach the good news to all creation. Whoever believes and is baptized will be saved, but whoever does not believe will be condemned. And these signs will accompany all those who believe: In my name they will drive out demons; they will speak in new tongues; they will pick up snakes with their hands; and when they drink deadly poison, it will not hurt them at all. They will place their hands on sick people and they will get well. (Mark 16:15–18)*

The Words of the above Scripture are words the Lord Jesus intended for every believer, and we should be willing to accept and act upon it.

*"Faith comes by hearing and hearing by the Word of God."* *(Romans 10:17)* So we must let the Word of God permeate the depths of our beings by reading and meditating upon it; by memorizing and speaking it aloud, we will have enough faith to act upon it. David said this about the future Messiah:

*Posterity will serve him; future generations will be told about the Lord. They will proclaim his righteousness to a people yet unborn—for he has done it. (Psalm 22:30–31)*

There is much work to be done and many babies to be delivered; the Lord loves us all so very much. It's time to diligently serve the Lord, for the time of His return is very much at hand!

# Chapter 14

# NEAR DEATH

———∞∞∞———

N ow I was permitted to see a rather close-up view of the forearm and hand of an individual who seemed to be reclining on a couch of sorts. I could see a part of the right side of the body but I could not see the face. The person's right arm lay limply on the edge of the couch and both the hand and forearm were extremely pale, giving the appearance of death or near death.

Above where this seriously ill person lay, I could see a beautiful pure white dove flying around in the room. Several times I saw the dove fly very close to where this sick person lay.

I knew immediately that this dove represented the precious Holy Spirit.

Suddenly the beautiful white bird flew slowly, very close to the hand of this sick person, and appeared to be inviting the hand to rise up and take hold of it. As I watched, it became obvious that healing and health to this desperately sick being would come, only if the individual would reach out, grasp the dove, and keep holding onto it. This was obviously an issue of life or death.

As the gentle dove flew by again it seemed to be silently urging the person to reach out and take hold of it. Finally the fingers moved ever so slightly making a couple of feeble attempts to catch the dove.

The bird now flew deliberately into the hand of the person who weakly grasped it this time, but held on for only an instant. In fact the grasp was so loose that it was very apparent there was no actual desire or inclination, within the person to retain contact with the bird, which then easily slipped through the fingers.

The dove circled around again; one more time the beautiful bird flew directly and intentionally into the grasp of this disinterested person. The fingers draped over it with the same loose indifference as before, and the dove once more moved right through the fingers of this clearly unwilling person.

As the hand let go of the bird for the second time, I was suddenly able to see the entire form of the individual who was lying on the couch. The person was dressed in extremely rich, robe-type attire and reclined on a very luxurious couch. The head of the person rested on ornately embroidered, red and gold colored pillows. I could not see the face clearly, but I was impressed that it was a man of advanced age. It was obvious from the person's attire and surroundings, that this individual was exceedingly wealthy.

Having been rejected a third time, the gentle dove, with a sense of great sadness, flew slowly away from the person on the couch, never to return again. As soon as this happened, I was horrified to see this rich individual suddenly disintegrate and turn into a skeleton. All the rich garments fell away from the body and only a bony skeleton remained upon the couch.

Filled with despair, I prayed earnestly for understanding of what all this could mean; then the Lord explained. He said, "This sick person is a picture of every congregating church body that chooses to reject the power and the presence of the Holy Spirit." It is the Holy Spirit, He said, who empowered the Church on the day of Pentecost, and it is simply not possible for a Church to survive without the Holy Spirit. At this point the numerous denominations that do not believe in the importance of the presence and Person of the Holy Spirit began to cross my mind. Jesus told us clearly while He was on earth, " . . . the **Counselor, the Holy Spirit,** *whom the Father will send in* *my name, **will teach you all things and will remind you of everything I have said to you"** (John 14:26).*

I saw the dove flying three times into the hand of the ailing one on the lavish couch before finally leaving. This made it obvious that God gives ample time, and extends numerous opportunities and invitations to individuals or churches, to receive His Spirit, but when all His gracious offers are rejected, and treated with disinterest, lethargy, and unwillingness to receive Him, the Holy Spirit finally withdraws and the church or individual eventually dies spiritually.

Paul gives us an idea of what a church that is alive to God and led by the Spirit of God should be. Paul says:

> ***Love must be sincere. Hate what is evil; cling to what is good.*** *Be devoted to one another in brotherly love. Honor one another above yourselves.* ***Never be lacking in zeal, but keep your spiritual fervor, serving the Lord. Be joyful in hope, patient in affliction, faithful in prayer.*** *Share with God's people who are in need. Practice hospitality.* ***Bless those who persecute you; bless and do not curse.*** *Rejoice with those who rejoice; mourn with those who mourn.* ***Live in harmony with one another. Do not be proud, but be willing to associate with people of low position.*** *Do not be conceited.* ***Do not repay anyone evil for evil. Be careful to do what is right in the eyes of everybody. If it is possible, as far as it depends on you, live at peace with everyone. Do not take revenge, my friends, but leave room for God's wrath, for it is written: "It is mine to avenge; I will repay," says the Lord.*** *On the contrary: "If your enemy is hungry, feed him; if he is thirsty, give him something to drink. In doing this, you will heap burning coals on his head."* ***Do not be overcome by evil, but overcome evil with good.*** *(Romans 12:9–21)*

The Book of Revelation speaks a warning to the church at Sardis and to all Sardis-type churches.

*To the angel of the church in Sardis write: These are the words of him who holds the seven spirits of God and the seven stars.* **I know your deeds; you have a reputation of being alive, but you are dead. Wake up! Strengthen what remains and is about to die, for I have not found your deeds complete in the sight of my God.** *(Revelation 3:1–2)*

Even though the Church in Sardis had a great reputation of being alive and well, it was dead by Lord's standards. *Matthew Henry's Commentary* has this to say about the church in Sardis.

. . . the church of Sardis, an ancient city of Lydia, on the banks of the mountain Tmolus, said to have been the chief city of Asia the Less, and the first city in that part of the world that was converted by the preaching of John; **and, some say, the first that revolted from Christianity, and one of the first that was laid in its ruins, in which it still lies, without any church or ministry.**

We should note that when the Lord spoke to the Church in Sardis, He is referred to as having the seven Spirits of God. John 3:34 states that Jesus Christ has the Spirit without measure. When the Lord Jesus addressed each church, and in this case the church at Sardis, He spoke as One who had a perfect perception of everything concerning it. We mentioned earlier the possibility that these seven churches in Asia might actually characterize every church upon the face of the earth, from the day of Pentecost until the Lord returns to take the Church home.

Matthew Henry's Commentary puts it this way:

He has seven Spirits, that is, the Holy Spirit, with his various powers, graces, and operations; for he is personally one, though efficaciously various, and maybe said here to be seven, which is the number of the churches, and of the angels of the churches, to show to every minister and every church, there is a dispensation and measure of the Spirit for them to profit withal—A stock of spiritual influence for that minister and church to improve, both for enlargement and continuance, *which measure of the Spirit is not ordinarily withdrawn from them, till they forfeit it by misimprovement.*

The Church at Sardis had a reputation of being alive, but the Lord Jesus said,

**You are dead.** *"Wake up! Strengthen what remains and is about to die, for I have not found your deeds complete in the sight of my GOD.* **Remember therefore, what you have received and heard; obey it, and repent. But if you do not wake up, I will come like a thief and you will not know at what time I will come to you.** *(Revelation 3:1–3)*

Even though He declared this church dead, the Lord still graciously encouraged them to wake up and repent—to return to Him and obey what they had heard, namely His Word. It can be clearly seen from the words of Jesus that the Holy Spirit continues to work within each church to achieve His purpose for that body. However, if they consistently choose not to obey Him or cling to Him, He will withdraw His presence and that body will die, as indeed was the case with the church at Sardis.

Matthew Henry further had to say about the Church at Sardis.

This church had a great reputation; it had a name and a very honorable one, for a flourishing church, a name for vital lively religion, for purity of doctrine, unity among themselves, uniformity in worship and everything appeared to be well as to what falls under the observation of men. **The church was not what it was reputed to be. They had a name to live, but they were dead; there was a form of godliness, but not the power, a name to live but not a principle of life. If there was not a total privation of life, yet there was great deadness in their souls and in their services, a great deadness in the spirits of their ministers and a great deadness in their ministrations, in their praying, in their preaching, in their converse, and a great deadness in the people hearing, in prayer and in conversation; what little life was yet left among them was in a manner, expiring, ready to die.**

This summarizes the Church symbolized by the rich but dying person I saw. The Bible warns,

*Serve the LORD with fear and rejoice with trembling. Kiss the Son, lest he be angry and you be destroyed in your way, for his wrath can flare up in a moment. Blessed are all who take refuge in him. (Psalm 2:11–12)*

The Lord in His great love is amazingly patient and not willing that any should perish, but the existence of pride and apathy are a very dangerous combination for any Church body, or any individual for that matter. Jesus said to His disciples,

*I have much more to say to you, more than you can now bear. **But when he, the Spirit of truth, comes, he will guide you into all truth. He will not speak on his own; he will speak only what he hears, and he will tell you what is yet to come. He will bring glory to me by taking from what is mine and making it known to you.** All that belongs to the Father is mine.*

*That is why I said the Spirit will take from what is mine and make it known to you. (John 16:12–15)*

There are at least four vitally important things that happen when the Holy Spirit is present among a body of believers.

1. He guides into all truth.
2. He speaks whatever He hears.
3. He reveals what is to come.
4. He glorifies Jesus by taking what belongs to Him and disclosing it to the believers.

This then suggests that a Church that chooses to reject the Holy Spirit will certainly miss out on all these blessings that both supply and maintain life. First, without the Holy Spirit such a church will not be able to operate in Truth because according to Jesus, it is the Holy Spirit who leads and guides into all Truth. Without the presence of the Holy Spirit, error and false doctrine will abound. The Holy Spirit speaks whatever He hears and reveals what is to come. If the Holy Spirit is not present, it would be impossible to bring glory to Jesus because there would be no revelation knowledge.

Furthermore it is the Holy Spirit who convicts believers of sin in their lives. It is He who inspires our desire to be conformed to the image of Christ.

A church that rejects the Holy Spirit is also one that will not be convicted of sin; therefore the sins of the people remain unconfessed and unforgiven.

*If we confess our sins, he is faithful and just and will forgive us our sins and purify us from all unrighteousness. (1 John 1:9)*

The fruit of the Spirit is, love, joy, peace, patience, kindness, goodness, faithfulness, gentleness and self-control.

These beautiful attributes are blessings that come from the very heart of Jesus, and they can only manifest in the lives of believers through the abiding presence of the Holy Spirit. Paul the apostle tells us,

*If you live by the sinful nature you will die;* ***but if by the Spirit you put to death the misdeeds of the body, you will live, because those who are led by the Spirit of God are sons of God.*** *(Romans 8:13–14)*

It is basically impossible to reject God the Holy Spirit and yet continue to live an acceptable Christian life. According to God's Word, it is only those who are led by the Spirit of God who can be called the sons of God. Jesus said,

*. . .* ***If anyone is thirsty, let him come to me and drink****. Whoever believes in me as the Scripture has said, streams of Living Water will flow from within him.* ***By this he meant the Spirit, whom those who believed in him were later to receive.*** *(John 7:37–39)*

Those who are not thirsty for Jesus will refuse to come to Him and drink and so the Holy Spirit—the Living Water—will be absent in their lives.

Ezekiel had a beautiful vision of the millennial Temple and the River of Life. Before we go deeper into Ezekiel's vision, let's remember the question Paul the Apostle asked as he tried to help us to understand who we really are in Christ. He said,

***Do you not know that your body is a temple of the Holy Spirit, who is in you, whom you have received from God?*** *You are not your own; you were bought at a price. Therefore honor God with your body. (1 Corinthians 6:19–20)*

Paul referred to our bodies as temples of the Holy Spirit whom we received from God. Paul recommends that we

237

remember that we are not our own, but we were bought with the precious Blood of Jesus. Keeping all this in mind, let's read what Ezekiel saw in his vision, and embark on a spiritual journey with him.

The Holy Spirit is referred to as "Living Water," so let's wade out with Ezekiel.

*The man brought me back to the entrance of the temple, and I saw water coming out from under the threshold of the temple toward the east (for the temple faced east). The water was coming down from under the south side of the temple, south of the altar. He then brought me out through the north gate and led me around the outside to the outer gate facing east, and the water was flowing from the south side. As the man went eastward with a measuring line in his hand, he measured off a thousand cubits and then **led me through water that was ankle-deep.** He measured off another thousand cubits and **led me through water that was knee-deep.** He measured off another thousand and **led me through water that was up to the waist.** He measured off another thousand, **but now it was a river that I could not cross, because the water had risen and was deep enough to swim in-a river that no one could cross.** He asked me, "Son of man, do you see this?" Then he led me back to the bank of the river. When I arrived there, I saw a great number of trees on each side of the river. He said to me, **"This water flows toward the eastern region and goes down into the Arabah, where it enters the Sea. When it empties into the Sea, the water there becomes fresh. Swarms of living creatures will live wherever the river flows. There will be large numbers of fish, because this water flows there and makes the salt water fresh; so where the river flows everything will live.** Fishermen will stand along the shore; from En Gedi to En Eglaim there will be places for spreading* *nets. The fish will be of many kinds-like the fish of the Great Sea.* ***But the swamps and marshes will not become fresh; they will be left for salt. Fruit trees of all kinds will grow on both banks of the river. Their leaves will not wither, nor will their fruit fail. Every month they will bear, because the water from the sanctuary flows to them. Their fruit will serve for food and their leaves for healing.*** *(Ezekiel 47:1–12)*

So let's get into the water with Ezekiel and journey with him, relating the facts of his vision to our own spiritual lives. We will begin by wading into the river, which equates submitting to the Holy Spirit. As we step out in faith and go deeper and deeper with the Lord, we will be doing as Ezekiel did when he submitted to the celestial being who was leading him. At the first thousand cubits measured by the angel, Ezekiel was only ankle deep. The thousand cubits speaks of both time and depth of submission. This is the same process we will experience as we submit just a little at a time, going only ankle deep at first. Obviously it takes time for our relationship with the Holy Spirit to mature, not on His part, but on ours. However, as we will see, time creates greater trust and deeper intimacy.

The angel now measured off another thousand cubits which speaks of another period of time and depth. Now just as Ezekiel went deeper, when we begin to trust the Holy Spirit more, it becomes easier to submit to a greater degree. So we surrender and go yet deeper, yielding more to Him, and as Ezekiel did, we now find ourselves at a level that is knee deep. At the next level of submission, a thousand cubits further as measured by the angel, we move to a waist-deep level of surrender to the awesome Holy Spirit. At this point we find ourselves half surrendered but totally ready to go all the way. Finally, a thousand cubits further, comes the moment of total surrender. Now it is no longer possible to desire to do anything by ourselves, because we have reached a point of total dependence on the Holy Spirit. To swim, one must be submerged, and so it is in our relationship with the Holy Spirit.

We must trust, obey, and yield to Him completely, not unlike an experienced swimmer who relaxes and floats in the water. It is at this point that the Holy Spirit engulfs and carries us.

When Ezekiel was taken back to the bank of the River he could see that everything the River touched became abundantly alive. This is exactly what happens through the life of a yielded believer. Listen to Jesus:

> *On the last day, that great day of the feast, Jesus stood and cried out, saying, **"If anyone thirsts, let him come to Me and drink. He who believes in Me, as the Scripture has said, out of his heart will flow rivers of living water." But this He spoke concerning the Spirit, whom those believing in Him would receive;** for the Holy Spirit was not yet given, because Jesus was not yet glorified. (John 7:37–39)*

Ezekiel saw water coming from under the threshold of the Temple, and like this flowing water, a person who is filled with the Holy Spirit will overflow with the things of the Spirit of God. Ezekiel said, when the *River* emptied into the *Sea,* the waters became fresh.

The *sea* in our journey represents the masses of people we encounter daily. The Spirit of God flows through us to touch them and they come to life in the Lord. Swarms of living creatures (believers) will throng wherever the River (the Holy Spirit) flows, and there will be large numbers of *fish*—those who will be saved, because the flow of the Holy Spirit through believers makes the saltwater fresh; *"Come, follow me," Jesus said, "and I will make you fishers of men" (Matthew 4:19).*

Those who believe and surrender to Jesus are the fishermen—soul winners. We will stand along the shore as fishers of men, and people from every tribe and tongue and nation will be saved. However, the swamps and marshes—churches and individuals—that will not receive or submit to the Holy Spirit, *the River that brings Life,* will not become fresh. When the River is rejected, life will ebb away as was the case with the church at Sardis.

Those totally surrendered to the Holy Spirit will be like trees planted by the River. They will bear much fruit. Water, the power of the Holy Spirit, that flows from these temples (the very inmost beings of these surrendered individuals) produces fruit, and the lost and dying receive the food and healing that comes from the Holy Word of God.

Jeremiah referred to those who genuinely trust and serve the Lord, as trees planted by the Water.

*Blessed is the man who trusts in the LORD, whose confidence in Him. He will be like a tree planted by the water that sends out its roots by the streams*. *It does not fear when heat comes; its leaves are always green. It has no worries in a year of drought and never fails to bear fruit. (Jeremiah 17:7–8)*

This Scripture perfectly describes the lives of all believers who willingly and obediently trust the Lord and submit to the Holy Spirit, permitting Him to totally fill them. Believers such as this continually bear much fruit; they continue to speak words of healing and salvation to the lost and dying.

So then, what is to be said of the ones that do nothing but merely attend churches that in turn do nothing for the cause of Christ but follow their own traditions and rules?

Sadly, these would be the swamps where the fresh and pure water of the Holy Spirit is not accepted. These would also be the ones that remain stagnant. These dead churches are the ones that were represented by the lavishly rich, but deathly ill individual I saw. They were the ones that would not grab hold of the life-giving Holy Spirit, because of disinterest and apathy. The absence of life leaves only one thing— death. Death in turn leaves only one thing too—a skeleton. This was the dismal but very real picture the Lord showed me. How sad the Holy Spirit was to see the disintegration of the individual—the church that perished as He departed. The Lord does all He can to save them, but they refuse His love and care.

We are told: *"Seek the LORD while he may be found; call on him while he is near" (Isaiah 55:6).*

No doubt Jesus weeps over such churches and individuals as He wept over Jerusalem when they rejected Him. He wept because He knew the terrible things that were about to come upon them for the hardness of their hearts. Jesus wept as He said,

> *O Jerusalem, Jerusalem, you who kill the prophets and stone those sent to you, how often I have longed to gather your children together, as a hen gathers her chicks under her wings, **but you were not willing.** Look, your house is left to you desolate. For I tell you, you will not see me again until you say, 'Blessed is he who comes in the name of the Lord.' (Matt 23:37–39)*

Strongly emphasizing the importance of the presence of the Holy Spirit Jesus said this to His disciples:

> *But I tell you the truth: It is for your good that I am going away. **Unless I go away, the Counselor will not come to you; but if I go, I will send him to you. When he comes, he will convict the world of guilt in regard to sin and righteousness and judgment:** in regard to sin, because men do not believe in me; in regard to righteousness, because I am going to the Father, where you can see me no longer; and in regard to judgment, because the prince of this world now stands condemned. (John 16:8–11)*

Without the Holy Spirit there will never be conviction of guilt and so sin will remain and the body will perish because there is no repentance. The Bible tells us *the wages of sin is death.*

The Church that Jesus built was empowered when the disciples were obedient to His specific command. Jesus told them;

*Do not leave Jerusalem, but wait for the gift my Father promised, which you have heard me speak about. For John baptized with water, but in a few days you will be baptized with the Holy Spirit."* Jesus further said to them, *". . . **But you will receive power when the Holy Spirit comes on you; and you will be my witnesses in Jerusalem, and in all Judea and Samaria, and to the ends of the earth.** (Acts 1:4–8)*

These next few words I am writing are of vital importance. I am writing them by the command of the Lord, so that those who have so far refused the person, the presence, the works, and the gifts of the Holy Spirit, might invite Him in to their lives. It is my prayer that many will step into the life-giving River that flows, going deeper and deeper until they are completely submerged in the power and presence of the precious Holy Spirit; that they will take a hold of Him and never let go again. Those who do will live, but those who refuse to will not.

There is a River that flows from the throne of God that is identical to the one Ezekiel saw. John the Apostle saw it and said,

***Then the angel showed me the river of the water of life, as clear as crystal, flowing from the throne of God and of the Lamb down the middle of the great street of the city.*** *On each side of the river stood the tree of life, bearing twelve crops of fruit, yielding its fruit every month. And the leaves of the tree are for the healing of the nations. No longer will there be any curse. The throne of God and of the Lamb will be in the city, and his servants will serve him. They will see his face, and his name will be on their foreheads. There will be no more night. They will not need the light* *of a lamp or the light of the sun, for the Lord God will give them light. And they will reign forever and ever. (Revelation 22:1–5)*

This promise from God is the ultimate, glorious destination and reward, that all who receive the Precious Holy Spirit have to look forward to. The River of Life that flows from the Throne of God is the Life Giver; Jesus called Him the Holy Spirit. The first Church needed the Holy Spirit, and so does every subsequent one. The first Church was made up of individuals that desperately desired the abundant life Jesus Christ offers, and this should be the burning desire of everyone in the Church today.

To honor and obey the Holy Spirit we must live with a great awareness of His presence in our lives, and if we totally submit to Him, we will clean up our actions. Paul advises the Ephesian Church,

*Do not let any unwholesome talk come out of your mouths, but only what is helpful for building others up according to their needs, that it may benefit those who listen. **And do not grieve the Holy Spirit of God, with whom you were sealed for the day of redemption.** Get rid of all bitterness, rage and anger, brawling and slander, along with every form of malice. Be kind and compassionate to one another, forgiving each other, just as in Christ God forgave you. (Ephesians 4:29–30)*

Unwholesome words that come from our mouths, unholy actions, nursed grievances, unforgiving attitudes and the likes, grieve the Holy Spirit with whom we are sealed for the day of redemption. Our love for Him and the thought of His pain should compel us to change our ways.

Any church body that ignores or rejects the Holy Spirit should seriously reconsider their acceptability to Christ, because according to Paul, it is the Holy Spirit who actually seals us for the day of redemption! Paul gives this important instruction to the Thessalonians, and all Christians should remember to take it very seriously. Paul warns us to be careful not to put out the Spirit's fire and here's how we can avoid doing that.

*Be joyful always; pray continually; give thanks in all circumstances, for this is God's will for you in Christ Jesus. Do not put out the Spirit's fire;* do *not treat prophecies with contempt. Test everything. Hold on to the good. Avoid every kind of evil. May God himself, the God of peace, sanctify you through and through. May your whole spirit, soul and body be kept blameless at the coming of our Lord Jesus Christ. The one who calls you is faithful and he will do it. (1 Thessalonians 5:16–24)*

Paul ends this great piece of advice with a blessing. He prays that God Himself would completely sanctify us and that our spirits, souls and bodies would be kept blameless at the coming of our Lord Jesus Christ. Paul goes on to state that the One who called us is faithful and He will do it. What an awesome promise this is. Jesus Christ the faithful and True will help us in our daily walk by strengthening us with the presence of the Holy Spirit. He will preserve us blameless until He returns.

In the Book of Acts, Stephen said to the Jews, *"You always resist the Holy Spirit" (Acts 7:51).* Resisting the Holy Spirit occurs when the truth of the Gospel of Jesus Christ is denied and rejected. Stephen lost his life at the hands of the very ones he was trying to exhort and lead to the Lord. The possibility of losing his life did not stop Stephen from boldly declaring the truth. It is possible that we may find ourselves in Stephen's position. Are we ready to take that challenge?

As followers of Jesus Christ would we be willing and bold enough to proclaim the truth even in the face of certain death? Jesus once said to his disciples,

*If anyone would come after me, he must deny himself and take up his cross and follow me.* **For whoever wants to save his life will lose it, but whoever loses his life for me will find it.** *What good will it be for a man if he gains the whole world, yet forfeits his soul? Or what can a man give in exchange for his soul? For the Son of Man is going to come in his Father's glory with his angels, and then he will reward each person according to what he has done. (Matthew 16:24–27)*

We have seen that it is possible to put out the fire of the Holy Spirit, to grieve and resist Him; the danger of such actions cannot be overemphasized. The Bible is filled with instructions and warnings, and we will either receive them and live, or reject the outstretched Hand of God and perish.

**It is time to wake up!**

Love is the chief ingredient by which a body of faithful believers in Jesus Christ could be identified—a vibrant love for Jesus, each other, and the lost and dying. True and sincere love among believers will keep the Holy Spirit from being grieved, because love is the very first fruit of the Spirit. Jesus said, *"By this all men will know that you are my disciples, if you love one another (John 13:35).*

On the other hand, cold, austere, indifferent religious environments or those that promote the feel-good, anything-goes atmosphere declare the absence of the Holy Spirit. If you find yourself in a church setting of this type, and you are hurting because of it, remember, Jesus cares deeply for you. He will help and protect you and if you will permit Him to. The Holy Spirit Himself will gently lead you to a congregation where He is welcomed. The Bible says,

*A bruised reed He will not break, and a smoldering wick He will not snuff out till He leads justice to victory . . . (Matthew 12:20).*

Don't waste any more precious time, as you are strengthened by the Lord; go out and serve, being careful not to break any bruised reeds or snuff out a smoldering wicks. Instead, do what Jesus did for you and strengthen those with flickering faith, and edify and build them up in the Lord. Jesus said, to the church at Sardis,

> ***Yet you have a few people in Sardis who have not soiled their clothes. They will walk with me, dressed in white, for they are worthy.*** *He who overcomes will, like them, be dressed in white. I will never blot out his name from the Book of life, but will acknowledge his name before my Father and his angels. He who has an ear, let him hear what the Spirit says to the churches. (Revelation 3:4–6)*

Beloved, you might be one who has not soiled your clothes, but will walk with Jesus dressed in white. However, you may be feeling uncertain in your present church and want to know if you are in the right place and doing the right thing. Seek the Lord and do as He leads. If the church you're in has quenched the fire of the Holy Spirit or rejected Him you might have to move. Be sure the Lord will lead you in the right direction as you sincerely seek Him in prayer. Your unrest might be an indication that it is time to go where the Holy Spirit flows.

As we mentioned before, there are many so-called churches that even deny that Jesus Christ is Lord. They deny that He is the only Way to the Father. A short trip on the Internet will very quickly identify multitudes of these organizations. The Bible tells us:

> ***They claim to know God, but by their actions they deny him.*** *They are detestable, disobedient and unfit for doing anything good. (Titus 1:16)*

Listen to what the Apostle John says, it will shed much light and help bring you peace.

*We know that those who have become part of God's family do not make a practice of sinning, for God's Son holds them securely, and the evil one cannot get his hands on them. We know that we are children of God and that the world around us is under the power and control of the evil one. **And we know that the Son of God has come, and he has given us understanding so that we can know the true God. And now we are in God because we are in his Son, Jesus Christ. He is the only true God, and he is eternal life. Dear children, keep away from anything that might take God's place in your hearts.** (1 John 5:18-21)*

Paul said:

*So I want you to know how to discern what is truly from God: No one speaking by the Spirit of God can curse Jesus, **and no one is able to say, "Jesus is Lord," except by the Holy Spirit.** (1 Corinthians 12:3)*

By knowing this you can also know if you are in a church that is being obedient to the Holy Spirit. Remember that to deny the Holy Spirit is also to deny the Lord Jesus. So pray, study your Bible, focus especially on what Jesus said to the seven churches in Asia as recorded in the Book of Revelation, and depend completely on the Holy Spirit. What He says and does always lines up with God's Word, and always points to Jesus Christ as Lord and Savior.

Great wisdom and understanding from the Scriptures come from listening to the Holy Spirit. He is the author of the Bible and He alone can help us to deeply understand His Word in a manner that enables us to fully obey Jesus.

When Jesus was only twelve years old, He spent time in the Temple, listening to the teachers of the Law and asking questions of them. Jesus was obviously trying to stimulate these men of great earthly education to think as God does. The Bible tells us, *"And all who heard him were astonished at his understanding and answers" (Luke 2:47).* Jesus asked his parents who had been searching for him, *"Did you not know that I must be about My Father's business?" (Luke 2:49).* It is noteworthy that even from such a tender age Jesus was always doing what His Heavenly Father had instructed Him to do.

As we walk in the wisdom and guidance of the Holy Spirit, many will be astonished at our own understanding and answers as well. The answers we give will not be our own, but those that come through revelation from the Holy Spirit.

Jesus was constantly about His Father's business, and so must we. Our job is to try to bring as many as possible into the Kingdom of God. This is what bearing fruit is all about, but it cannot be done without the Holy Spirit—the Living Water. All seven churches of Asia received this counsel from Jesus, *"He who has an ear, let him hear what the Spirit says to the Churches."* Our spiritual ears must be constantly listening to the voice of the Holy Spirit.

It is interesting to note, that the very last time the Holy Spirit is mentioned in the Bible, He is with the Bride—the Church, offering an invitation to whoever wishes to take of the free gift of the water of life.

> *The Spirit and the Bride say, 'Come!' And let him who hears say 'Come!' Whoever is thirsty, let him come; and whoever wishes, let him take the free gift of the water of life. (Revelation 22:17)*

This call from the Lord is to every church. So wake up and drink deeply from the River of God—the precious Holy Spirit—for He alone leads us into all Truth.

The time truly is at hand.

# Chapter 15

# THE GREAT PROSTITUTE

⸺⦿⸺

I was now shown a brazen-looking woman attired in a flashy and revealing, purple gown. She was decked in gaudy jewels that spoke of much opulence. She was standing nonchalantly with a cigarette dangling from her fingers, and her entire posture exuded worldliness, arrogance, and sin. I wondered who she might be, so I asked the Lord and He opened my understanding to the fact that I was being shown the great prostitute of the Book of Revelation. The Apostle John who saw this vision said,

*One of the seven angels who had poured out the seven bowls came over and spoke to me. "Come with me," he said, "and I will show you the judgment that is going to come on the great prostitute, who sits on many waters. The rulers of the world have had immoral relations with her, and the people who belong to this world have been made drunk by the wine of her immorality." So the angel took me in spirit into the wilderness.* **There I saw a woman sitting on a scarlet beast that had seven heads and ten horns, written all over with blasphemies against God. The woman wore purple and scarlet clothing and beautiful jewelry made of gold and precious gems and pearls. She held in her hand a gold goblet full of obscenities and the** *impurities of her immorality. A mysterious name was written on her forehead: "Babylon the Great, Mother of All Prostitutes and Obscenities in the World." I could see that she was drunk—drunk with the blood of God's holy people who were witnesses for Jesus. I stared at her completely amazed. (Rev 17:1-6)*

This harlot embodies all idolatrous religious organizations that have masqueraded as the Church but have never really been faithful to the Lord Jesus Christ. This unfaithful institution is allied with the political leaders and rulers of the world and commits spiritual adultery with them.

The great prostitute church, comprised of all its affiliates, is so filled with the world and the things of it, that the two are indistinguishable. The various apostate churches that agree with the philosophies and the deceitful thought patterns of the world, elevate these things above Almighty God and His Holy Word. Paul said to the true Church of Jesus Christ:

*We demolish arguments and every pretension that sets itself up against the knowledge of God, and we take captive every thought to make it obedient to Christ. (2 Corinthians 10:5)*

The harlot church denies the God-breathed inerrant truth of the Bible and accepts, agrees, and mingles itself with the false religions of the world under the guise of being tolerant. Sadly, many confuse this great assembly of false churches with the Church of Jesus Christ, but it is an organization steeped in spiritual adultery. It is the system that has a reputation of being alive but in reality is dead.

As John the Apostle stated, this church has a world-wide influence; multitudes, peoples, nations, and tongues are affiliated with this deviant church. The sheer magnitude of the dominion of this deceitful religious system is too staggering to perceive. Millions have and many more millions will blindly go along with this harlot church. Consequently, these multitudes will eventually find themselves not only trapped in her clutches, but also judged by God as she is judged.

Jesus warned:

*Enter through the narrow gate. **For wide is the gate and broad is the road that leads to destruction, and many enter through it.** But small is the gate and narrow the road that leads to life, and only a few find it. (Matthew 7:13–14)*

It is obvious that the clear biblical mandate, spoken of by John, has very little bearing on this apostate giant. John said:

***Do not love the world or anything in the world. If anyone loves the world, the love of the Father is not in him. For everything in the world-the cravings of sinful man, the lust of his eyes and the boasting of what he has and does-comes not from the Father but from the world.*** *The world and its desires pass away, but the man who does the will of God lives forever. (1 John 2:15–17)*

The words and actions of the multitudes within this adulterous entity speak for themselves. They agree with the world and reject the word of God. The Bible inquires of us,

*You adulterous people, don't you know that friendship with the world is hatred towards God? Anyone who chooses to be a friend of the world becomes an enemy of God. (James 4:4)*

It becomes clear at this point, that every person who has ever walked this earth in the past, those who are presently here, and those who will come in the future, will find themselves in one camp or the other—God's or Satan's. This of course will be determined by what each one has personally chosen.

All who love, obey, and serve the Lord with all their hearts belong to the Church of Jesus Christ, and are called His Bride. These believers are Blood-bought, sanctified, and redeemed. They will be clothed by the Lord Jesus in beautiful, spotless bridal attire, bright, shiny, and pure. They will have their names in the Lamb's Book of Life. Those on the other hand, who choose to be unfaithful to the Lord will find to their ultimate dismay that they have their names on Satan's list. The apostate church—Satan's harlot—will be clothed in the gaudy garments of unbelief, blasphemy, and disobedience to God. In addition to their own sins they will be held accountable for the souls of the scores of people they led astray through false doctrine. John puts it this way,

*With her the kings of the earth committed adultery and the inhabitants of the earth were intoxicated with the wine of her adulteries. (Revelation 17:2)*

Unfortunately for these people, none of them will be able to claim ignorance for what they did, because Jesus Christ Himself has forewarned them. The Lord said, *"I am the way the truth and the life. No one comes to the Father except through me" (John 14:6).*

In the meantime the haughty, sinful harlot pridefully boasts:

*. . . I sit as queen; I am not a widow, and I will never mourn. **Therefore in one day her plagues will overtake her: death, mourning, and famine. She will be consumed by fire, for mighty is the Lord God who judges her.** (Revelation 18:7–8)*

In all this we see the Lord's amazing patience. He still loves and calls to those who are caught up in this harlot church. He pleads with them:

**Come out of her, my people, so that you will not share in her sins, so that you will not receive any**

*of her plagues; for her sins are piled up to heaven, and God has remembered her crimes. Give back to her as she has given; pay her back double for what she has done. Mix her a double portion from her own cup. Give her as much torture and grief as the glory and luxury she gave herself. (Revelation 18:4–7)*

Jesus longs for you to know that you don't have to remain a slave in the domain of darkness. He wants you to know that you can exchange the gaudy garments of sin for a pure and spotless bridal gown, and you can do this by yielding to the loving voice of the Good Shepherd. Faith in Jesus Christ and obedience to His Word will immediately bring you out of the horrors of sin and into the Kingdom of the King of kings and Lord of lords.

Dear beloved friends, the purpose of this book is to implore you; to call to you in the words of the Lord Jesus Christ, to wake up and come out of this sinful organization. Come as a little child to Jesus, believe His word; and be saved, redeemed, and set free. The Lord warned us through Peter:

*But there were also false prophets among the people, just as there will be false teachers among you. They will secretly introduce destructive heresies, even denying the sovereign Lord who bought them-bringing swift destruction on themselves. **Many will follow their shameful ways and will bring the way of truth into disrepute. In their greed these teachers will exploit you with stories they have made up. Their condemnation has long been hanging over them, and their destruction has not been sleeping.** (2 Peter 2:1–3)*
*. . . **They promise them freedom, while they themselves are slaves of depravity-for a man is a slave to whatever has mastered him.** (2 Peter 2:19–20)*

Jesus promised to set you free if you come to Him.

*I tell you the truth, everyone who sins is a slave to sin. Now a slave has no permanent place in the family but a son belongs to it forever. So if the Son sets you free, you will be free indeed. (John 8:34–36)*

Jesus alone gave His precious life to save us, so run to Him. The Bible declares,

*Salvation is found in no one else, for there is no other name under heaven given to men by which we must be saved. (Acts 4:12)*

It doesn't matter if you call yourself a Christian, if you continue to live as the world does you will receive the judgment that comes to the world. If you truly accept Jesus Christ into your heart, and choose to obey His word and His way your reward will be great. The Bible informs us, *"Do not merely listen to the word, and so deceive yourselves. Do what it says"* (James 1:22).

The Kingdom of God is a glorious place to be in! David said,

*But let all who take refuge in you be glad; let them ever sing for joy. Spread your protection over them, that those who love your name may rejoice in you. For surely, O LORD, you bless the righteous; you surround them with your favor as with a shield. (Psalm 5:11–12)*

The heart of the Father aches for all those who have not come to Him; His heart aches for those who believe they are spiritually well, only to have to learn in the end that they were wrong. To all who will listen, this is what the Father says.

*Come now, let us reason together, says the LORD. Though your sins be as scarlet they shall be as white as snow, though they are red as crimson they shall be like wool. If you are willing and obedient*

*__you will eat the best from the land;__ but if you resist and rebel you will be devoured by the sword. __For the mouth of the LORD has spoken.__ (Isaiah 1:18–20)*

The LORD is so amazingly gracious and forgiving. It is hard to conceive why anyone would turn away from this awesome, loving, all-powerful, and compassionate God. The Bible tells us,

*Praise the LORD, O my soul; all my inmost being, praise his holy name. Praise the LORD, O my soul, and forget not all his benefits—who forgives all your sins and heals all your diseases, who redeems your life from the pit and crowns you with love and compassion, who satisfies your desires with good things so that your youth is renewed like the eagle's. (Psalm 103:1–5)*

Why would anyone refuse all these wonderful blessings from the LORD we might ask? The answer would once again be found in the Scriptures. The Apostle Paul said,

*If the Good News we preach is veiled from anyone, it is a sign that they are perishing. Satan, the god of this evil world, has blinded the minds of those who don't believe, so they are unable to see the glorious light of the Good News that is shining upon them. They don't understand the message we preach about the glory of Christ, who is the exact likeness of God. (2 Corinthians 4:3–4)*

As conditions on the earth grow darker, and those in sin get more resolute in their disobedience to the God who created them, the true Church of Jesus Christ will begin to shine more brightly. Believers will become steadfast in prayer and will constantly live in the Word and in submission to Jesus.

While the world desperately seeks to snuff out the things of the Lord and to erase even the remembrance of His holy name, we, the Church, must remember to always be faithful, always praying and always thankful to God for who He is. We must not lose sight of His great and awesome power. We must love the Lord with all our hearts, souls, minds, and strength and fervently love each other. The words of the psalmist should be our cry and hope in our God.

> *Blessed is the nation whose God is the LORD, the people he chose for his inheritance. **From heaven the LORD looks down and sees all mankind; from his dwelling place he watches all who live on earth— he who forms the hearts of all, who considers everything they do.** No king is saved by the size of his army; no warrior escapes by his great strength. A horse is a vain hope for deliverance; despite all its great strength it cannot save. **But the eyes of the LORD are on those who fear him, on those whose hope is in his unfailing love, to deliver them from death and keep them alive in famine. We wait in hope for the LORD; he is our help and our shield. In him our hearts rejoice, for we trust in his holy name. May your unfailing love rest upon us, O LORD, even as we put our hope in you.** (Psalm 33:12–22)*

We should never forget who we are in Christ. Peter reminds us:

> **But you are a chosen people, a royal priesthood, a holy nation, a people belonging to God,** *that you may declare the praises of him who called you out of darkness into his wonderful light. (1 Peter 2:9)*

Those in the worldly church should be reminded that though the Lord is patient, His patience will not last forever. The clarion call of the Lord of Hosts is, "*Come out!*" We are to come out of everything that is in disobedience to God's Word and His way. It does not matter how many educational degrees any man has, his opinion remains as it always will be—only his opinion. Anything that opposes God's Word is a lie. The Apostle Paul asks,

> *What if some did not have faith?* **Will their lack of faith nullify God's faithfulness? Not at all! Let God be true, and every man a liar.** *(Romans 3:3–4)*

Every person who is caught up in the doctrines of the world is walking in error and is in great spiritual danger. *Keep in mind you are one heart-beat away from eternity. Where will you spend it?* Jesus said, *"**All that the Father gives me will come to me, and whoever comes to me I will never drive away.**" (John 6:37)*

The church today is full of unbelief concerning the return of Jesus Christ for His Church. Preachers scoff and make fun of those who believe in the Rapture. But this is to be expected. Peter informed us that this would happen in the last days.

> *First of all, you must understand that **in the last days scoffers will come**, scoffing and following their own evil desires. They will say, **"Where is this 'coming' he promised?** Ever since our fathers died, everything goes on as it has since the beginning of creation. (2 Peter 3:3–4)*

Many who call themselves evangelicals deny this great and imminent event; but listen to the Apostle Peter once more.

> **The Lord is not slow in keeping his promise, as some understand slowness. He is patient with you, not wanting anyone to perish, but everyone to come to repentance.** *But the day of the Lord will come like a thief. The heavens will disappear with a roar; the elements will be destroyed by fire, and the earth and everything in it will be laid bare. (2 Peter 3:9–10)*

The day of the Lord will come as a thief to those who are not watching or expecting His return, so Jesus told us to keep watch and be ready for His coming.

> ***Therefore keep watch, because you do not know on what day your Lord will come.*** *But understand this:* ***If the owner of the house had known at what time of night the thief was coming, he would have kept watch and would not have let his house be broken into.*** *So you also must be ready, because the Son of Man will come at an hour when you do not expect him.* (Matthew 24:42–44)

Unfortunately, the giant global church will walk in its own way as it denies, scoffs, and makes fun of the prospect of the Lord's return for His Church, even though the Bible is absolutely clear about it. Consequently, they will not go with Him in the Rapture, but instead will slip into the tribulation hour, during which time they will experience immense difficulties and calamities. Sadly, they will not be able to claim that they were not warned, because the Bible has revealed these truths all along.

Those on the other hand who believe, keep watch, and pray for the coming of the Lord have this glorious event to look forward to. Listen to the Apostle Paul:

> *Brothers, we do not want you to be ignorant about those who fall asleep, or to grieve like the rest of men, who have no hope.* ***We believe that Jesus died and rose again and so we believe that God will bring with Jesus those who have fallen asleep in him. According to the Lord's own word, we tell you that we who are still alive, who are left till the coming of the Lord, will certainly not precede those who have fallen asleep. For the Lord himself will come down from heaven, with a loud command, with the voice of the archangel and with the trumpet call of***

**God, and the dead in Christ will rise first. After that, we who are still alive and are left will be caught up together with them in the clouds to meet the Lord in the air. And so we will be with the Lord forever. Therefore encourage each other with these words.** *(1 Thessalonians 4:13–18)*

Paul exhorts us to encourage each other with the promise of the return of the Lord. We are in no wise to be doubters or mockers.

After the faithful church from every tribe and tongue and nation and every denomination has been taken home to be with Jesus, this huge ecumenical religious system of worldly persuasion will appear to flourish for a short period of time during the tribulation. It will be well-liked by the systems of government and commerce. This false church will be made up of the multitudes that were left behind at the coming of the Lord for His Church. This harlot church made up of great numbers, will eventually come to an end at the hand of the very one to which she sold herself—the antichrist. The Apostle John said of the great prostitute,

Then the angel said to me, 'The waters you saw, where the prostitute sits are peoples, multitudes, nations, and languages. **The beast and the ten horns you saw will hate the prostitute. They will bring her to ruin and leave her naked; they will eat her flesh and burn her with fire.** For God has put it into their hearts to accomplish his purpose by agreeing to give the beast their power to rule, until God's words are fulfilled. **The woman you saw is the great city that rules over the kings of the earth.** *(Revelation 17:15–18)*

Finally this sinful religious system in combination with the commercial and political systems of the day, referred to as Babylon, will be destroyed by God. *"Woe! Woe, O great city,*

*Babylon, city of power! In one hour your doom has come!"*
*(Revelation 18:10)*

The lament of those who committed adultery with her will be great. Every person who rejected Jesus Christ and clung to the ways of the world will suffer great loss and misery.

> *Woe! Woe, O great city, dressed in fine linen, purple and scarlet, and glittering with gold precious stones and pearls! In one hour such great wealth has been brought to ruin! (Revelation 18:16–17)*

Those who choose wealth, power, luxury, and false religion over Jesus Christ and His Word will lose everything in one hour, and their lament will be very great. There will be nothing to look forward to except pain, despair, and carnage. The torment and horror of the religious prostitute, and the commercial and political systems will now reach its apex. The people will weep and mourn and cry out:

> *Woe! Woe, O great city, where all who had ships on the sea became rich through her wealth!* **In one hour she has been brought to ruin!** *Rejoice over her, O heaven! Rejoice, saints and apostles and prophets!* **God has judged her for the way she treated you.** *(Revelation 18:19–20)*

While all this is happening on earth, the saints will be rejoicing in the presence of the Lord in heaven. Because of their faith and their loyalty to Jesus many of them would have lost their lives on earth, at the hands of the unfaithful ones, now in misery. The time now had finally arrived when God avenges His faithful children.

Dear people, the God of the Bible has told you everything that is to come, in advance. Will you believe His Holy Word and save yourselves from the certain horrors and devastation before it is too late? The Lord has a word for you; *it is His will for you to hear His call and live, but this is the day to do it.* You have no guarantee of another year, month, week, day, hour or even another minute.

> **As God's partners, we beg you not to reject this marvelous message of God's great kindness.** *For God says, "At just the right time, I heard you. On the day of salvation, I helped you."* **Indeed, God is ready to help you right now. Today is the day of salvation.** *(2 Corinthians 6:1–2)*

If the Lord has tarried by the time you are reading this, He has been merciful not willing that any should perish, and the Lord Jesus Christ keeps calling to you,

> *Come out of her, my people, so that you will not share in her sins, so that you will not receive any of her plagues; for her sins are piled up to heaven, and God has remembered her crimes. (Revelation 18:4–5)*

Dear friends, please hear the voice of the Lord; listen to His call and obey Him. The God you need to seek and know is found within the pages of the Holy Bible, and His name is Jesus.

- He is the Word. *(John 1:1)*
- He is the author of the Word. *(2 Timothy 3:16)*
- He is the Savior. *(John 3:16)*
- He is the Bridegroom. *(Matthew 25:6)*
- He is also the soon coming King to whom His Bride says *"Amen. Come Lord Jesus." (Revelation 22:20)*

Call to the Lord today. Pray this simple prayer:

> Lord Jesus, I have sinned and messed up, please forgive me, I believe that you are the Christ the Son of the living God. Thank you for dying on the cross for me. Please come into my heart, be the Lord of my life and I will serve you forever.

Dear friend, if you prayed that simple prayer and believed it with all your heart you are saved and you will go with Jesus in the Rapture. You will never have to go through the tribulation and suffer the extreme horror, great persecution, or the loss of your soul.

Start praying regularly to God your Father through Jesus Christ your Savior. Prayerfully read your Bible every day, and go to a good Bible-believing Church to which the Holy Spirit leads you. Be faithful to Jesus, and watch for His return.

If you refuse to hear the call of the Savior and do not respond to Him you will have no excuse. The Lord God spoke these words to the Israelites through Moses, and He gives us the same choice and instruction. Will you choose Him and live?

*This day I call Heaven and earth as witness against you that I have set before you life and death, blessings and curses. Now choose life so that you and your children may live and that you may love the LORD your God, Listen to his voice and hold fast to him, for the LORD is your life . . . (Deuteronomy 30:19–20)*

The Lord also spoke the following words through Paul and Barnabas to the Jewish leaders who rejected the Gospel.

*Then Paul and Barnabas spoke out boldly and declared, "It was necessary that this Good News from God be given first to you Jews. **But since you have rejected it and judged yourselves unworthy of eternal life—** well, we will offer it to Gentiles. (Acts 13:46)*

God sent His angels to warn Lot and his family of impending danger.

*At dawn the next morning the angels became insistent. "Hurry," they said to Lot. "Take your wife and your two daughters who are here. Get out of here right now, or you will be caught in the destruction of the city. (Genesis 19:15)*

God loves us and warns us, those who listen and obey Him will live with him is Glory. Wake up; the hour is late, and the time is at hand.

# Chapter 16

# THE TUNNEL OF LIGHT

—⚬⚬⚬—

The Lord now revealed to me a lighted tunnel. I could see a passageway inside the tunnel which was ablaze with brilliant light. This light was extremely bright but warm and inviting. As beautiful as the tunnel was on the inside, the entrance to it was encircled by thick bramble. Very sharp, spiny thorns protruded from thick vines, causing the entry way of the tunnel to appear much smaller than it actually was.

In addition to the bramble which entwined the entrance of the tunnel, the outer walls of it were covered by these vicious vines as well, which camouflaged and completely obscured its existence. As I gazed at the passageway within the tunnel, I realized there was only one way a person could ever know this wonderful place existed, and this would be if he or she was to come straight up, face to face with the light that shined through the entrance. There was no way to see this tunnel from any other angle, because of the thick thorns and brier that covered it.

It was obvious that, because of the prickly shrubs encircling the entrance, in order for someone to enter this beautiful place, they would of necessity have to stoop to a bowed position. Any attempt to enter the tunnel in upright posture would cause the head of the person to be seriously pierced by the sharp thorns. The only ones who would have success in entering in an upright position would be little children no older

265

than the age of about five or six so as to correspond with the height of the doorway of the tunnel. Jesus once said;

> *Let the little children come to me, and do not hinder them, for the kingdom of God belongs to such as these. I tell you the truth, anyone who will not receive the kingdom of God like a little child will never enter it. (Luke 18:16–17)*

Clearly this picture showed the need for humility, and the Lord made me understand that the lighted passage way portrayed the entrance to the Kingdom of God. The the point of paramount significance was, there is *only one entrance* to the Kingdom and God, and His name is Jesus.

> *Then Jesus said to them again, "Most assuredly, I say to you, I am the door of the sheep. (John 10:7)*

We know that to gain entrance to the Kingdom of God one must submit to Jesus in a spirit of humility.

> *Jesus called a small child over to him and put the child among them. Then he said, "I assure you, unless you turn from your sins and become as little children, you will never get into the Kingdom of Heaven. Therefore, anyone who becomes as humble as this little child is the greatest in the Kingdom of Heaven. (Matthew 18:2–4)*

Prideful people tend to strut; they usually do not acknowledge their sins but walk with their noses in the air. These ones will not gain access to the Kingdom of God. The devil blinds prideful people to the presence of the Kingdom of God, and they disbelieve and reject the Bible. It is this blindness the thorns represented. The very Scripture they reject tells us:

> *In the paths of the wicked lie thorns and snares, but he who guards his soul stays far from them. (Proverbs 22:5)*

When a person humbles himself, he or she becomes able to see the sinful condition of their lives and it is at this point that they see their need for the Savior and come submissively to Him. Jesus said *"those the Father has given me will come to me, and I will never reject them" (John 6:37).*

When a person recognizes sin in his or her life, they will willingly bow at the feet of Jesus and cry out for mercy. Those who remain prideful and unrepentant will bow nevertheless, at some point, for it is written;

> *Therefore God exalted him to the highest place and gave him the name that is above every name, that at the name of Jesus every knee should bow, in heaven and on earth and under the earth, and every tongue confess that Jesus Christ is Lord, to the glory of God the Father. (Philippians 2:9-11)*

Because the threshold of the tunnel was covered with spiny thorns, it meant one would have to step very carefully over the thorns to avoid being pierced in the feet. No doubt this indicated that anyone who desired to enter the tunnel would have to put out a very careful and determined effort to do so. Jesus said, *"Make every effort to enter through the narrow door. . ."* *(Luke 13:24)*. When Jesus said this He was actually telling the people of His day, and us, that we should spare no effort to enter the Kingdom of God. Any wishy-washy attempt to enter the Kingdom will not work, and pain and disillusionment will be the end result.

I began to wonder why the Lord had shown me the tunnel of light camouflaged by thorns and thistles on every side, and then Jesus enlightened me. Thorns and thistles first appeared as a form of judgment that was placed upon Adam and Eve, by God. As we know this judgment came because Adam received the word of the serpent, the devil, and acted in accordance with it. When Adam received the word of the serpent he ingested a lie and rejected the truth of God's Word.

This was the lie of pride and self-will which says, I know best. God said to Adam,

> *Thorns also and thistles shall it bring forth for you, and you shall eat the plants of the field. In the sweat of your face shall you eat bread until you return to the ground, for out of it you were taken; for dust you are and to dust you shall return. (Genesis 3:18–19, AMP)*

Every false religion teaches the lie of the devil that there are many ways into the Kingdom of Heaven but the Lord Jesus said:

> *Most assuredly, I say to you, **I am the door of the sheep.** All who ever came before me are thieves and robbers, but the sheep did not hear them. I am the door. If anyone enters by me, he will be saved, and will go in and out and find pasture. (John 10:7–9)*

Jesus bore the intense pain of a crown of thorns upon His holy brow. He did this to take the punishment for all prideful thoughts that began in the Garden and have continued on to this day. Kings are known for pride and pomposity. This mindset is the absolute antithesis of the mind of Jesus Christ, the King of Kings, and Lord of lords, Yet He paid the painful price.

> *They stripped him [Jesus] and put a scarlet robe on him, **and then twisted together a crown of thorns and set it on his head. They put a staff in his right hand and knelt in front of him and mocked him. "Hail, king of the Jews!" they said. They spit on him, and took the staff and struck him on the head again and again.** After they had mocked him, they took off the robe and put his own clothes on him. Then they led him away to crucify him. (Matthew 27:28–31)*

Sharp thorns and bramble are emblems of the painful consequences of dabbling in false religions. Those who refuse God's Word and take another route remain trapped and ensnared. They do not see the light because they try to enter God's Kingdom in ways other than through the Lord Jesus Christ, *the Door.* So they are destroyed and blinded as they seek God in the delusions of their own prideful minds. No matter how terribly many of these people suffer, they will not accept that there is only *one way* to God and His name is *Jesus.*

The Lord now reemphasized to me many specific things He has spoken to us in His Word with statements such as this:

*Then Jesus went through the towns and villages, teaching as he made his way to Jerusalem. Someone asked him, "Lord, are only a few people going to be saved?" He said to them, **"Make every effort to enter through the narrow door, because many, I tell you, will try to enter and will not be able to.** (Luke 13:22–24)*

The "many" Jesus was speaking of, are those who try to enter the Kingdom by some means other than the Lord Jesus Christ. As mentioned I earlier, the entrance to the tunnel appeared much smaller than it really was because of the thorns encircling it. Listen to the Lord's description of the entrance to the Kingdom. Jesus said,

*Enter through **the narrow gate**. For wide is the gate and broad is the road that leads to destruction, and many enter through it. **But small is the gate and narrow the road that leads to life, and only a few find it.** (Matthew 7:13–14)*

Jesus said plainly,

*I am the light of the world. Whoever follows me will never walk in darkness, but will have the light of life. (John 8:12)*

These Scriptures make it absolutely clear that Jesus alone is the door and the light. It was His light that shined through the door of the tunnel, for He is the Light of the world. No doubt the Lord Jesus was reminding us:

*I am the way and the truth and the life. No one comes to the Father except through me. (John 14:6)*

Jesus spoke the words referred to in the above Scriptures, to help us to understand many important truths. He invites us to follow Him, but He never promised that it would be an easy journey. The Lord was clear and direct when someone asked to follow Him. He explained, that to follow Him meant that one must be willing to lay down all else. There had to be a total willingness to put Him first, to completely surrender to Him, and to keep on steadfastly following Him.

*"Follow me,"* Jesus said to His disciples, and they did, leaving all else behind.

It is logical to conclude that if you intend to follow someone who knows the way to a given destination, your eyes should be fixed upon that person so as to not lose view of your leader, and your way. Unfortunately, too often, many Christians make the unrealistic choice of keeping their eyes on the world while attempting to follow Jesus. Naturally they lose their way and many times don't even realize it. A person, who does not listen to the voice of God through prayer and study of the Bible, listens to a voice that is not God's. This happens with or without the individual's knowledge.

It doesn't take much to figure out whose that other voice might be. Those who spend little or no time in Bible study or prayer are likely to find to their great surprise one day, that Jesus had actually been leading north while the whole time they themselves were heading south, falsely assuming that they were right behind Him. The acceptance of situation ethics and the rejection of moral absolutes is one example of this.

We could all learn a worthy lesson from a lowly little moth. When a moth sees a light, nothing, in fact not one thing will keep it from flying straight to that light. In the process, many times the little moth loses its life in the flame. This could be an excellent parallel for our Christian walk! Just as the little moth focuses on the light, we too should become so focused on the glorious light of Jesus, that absolutely nothing would keep us from Him. Like the little moth, we too should be willing to lose our own lives in the light of the Lord. We should be willing to lose our lives so as to receive His Life. Jesus said, *". . .whoever loses his life for my sake will find it" (Matthew 10:39).* What an awesome promise this is from the Lord! Come to me, He says, lose your life for My sake and you will find it.

We have a tendency to allow our lives to become so cluttered and allow a gazillion things to hinder us from the abundant life Jesus offers. The thorns and bramble we've been discussing represent the many worldly hindrances that are thrust into our paths by the enemy. The devil deliberately does this to keep us from ever finding or entering God's Kingdom.

Going back to Adam for a moment, let's keep in mind that, instead of obeying God, he chose to listen to the voice of his wife Eve—the one closest to him. Adam should have acted as Job did. When Job noticed that his wife was speaking a message different from what he knew to be true of God, he rebuked her.

*His [Job's] wife said to him, "Are you still holding on to your integrity? Curse God and die!" He replied, "You are talking like a foolish woman. Shall we accept good from God, and not trouble? (Job 2:9–10)*

Adam on the contrary, chose to listen to the misguided words of his wife; he willingly accepted the word that came from the enemy through Eve. The lying word from the devil enticed Eve to eat from the tree God had clearly forbidden. Unfortunately, Adam chose to agree with the word of that serpent, the devil, and acted in direct disobedience to the command of God. Sadly, he ate the fruit along with Eve.

The devil for some reason seems to have a passion for going after people through the medium of food. Notice he even tried to get Jesus Christ with this same temptation.

*And when He had fasted forty days and forty nights, afterward He was hungry. Now when the tempter came to Him, he said, "If You are the Son of God, command that these stones become bread." But He answered and said, **"It is written, 'Man shall not live by bread alone, but by every word that proceeds from the mouth of God.'** (Matt 4:2–4)*

Jesus made one thing exceedingly clear; *we are to live by every word that proceeds from the mouth of God.*

The Bible calls the voice of evil enticements, "the world." The voice of the world speaks loudly and sometimes through the ones closest to us: those who appear to be our friends, or family at times, become mouthpieces for the enemy as in the cases of Adam and Job. All worldly desires, false religions, thought patterns and everything that goes contrary to the Word of God is the voice of the world. *The world* is a synonym for Satan's kingdom. Jezebel was an outstanding example of the voice of the world. She continually led Ahab down the path of evil. This is why the Bible says,

*You adulterous people, don't you know that friendship with the world is hatred toward God? Anyone who chooses to be a friend of the world becomes an enemy of God. (James 4:4)*

We all know Satan is God's enemy, and he is called the prince of this world. If we listen, agree with, and obey the reasoning of the world, we are doing nothing other than agreeing with and obeying the enemy of God. This automatically makes us enemies of God. It is truly amazing to see those who identify themselves as Christians, turn around and agree with and endorse a politician whose views and agendas diametrically oppose the Word of God!

The desire to follow any other path than the biblical one stems from a deep-down lack of relationship with the Creator. This again takes us right back to Adam and Eve in the Garden. They decided that they couldn't trust God, based upon the diabolical lies of the serpent. They felt that God was somehow depriving them of something to be desired.

Friends, how often we make the same mistake of trusting our own thoughts and judgments, or the voice of someone else, to get us what we want. When we doubt God's willingness and ability to supply all our needs according to His riches in glory through Christ Jesus, then like Adam and Eve we too find ourselves listening to the voice of the enemy instead of the voice of God.

What a terrible surprise Adam and Eve must have had once they indulged their appetites for the forbidden fruit! Instead of becoming wise and like God as they imagined they would, they wound up naked, ashamed, filled with fear, and headed for lives of endless misery. As we know, this deadly mistake not only brought guilt and condemnation upon them but also to every individual of every subsequent generation on planet earth!

Thorns, bramble, and brier cause only one thing. Excruciating Pain! Sin causes excruciating pain as well!

The condition of spiritual, mental, and physical confusion, and the misery that comes with sins of all kinds, continues in the lives of each person until he or she comes straight up with the Light of the World and becomes willing to humbly bow before the Lord Jesus Christ, and confess Him as Lord and Savior of their lives. It is then and only then that relationship between God and that individual can be restored. It isn't until we are willing to love Jesus more than anything or anyone else that we will proceed to walk in the abundant life that God so willingly offers us. Jesus said:

*Anyone who loves his father or mother more than me is not worthy of me; anyone who loves his son or daughter more than me is not worthy of me; and anyone who does not take up his cross and follow me is not worthy of me. (Matthew 10:37–38)*

When we understand that the Lord cares more for us than we could ever care for ourselves we will surrender completely and lose ourselves in the light of His love. Jesus promised,

*And everyone who has left houses or brothers or sister or father or mother or children or fields for my sake will receive a hundred times as much and will inherit eternal life. But many who are first will be last, and many who are last will be first. (Matthew 19:29–30)*

"Many who are first will be last, and many who are last will be first." Couldn't this statement made by Jesus, apply to the multitudes of seasoned believers who have become listless, sluggish, and lethargic in their Christianity? Is it not possible for a believer to have reached a place of such deep complacency that his or her eyes have shifted dangerously away from the Savior? Is it not equally possible for such a person or persons to be so otherwise engaged, that the drift of their direction has turned exactly opposite to that of the Lord's, and they aren't even aware of it? Could it just not also be that these very ones who although they were first, are now last?

It's time for a heart check, dear friends. What consumes your thought life? What consumes your desires, your time, and your everyday activities? What's the first thing on your mind and mine in the morning and the last thing at night? What do we think about during the day? Is it Jesus and the wisdom of His word? Is it our overwhelming desire to please Him or is there little or no time for such thoughts as these? "Make every effort to enter through the narrow gate" Jesus said, but is it not possible for a believer to get so tangled in the fierce brambles of circumstances, things, position, appearance, pride, and so on, that he or she becomes unable to even see the light anymore?

Focusing on worldly things will cause us to become sluggish in seeking and pursuing the Kingdom of God. Listen to Solomon, *"The way of the sluggard is blocked with thorns, but the path of the upright is a highway" (Proverbs 15:19).*

Remember it was Jesus, who said,

> *But seek first his kingdom and his righteousness, and all these things will be given to you as well. (Matthew 6:33–34)*

It used to be only those who classified themselves as nonbelievers in Jesus Christ who thought they could enter the Kingdom of God through a plethora of doors. However, now as appalling as this may seem, according to which survey you choose to believe, more than fifty percent of those who claim to be evangelicals have stumbled down the same thorny, many-door path of deception.

Whether they know it or not, these deluded people have chosen to take a bite from the fruit of the Tree of the Knowledge of Good and Evil. Even though they once knew the truth, they again chose to receive lying words from the mouth of the serpent—the devil—just as Adam did. Consequently these so-called Christians have convinced themselves, *contrary to the Scriptures* that there are more ways than one to heaven. They once more deliberately chose a word that goes contrary to the Bible, thereby contradicting the word spoken by the Lord Jesus Christ.

> *Most assuredly, I say to you, I am the door of the sheep. All who ever came before me are thieves and robbers, but the sheep did not hear them. I am the door. If anyone enters by me, he will be saved, and will go in and out and find pasture. The thief does not come except to steal, and to kill, and to destroy. I have come*

*that they may have life, and that they may have it more abundantly. (John 10:7–10)*

We must note that according to Jesus there is only *one way*. Again according to Jesus it is only His sheep that will listen to His voice and come to this Door called *Jesus*. Shepherds would usually lie down at the entrance to the sheep pens and nothing could get to the sheep without first having to encounter the shepherd. Jesus is the Good Shepherd!

*My sheep listen to my voice; I know them, and they follow me. I give them eternal life, and they shall never perish; no one can snatch them out of my hand. My Father, who has given them to me, is greater than all; no one can snatch them out of my Father's hand. I and the Father are one. (John 10:27–30)*

It doesn't matter how messed up you are, if you come to this single Door at the entrance to the tunnel of light we have been discussing, and if you humble yourself to the Lord, and determinedly enter in through *Jesus* the Door, He calls you His sheep and you will be saved.

Those who guard their souls stay far from the thorns and snares of the devil, they recognize the web of lies and deceit spun by Satan because they know and believe the word of God. *In the path of the wicked lie thorns and snares, but he who guards his soul stays far from them (Proverbs 22:5).*

Thorns and briars, in the pathway of all who stumble onto them, are representative of any word that goes opposite to God's Word. Those who do not guard their souls through the *Word of God* will become ensnared by the huge and painful thorns prepared for them by the arch deceiver, the devil. These will pierce them, causing unbearable pain both physically and spiritually. The Lord implored us through Solomon:

*O My son, pay attention to what I say; listen closely to my words. Do not let them out of your sight, keep* *them within your heart; for they are life to those who find them and health to a man's whole body. **Above all else, guard your heart, for it is the wellspring of life.** (Proverbs 4:20–23)*

Who the Lord classify as the wicked, we might ask. They are the ones who refuse and reject His Word and His blessing of salvation through Jesus Christ His holy Son. The wicked are all those who have chosen to follow the way of the world—their own thoughts, desires, and ways.

Those who take this route are prideful and deluded people, who will ultimately end up stuck in the briar of sin from which they can't get free. Unfortunately the more intensely they feel the pain of the massive thorns of Satan's deceptions, the harder they struggle, piercing themselves to an even greater extent. They do this by grasping onto increasingly more sinful things in their quest for some form of relief from their pain. Drugs, alcohol, sex, witchcraft, or whatever else they can find to indulge in, becomes their way of life as a means of alleviating the unbearable torture they live with.

In the natural, the harder you grab at a thorn, the deeper it will pierce your hand causing more pain. So it is in the spiritual realm. Sin causes unbearable pain, and everything that goes opposite and contrary to God's word are huge thorns that pierce the souls. These thorns are those of depression, sickness, despair, hopelessness, and total misery. This is why Jesus Christ received a crown of massive thorns upon His holy head to pay the price for all the terrible transgressions of us all. Those who receive His sacrifice will immediately be set free from all the agony of their own sins. The Bible tells us:

*They stripped him* [Jesus] *and put a scarlet robe on him, and then twisted together a crown of thorns and set it on his head. They put a staff in his right hand and knelt in front of him and mocked him. "Hail, king of the Jews!" they said. They spit on him, and took the staff and struck him on the head again and again. After they had mocked him, they took off the robe and put his own clothes on him. Then they led him away to crucify him. (Matthew 27:28–31)*

Believers in the Lord are called to be light-bearers to those in darkness. Jesus cares greatly for the lost and dying and He commissions all His true followers to share the Good News of His saving grace with all who will hear and believe.

*All authority in heaven and on earth has been given to me. Therefore go and make disciples of all nations, baptizing them in the name of the Father and of the Son and of the Holy Spirit, and teaching them to obey everything I have commanded you. And surely I am with you always, to the very end of the age. (Matthew 28:18–20)*

Those who glimpse the glorious light of the Gospel, and come to Jesus, will find that He is the only One who can and will extricate them from painful bramble that ensnares their souls. He will heal their wounds and carry them over the thorny threshold as His Bride, into the glorious light of His Kingdom. *"So if the Son sets you free, you will be free indeed" (John 8:36).*

According to various and diverse surveys, more than fifty percent of those who call themselves evangelical Christians have gone down the slippery slope of deception, believing that "good people," no matter what their religion, are going to heaven.

For these deceived ones who have stumbled once more onto the broad road that Jesus described, there will be no light, peace, or joy. They will stagger and reel under the pressure of the oppressor, and their darkened hearts and minds will grow even darker. Many of these unfortunate people will remain ensnared head, hand, and foot until they perish because they have rejected the way of the Lord Jesus Christ and chosen the path of Satan. The Bible says:

*It is impossible for those who have once been enlight-
ened, who have tasted the heavenly gift, who have
shared in the Holy Spirit, who have tasted the goodness of the word of God and the powers of the coming
age, if they fall away, to be brought back to repentance,
because to their loss they are crucifying the Son of God
all over again and subjecting him to public disgrace.
(Hebrews 6:4–6)*

Meanwhile the Lord still lovingly calls to all who will listen:

*Come to me, all you who are weary and burdened, and
I will give you rest. Take my yoke upon you and learn
from me, for I am gentle and humble in heart, and you
will find rest for your souls. For my yoke is easy and my
burden is light. (Matthew 11:28–30)*

Felix, the governor from the Book of Acts, is an example of
one who was ensnared by the thorns of power, pride, positions,
and status in life. The Apostle Paul, the light-bearer, was sent
to him by Jesus, and Paul did his best to help Felix see the
light. Felix is referred to as one who was *". . . well acquainted
with the Way" (Acts 24:22)*. This meant that Felix knew well
about salvation through Jesus Christ, but it is obvious that he
had no desire to accept the light of the Gospel. Listen to what
we are told:

*Several days later Felix came with his wife Drusilla,
who was a Jewess. He sent for Paul and listened to
him as he spoke about faith in Christ Jesus. **As Paul
discoursed on righteousness, self-control and
the judgment to come, Felix was afraid and said,
"That's enough for now! You may leave. When I
find it convenient, I will send for you."** At the same
time he was hoping that Paul would offer him a bribe,
so he sent for him frequently and talked with him.
(Acts 24:24–26)*

279

Too many people have made Felix's mistake. Fear of the truth and the lack of willingness to change one's lifestyle causes them like Felix to say, *"That's enough for now! You may leave, when I find it convenient, I will send for you."* Felix rejected salvation even though he spoke often with Paul. He made the mistake many people do. He was looking for a bribe; he desired money over the true treasures of God's Kingdom. There is no indication in the Bible that Felix was ever saved. As in Felix's case, a convenient time may never come. Multitudes who postpone their face-to-face moment with the Light may never ever see Him again. No wonder Jesus said:

> *"No one can serve two masters. Either he will hate the one and love the other, or he will be devoted to the one and despise the other. You cannot serve both God and Money. (Matt 6:24)*

When someone comes to Jesus, there can be no room for pride. Anyone who approaches Him in pride will never become His follower. The Matthew 19 story of the rich young ruler proves this to be true. He never became a follower of Jesus because he could not let go of his love for his wealth and all that it offered him. He went away sadly, the Bible tells us. Pride and greed go hand in hand.

True peace is found in Jesus Christ alone, and the only way to Jesus is to go directly to Him just as a moth flies directly to a light. Faith does not mix with pride. Jesus once called some children to him and he blessed them and said,

> *Let the little children come to me, and do not hinder them, for the kingdom of God belongs to such as these.* ***I tell you the truth, anyone who will not receive the kingdom of God like a little child will never enter it.*** *(Luke 18:16–17)*

As I mentioned earlier, the tunnel of light I saw was encircled by thorny bramble. This is how the Lord explained the meaning of the scene. The size of the entrance interprets the humility of a small child. Little children are humble and trusting; they don't have any problem believing Jesus, so the only ones who will enter His Kingdom are those who are willing to bow their hearts, minds, and knees to Him, humbling themselves as little children.

The time is coming when every human being will either bow now to Jesus Christ as Lord and Savior, or they will bow later to Him as King and Judge. The choice is only a matter of time.

The Bible lets us know quite clearly,

*Therefore God exalted him to the highest place and gave him the name that is above every name, that at the name of Jesus every knee should bow, in heaven and on earth and under the earth, and every tongue confess that Jesus Christ is Lord, to the glory of God the Father. (Philippians 2:9–11)*

Those who have bowed to Jesus as Savior should make sure they also bow to Him as Lord. Jesus has to become the Lord of our hearts; He cannot be not a guest; He has to be *the* owner. He must rule and we must obey.

*Do you not know that your body is a temple of the Holy Spirit, who is in you, whom you have received from God?* **You are not your own; you were bought at a price. Therefore honor God with your body.** *(1Corinthians 6:19–20)*

Apart from the Lord we have nothing to boast about. Jesus Christ purchased us with His life and His holy Blood. Jesus said ". . . *apart from me you can do nothing" (John 15:5).* As we can see, we have no reason at all to be prideful.

Humility must prevail in our hearts and the Lord's desire should be our command. Jesus never asks us to do anything He hasn't first done Himself. Take a look at Jesus' attitude, Paul described it as follows.

*Your attitude should be the same as that of Christ Jesus: Who, being in very nature God, did not consider equality with God something to be grasped, but made himself nothing, taking the very nature of a servant, being made in human likeness. And being found in appearance as a man, he humbled himself and became obedient to death- even death on a cross! Therefore God exalted him to the highest place and gave him the name that is above every name, that at the name of Jesus every knee should bow, in heaven and on earth and under the earth, and every tongue confess that Jesus Christ is Lord, to the glory of God the Father. (Philippians 2:5–11)*

Jesus humbled Himself and made Himself nothing, the Bible says. He gave up equality with Almighty God and became a servant even to death. He humbled Himself on the cruel cross to purchase our salvation with His own precious Blood.

It is amazing that every person doesn't fall at the beautiful feet of the Lord Jesus Christ and cover them with tears and kisses as the woman with the alabaster jar did. The only explanation would be pride and blindness: pride that comes from ignorance of God's Word and blindness from being entrapped in the thorny lies and deceit of the devil to whatever degree.

Jesus declared a very important thing about the Kingdom of Heaven. He said,

*From the days of John the Baptist until now, **the kingdom of heaven has been forcefully advancing, and forceful men lay hold of it.** (Matthew 11:12–13)*

What did Jesus mean by this statement? He meant that the Kingdom of Heaven is taken hold of by those with a strong and forceful desire for Him. There has to be a determined breaking away from the sinful ways and practices of the world and though the cost may be high for some, it should never be considered high enough to keep us from life eternal. Keeping our eyes solidly fixed on Jesus so that we will not lose our way, we must make every effort and endeavor to follow Him steadfastly, because our lives depend on Him.

Paul urges us:

*Fight the good fight for what we believe. Hold tightly to the eternal life that God has given you, which you have confessed so well before many witnesses. (1 Tim 6:12)*

According to Paul we are to fight, making every effort to win. He tells us to take hold of eternal life to which we were called. So take hold, grab on to Jesus Christ who is within you. When you want something badly enough you will do whatever it takes to secure it.

The cares of the world are thorns planted by Satan in the pathway of believers. He plants thorns to keep us from the Bible and the Kingdom of God. Worry about jobs, divorce, money, difficulties of various sorts, sickness, and every other difficulty that invades our lives are forms of fierce and painful thorns. The devil plants these thorns to stick the feet of all who hear the Word gladly and accept it at first, but in the end are overwhelmed by the cares of the world and the deceitfulness of riches. Spiritual growth becomes stifled, and these individuals remain pinned by thorns that pierce their feet, right at the very entrance of God's glorious kingdom. They don't enter because the thorns that stick their feet are called self-focus. Jesus said, *"But seek first his kingdom and his righteousness, and all these things will be given to you as well" (Matthew 6:33).*

Jesus gave us the cure for the cares of the world! He said,

*Come to me, all you who are weary and burdened, and I will give you rest. **Take my yoke upon you and learn from me, for I am gentle and humble in heart, and you will find rest for your souls. For my yoke is easy and my burden is light.** (Matthew 11:28–30)*

The way to win is to put on the whole armor of God.

*Finally, be strong in the Lord and in his mighty power. Put on the full armor of God so that you can take your stand against the devil's schemes. For our struggle is not against flesh and blood, but against the rulers, against the authorities, against the powers of this dark world and against the spiritual forces of evil in the heavenly realms. Therefore put on the full armor of God, so that when the day of evil comes, you may be able to stand your ground, and after you have done everything, to stand. (Ephesians 6:10–13)*

Paul says, we are to be strong in the Lord and in His mighty power by putting on the full armor of God, so that being fully protected, we can take our stand against the devil's schemes.

James tells us how to resist the devil "*So humble yourselves before God. Resist the Devil, and he will flee from you*" *(James 4:7)*. As we humble ourselves before God we become empowered to resist the devil, and when we do he has to flee from us. We are told, *God blesses those who are gentle and lowly, for the whole earth will belong to them. (Matthew 5:5)*

So now take up the sword of the Spirit which is the Word of God, and determinedly and systematically cut away the thorns and bramble, by faith-filled confessions of God's Word.

*So is My Word that goes forth from my mouth: It will not return to me empty but will accomplish what I desire and achieve the purpose for which I sent it. (Isaiah 55:11)*

We can always be sure that God's Word works when it is spoken in faith and so it is vitally important that we remain faithful in our thirst for knowledge that comes from the Word of God. It is crucial that we study, and meditate upon God's Word and fill ourselves with it. We must then use it as a sharp two-edged sword to chop away the thorny snares of doubt and fear that are planted in our souls by the devil. We should deliberately perform inward surgery by submitting to God in faith and willing obedience to Him.

*For the word of God is living and active. Sharper than any double-edged sword, it penetrates even to dividing soul and spirit, joints and marrow; it judges the thoughts and attitudes of the heart. (Heb 4:12)*

The importance of not allowing ourselves to become like the unfaithful servant who buried his talent should not be undermined. He was one who had his feet stuck in thorns of laziness and fear.

*You wicked and lazy servant . . ."* said his Master, *"Take the talent from him and give it to the one who has the ten talents. For everyone who has will be given more, and he will have an abundance. Whoever does not have, even what he as will be taken from him. And throw that worthless servant outside, into the darkness, where there will be weeping and gnashing of teeth. (Matthew 25:26–30)*

Could it be that many who once followed Jesus have been tagged "worthless" by the Lord and had their talents taken from them and given to another? Even though the Lord places victory in the hands of unfaithful ones, they choose to hide it and do nothing to profit the Lord's Kingdom. Consequently they become worthless to the Master, lose their position in the Kingdom, and end up being thrown into outer darkness. *"The path of the sluggard is blocked with thorns, but the way of the upright is a highway"* *(Proverbs 15:19)*. Laziness to study, to share the Gospel, and follow in the footsteps of Jesus, are ways to bury our talents. They are also thorns the enemy uses to block the way to the Kingdom of Heaven.

It is time for the Church to wake up and take heed. Jesus put it this way, *"He who has an ear, let him hear what the Spirit says to the Churches"* *(Revelation 2:7)*.

Let us consider the cost of failing to make every effort to enter the Kingdom of God. Obviously the unfaithful servant Jesus discussed, felt quite comfortable to return the Master's talent intact. He did not steal it or misuse it. However, He simply did not use it to gain any more. Surely he did not expect to be thrown into outer darkness for that! He had not committed any major crime, or so it may appear, but he had gravely neglected and disobeyed the Master's command, commonly known as the Great Commission.

The talent Jesus placed in this man's hands was unused, and it cost him his place in God's Eternal Kingdom. Jesus gave us salvation; He gave us His Word that through knowledge of it, lives of others might be purchased as well. He left us with understanding of His position and power; He also left us this command:

> ***Therefore go and make disciples of all nations,*** *baptizing them in the name of the Father and of the Son and of the Holy Spirit, and teaching them to obey everything I have commanded you. (Matthew 28:19–20)*

Surely Jesus never intended His Church to ignore or take lightly His final instruction before leaving this earth. One look at the first Church and their fervor in spreading the Gospel will clarify how seriously they took this command.

Let's now focus for a moment on the joy the Master felt at the work performed by the "five talent" and "two talent" servants who doubled what he had entrusted them with. The Lord applauded.

> *Well done good and faithful servant! You have been faithful with a few things; I will put you in charge of many things. Come and share your Master's happiness! (Matthew 25:21)*

It is time for those of us who think of ourselves as the Bride of Christ to wake up, for the time is at hand. Press into the Kingdom; be single-minded and focus upon serving the Lord with all your hearts. Study and meditate upon God's Word, and sow its message far and wide. Don't lose any opportunity to share the Gospel with anyone. The Word of God says, *"How beautiful are the feet of those who bring Good News" (Romans 10:15).* This is how Jesus feels about the good-ground-hearted servants; those who bring forth a thirty, sixty, and a hundred-fold return on His precious investment.

By no means do any of us want the surprise the unfaithful servant received. He had been one who knew the Master and had been accepted by Him as one of His household. Yet this man's focus was on himself. He took his Master's blessings for granted and did not fulfill what was expected of him. Note, his weak excuse was both accusatory and insulting to the Master, revealing his lack of relationship with him. Listen to him:

> **'Master,' he said, 'I knew that you are a hard man, harvesting where you have not sown and gathering where you have not scattered seed. So I was afraid and went out and hid your talent in the ground. See, here is what belongs to you.** *(Matthew 25:24–25)*

Sadly, this man not only did nothing with what he was entrusted, but he blamed his master for his own lack of service as well. This is preposterous! But it is what the man did, and consequently, he not only lost the talent that was given to him, but was thrown into outer darkness and torment. In other words, he lost his soul. How terrible! The man's condition was a heart issue. Jesus gave us this story so we would be warned.

> *Not everyone who says to me, 'Lord, Lord,' will enter the kingdom of heaven, but only he who does the will of my Father who is in heaven. (Matt 7:21)* Jesus also said, *"He who is not with me is against me, and he who does not gather with me, scatters. (Luke 11:23)*

Jesus said, He who is not with me is against me, and he who does not gather with me, scatters. You are either with Jesus or you aren't. You either do as Jesus did or you go against Him by doing exactly the opposite, by your inaction. Which will it be for you and me?

The time is at hand! The Lord said,

> **And behold, I am coming quickly, and my reward is with me, to give to everyone according to his work.** *I am the Alpha and the Omega, the Beginning and the End, the First and the Last."* **Blessed are those who do His commandments, that they may have the right to the tree of life, and may enter through the gates into the city. But outside are dogs and sorcerers and sexually immoral and murderers and idolaters, and whoever loves and practices a lie.** *(Revelation 22:12–15)*

All those on the outside of the city are the ones who specifically chose not to continue in the light of Jesus once having seen it. Included among them are all those who did not remain steadfast to His commission. They are the ones who allow themselves to get entangled once more in Satan's thorny brambles of sin, deceit, and laziness. These are also the ones referred to as dogs. Peter describes to us the reason such people are referred to as dogs:

> *It would have been better for them not to have known the way of righteousness, than to have known it and then to turn their backs on the sacred command that was passed on to them. Of them the proverbs are true:* **"A dog returns to its vomit,"** *and, "A sow that is washed goes back to her wallowing in the mud." (2 Peter 2:21–22)*

Everyone who chooses to neglect the many warnings given to us in God's Word unfortunately puts themselves in the frightening position of being left outside the city when Jesus comes. What a terrible awakening that will be!

Just remember, the Lord Jesus is still calling, *"He who has an ear, let him hear" (Revelation 13:9).* Wake up, dear ones, and heed the loving call of the Savior, while there still is time.

The time is at hand!

# Chapter 17

# THE TORCH

—ⵓⵓ—

I mmediately following the lighted tunnel, I was shown a very muscular upper and lower arm of a male athlete, who was holding an Olympic torch.

I figured this could only mean one thing; run to win! As I was thinking on this, I saw the torch-bearer for the second time but now his image was followed by a picture of the same bramble-encircled tunnel of light that we have been discussing.

"Run" I could feel the Lord urging, "Continue to run your Christian race with the tenacity and focus of an Olympic contestant."

Olympic athletes spare absolutely no effort. They are focused, determined, disciplined, and consumed with the desire to win. They do all they must; they take no short cuts and leave little room for self-pampering. They push hard, make no excuses, and work until they literally hurt. They acquire all the knowledge and wisdom they possibly can for the task ahead and look for the most effective methods by which to accomplish their goal—a gold medal.

"Go for the gold" we've heard it said, and they go for nothing less. Single-minded, unbending, and uncompromising, these men and women remain dogged in their desire and focus. They certainly make every effort to win the gold; yes, they run with all their hearts, and yet, they run for an earthly, perishable gold medal.

How do we Christians run the race to which we are commissioned by the King of kings and Lord of lords? Yes, how do we run? Is it with the same fervor and unwavering determination as the Olympic athletes? Keep in mind they run to attain the perishable, but we run to attain the imperishable, heavenly gold! Paul says,

*Do you not know that in a race all the runners run, but only one gets the prize? Everyone who competes in the games goes **into strict training**. They do it **to get a crown that will not last forever**. Therefore **I do not run like man running aimlessly, I do not fight like a man beating the air, No, I beat my body and make it a slave so that after I have preached to others, I myself will not be disqualified for the prize**. (1 Corinthians 9:24–27)*

Paul's determination and tenacity came from his understanding of the great price Jesus paid for us; this price is beyond all human understanding. The seldom asked question is, how much of a price are we who are called by His name willing to pay in order to win the race we started when we said "Yes" to Jesus.

*"Go into all the world and preach the Gospel."* Jesus commanded, but how far do each of us really go? Do we venture next door or down the street—or does our race end no further than the couch we sit on while watching our favorite television show?

As we look in the face of Jesus Christ one day, perhaps we might desperately wish that Paul's words could be ours as well.

*. . . **when I preach the gospel, I cannot boast, for I am compelled to preach. Woe to me if I do not preach the gospel!** . . . Though I am free and belong to no man, I make myself a slave to everyone, to win as many as possible. To the Jews I became like a Jew, to win the Jews. To those under the law I became like one*

*under the law (though I myself am not under the law), so as to win those under the law. To those not having the law I became like one not having the law (though I am not free from God's law but am under Christ's law), so as to win those not having the law. To the weak I became weak, to win the weak.* **I have become all things to all men so that by all possible means I might save some. I do all this for the sake of the gospel, that I may share in its blessings.** *(1 Corinthians 9:16, 19–23)*

I often wonder what we would see in the beautiful eyes of Jesus when we stand before Him. Would we see joy or pain as He looks into ours?

How will we measure up? Have we, like Paul, become all things to all men so that by all possible means we could win some of the lost to Christ? *"I did not run aimlessly and I did not fight like a man beating the air!"* Paul said. Face to face with Jesus, would we wish that we could say that, too?

The thorny brambles of self-focus and the deceitfulness of the affairs of the world are *the* great blinders that keep us from the diligent focus that is required for the task set before us by the Lord. Somehow these words of Jesus seem overwhelmingly appropriate here.

*The one who received the seed that fell among the thorns is the man who hears the word, but the worries of this world and the deceitfulness of wealth choke it, making it unfruitful. (Matthew 13:22)*

Exacerbating the huge problem of the "I" syndrome which engulfs the hearts of many believers, are the many self-focusing sermons people receive in their churches. Jesus warned us of wolves who come in sheep's clothing. He said:

> **Beware of false prophets, who come to you in sheep's clothing,** but inwardly they are ravenous wolves. You will know them by their fruits. (Matthew 7:15–16)

Consistent with the warnings of Jesus, we find that at the core of too many sermons today is a self-gratifying message that feeds the insatiable desire for more and more worldly possessions. This is in steep contrast to the life-giving manna Jesus dispensed.

> **If anyone desires to come after Me, let him deny himself, and take up his cross, and follow Me. For whoever desires to save his life will lose it, but whoever loses his life for My sake will find it. For what profit is it to a man if he gains the whole world, and loses his own soul? Or what will a man give in exchange for his soul?** For the Son of Man will come in the glory of His Father with His angels, and then He will reward each according to his works. (Matthew 16:24–27)

The Holy Spirit says to us,

> **You adulterous people, don't you know that friendship with the world is hatred toward God?** Anyone who chooses to be a friend of the world becomes an enemy of God. (James 4:4)

Jesus asked what it would profit a man if he gained the whole world but lost his soul. Good question!

At one point, Jacob the patriarch could well have been one of the many who sit in pews today to get their "give me, give me more" appetites satiated each week. Jacob wanted much for himself too, to begin with. He was always planning and scheming to get what he desired. Notice that when he left his father Isaac's home as he ran from Esau, he made a conditional covenant with the Lord. The Bible tells us,

*Then Jacob made a vow, saying, "If God will be with me and will watch over me on this journey I am taking and will give me food to eat and clothes to wear so that I return safely to my father's house, **then the LORD will be my God and this stone that I have set up as a pillar will be God's house, and of all that you give me I will give you a tenth.** (Genesis 28:20–22)*

Basically Jacob said to God, "Lord, if you will give me all that I need, then You will be my God and I will give you a tithe." This was Jacob's mind set until he wrestled all night with the Lord. Clinging with all his might and strength to Him, Jacob desperately tried again to get something from the Lord. He cried out, *"I will not let you go unless you bless me" (Genesis 32:26).*

The Bible says, Jacob wrestled with the Lord and prevailed; and he certainly received a blessing, but it was a blessing that changed him from the inside out.

Jacob first received a name change. God called him Israel instead of Jacob. The name Israel pronounced Yis-ra-el in Hebrew means "He will be a prince of God." Jacob became the ancestor of the Messiah and his new name became the name of the nation to which the Messiah was born. During the process of wrestling, the Lord threw Jacob's hip out of joint by a mere touch. No longer would Jacob struggle to achieve his own selfish ends, but he would lean wholly upon the Lord!

Jacob learned that God is all-sufficient. Paul found this out first hand from the Lord. God said, *"My Grace is sufficient for you, for My power is made perfect in weakness . . ." (2 Corinthians 12:9).* These words from the Holy Spirit remained strong in Paul's spirit as he ran his race.

Jacob, now called Yis-ra-el, learned this important lesson. He began his new journey not depending on anything or anyone but the Lord. Limp, lean, limp, lean, went Jacob. In his new weakness, he progressed from *". . . Glory to Glory . . ." (2 Corinthians 3:18), even as Paul did.*

Dear friends, this is where we all need to be. We need to walk in the blessing of being able to lean on the Lord, submitting to Him in humility, even if it means limping for the rest of our lives as Jacob did. His limp was a medal of honor that came from wrestling with the Lord and prevailing. Yet, his prevalence was an act of submission to the One who was much greater than he. *""I will not let you go unless you bless me."*

Blessings come from one that is greater than the person who receives them. Jacob's intense craving for the blessing of the Lord came from his total recognition of the Almighty, the great I AM, and submission to His mighty power.

*Submit yourselves then to God."* the Holy Spirit says, *"Resist the devil and he will flee from you. Come near to God, and he will come near to you. Wash your hands you sinners and purify your hearts you double minded. Grieve, mourn and wail, change your laughter to mourning and your joy to gloom. Humble yourselves before the Lord and he will lift you up. Brothers do not slander one another. Anyone who speaks against his brother or judges him speaks against the law and judges it. When you judge the law you are not keeping it, but sitting in judgment on it. There is only one Law Giver and Judge, the One who is able to save and destroy. But you, who are you to judge your neighbor? (James 4:7–12)*

Our lack of submission to the Lord happens unknowingly many times. We tend to keep our attitudes, our mouths, and our tongues out of sync with our real purpose in life. The lack of understanding of who God really is, slows our run to glorify and serve Him. Somehow we fail to discern His awesome holiness. His justice, truth, and love seem to elude us as we pause to judge, slander, or speak against our brothers and sisters in Christ. We are also quick to take offence and react in ways that are not Christ-like.

If we do not take hold of the Holy Spirit in spiritual desperation, if we do not hang on to Him as Jacob clung to the Lord, we will find ourselves coming under a flood the devil relentlessly throws at us in the form of worldly attractions . The enemy's goal is to cause us to feel engulfed and defeated. He goes relentlessly after us with intent to bring about an eventual downward spiral into defeated and atrophied mindsets. This then leaves us totally unwilling and unable to accomplish what Jesus commissioned us to do.

Isaiah had a vision that should get our attention. He said:

*In the year that King Uzziah died, I saw the Lord seated on a throne, high and exalted, and the train of his robe filled the temple. Above him were seraphs, each with six wings: With two wings they covered their faces, with two they covered their feet, and with two they were flying. And they were calling to one another: "Holy, holy, holy is the LORD Almighty; the whole earth is full of his glory." At the sound of their voices the doorposts and thresholds shook and the temple was filled with smoke.* **"Woe to me!" I cried. "I am ruined! For I am a man of unclean lips, and I live among a people of unclean lips, and my eyes have seen the King, the LORD Almighty." Then one of the seraphs flew to me with a live coal in his hand, which he had taken with tongs from the altar. With it he touched my mouth and said, "See, this has touched your lips; your guilt is taken away and your sin atoned for."** *Then I heard the voice of the Lord saying, "Whom shall I send? And who will go for us?" And I said, "Here am I. Send me! (Isaiah 6:1–8)*

As soon as the guilt of Isaiah's lips was removed, he became more than willing to go and serve the Lord. Consider, it was just one bite of the forbidden fruit that caused Adam and Eve to become unclean. Our mouths have a lot to do with our spiritual condition both literally and metaphorically. Jesus once said to His disciples,

*. . . the things that come out of the mouth come from the heart and these make a man unclean. For out of the heart come evil thoughts, murder, adultery, sexual immorality, theft, false testimony, slander. These are what make a man unclean . . . (Matthew 15:18–20)*

When Isaiah saw the living God, he immediately became conscious of the sinful condition of his own lips and the lips those among whom he lived. The Bible tells us: *"The tongue has the power of life and death, and those who love it will eat its fruit" (Proverbs 18:21).*

The way we share the Gospel of Jesus Christ is by mouth; and to serve the Lord, our lips must of necessity be clean. If our lips are to become clean, our hearts must be clean, and there is only one way to achieve this. It is only when the glory and majesty, the beauty of the Lord Jesus Christ begins to unfold within us in a deep and personal way from the pages of His Holy Word that our hearts, our minds and our souls get cleansed by the Living Water.

*. . . Christ loved the church and gave himself up for her to make her holy, cleansing her by the washing with water through the word, and to present her to himself as a radiant church, without stain or wrinkle or any other blemish, but holy and blameless. (Ephesians 5:25–27)*

With cleansed lips we will now gladly be able to say as Isaiah did: "Here am I. Send me." Jesus stated,

*. . . Out of the overflow of the heart the mouth speaks. The good man brings good things out of the good stored up in him, and the evil man brings evil things out of the evil stored up in him. But I tell you that men will have to give account on the day of judgment for every careless word they have spoken. For by your words you will be acquitted and by your words you will be condemned. (Matthew 12:34–37)*

Hearts that are filled with the world bring forth worldly things. Worldly chatter flows easily from worldly hearts, but the things pertaining to the Lord come from hearts that have been cleansed by the Word. Many who are called believers spend much time discussing sports, movies, new fashions, and the list goes on; they do this on a daily basis, yet they never take time to share Jesus with a co-worker, a neighbor or anyone else. Truly from out of the overflow of the heart the mouth speaks.

The Most High God who has taken up residence in us deserves nothing less than the equivalent of Isaiah's heart. We also must see the Lord high and lifted up within the pages of the Bible, and when we do, the good things from God's Word stored up within us will begin to flow easily. This of course would mean sharing of the Gospel of Jesus Christ with the lost and dying as He commanded us to do.

Those in the world see and hear us each day in our places of work, or wherever we go. They should have the opportunity to see God's goodness and love operating in us, if they are to desire Him and be willing to give their lives to Him.

If we are to run to win this race set before us by Jesus, we must run according to His rules. Paul explains how he prepared for the race,

> *I beat my body and make it my slave so that after I have preached to others, I myself will not be disqualified for the prize. (1 Corinthians 9:27)*

As difficult as it might sound, our flesh must be crucified daily until we can finally say with Paul, *"I press on toward the goal to win the prize for which God has called me heavenward in Christ Jesus" (Philippians 3:14).*

Our God, who loves us so much, also blesses us with the ability to obey and serve Him. Paul advised the Church at Philippi.

> *. . . Continue to work out your salvation with fear and trembling, **for it is God who works in you to***

*will and to act accordingly to His good purpose. (Philippians 2:12)*

It is God who works in us to will and act according to His good purpose. He doesn't simply tell us to work out our salvation, but He tells us very simply how to accomplish it.

*Do everything without complaining and arguing so that you may become blameless and pure children of God without fault in a crooked and depraved generation in which you shine like stars in the universe, as you hold out the Word of Life . . . (Philippians 2:14–16)*

This is the key, this is the way! This is how we are to do what Jesus asked us to. We must stop complaining, stop arguing and slandering; the acts of judging and speaking against our brothers and sisters must go as well. Now we should just keep our eyes on the Lord and be on our way to doing everything as faithfully and willingly as Isaiah did, when he saw the LORD. David said, *"My eyes are always on the LORD for He rescues me from the traps of my enemies"* (Psalms 25:15).

The reward, yes now comes the reward! What is the reward for this life of submission and obedience?

> **We will become blameless and pure children of the Living God, without fault in a crooked and depraved generation in which we will shine like stars in the universe, as we hold out the Word of Life.**

It takes clean lips to be able to shine the light of Jesus into a world of darkness and filled with people of very unclean lips. Remember, Jesus spared no effort in the race He ran on earth to win and secure His Bride—the Church.

Paul summarizes it for us this way:

*Christ loved the church and gave himself up for her, to make her holy, cleansing her by the washing with water through the word, and to present her to himself as a radiant church without stain or wrinkle or any other blemish, but Holy and Blameless. (Ephesians 5:25-27)*

Jesus gave His all to purchase the church and we the church should respond with nothing less. We should be willing to shower upon Him all the love, effort, steadfast faithfulness and loyalty that He so richly deserves. No one displayed this ardent and thankful love for the Lord more than the woman with the alabaster box.

*. . . She brought an alabaster jar of perfume, and as she stood behind him at his feet weeping, she began to wet his feet with her tears. Then she wiped them with her hair, kissed them and poured perfume on them. (Luke 7:37–38)*

Love like this expresses deep gratitude. It is this kind of love and devotion Jesus seeks in each one of us when He cautions: *"Make every effort to enter through the narrow door."*

> The door to the Kingdom of God is narrow indeed, but we must run to win the prize of His high calling. We go for the true gold; the Kingdom of God, where the streets are paved with pure gold.
>
> We are to run this race making every effort to enter the narrow door, *a door only as wide as the loving outstretched arms of the Lord Jesus Christ upon the cross.* His precious bleeding hands and arms selflessly bore the heavy cross all the way to Calvary, only to be pierced in open welcome to all who would follow Him into His holy Kingdom.

Not every Olympic contestant wins a gold medal, but only those who lay down everything else in this life to achieve it.

Christ laid down His life so we might win, and we must lay down all else to receive that promised imperishable Gold that

He so yearns for us to have. There is however, only one way to run to win, and this is to do it with focus, keeping in mind that when we fall, His strength always picks us up. This is why Paul said, *"I can do all things through Christ who strengthens me" (Philippians 4:13).*

Jesus ensured our ability to make it to the finish line victoriously. He sent the Holy Spirit to come alongside of us. The Holy Spirit stays faithfully beside us, loving and encouraging us. He is our comforter and counselor. Many times He carries us, but we must determinedly surrender to Him if we are to win. Paul eloquently expressed this thought.

*Therefore, since we are surrounded by such a great cloud of witnesses, **let us throw off everything that hinders, and the sin that so easily entangles, and let us run with perseverance the race marked out for us. Let us fix our eyes on Jesus, the author and perfecter of our faith who for the joy set before him endured the cross, scorning its shame, and sat down at the right hand of the throne of God. Consider him who endured such opposition from sinful men, so that you will not grow weary and lose heart.** In your struggle against sin, you have not yet resisted to the point of shedding blood. (Hebrews 12:1–4)*

Those of us who have lived in the lap of ease and luxury, tend to whine and complain at the drop of a hat. We are seldom thankful to God for all the many blessings He has so generously poured out upon us as a nation, as His Church, and as individuals. Yet some of us arrogantly expect God to pop us into prominent positions of ministry. It is time, beloved brothers and sisters in Christ, to stop and take the humble road as Jesus and His disciples did.

If we could just keep our eyes on Jesus the author and perfecter of our faith instead of on ourselves, the gold will be ours and the race will be won. Paul said to the Church at Philippi:

*If you have any encouragement for being united with Christ, if any comfort from his love, if any fellowship with the Spirit, if any tenderness and compassion, then make my joy complete by being like-minded, having the same love, being one in spirit and purpose. **Do nothing out of selfish ambition or vain conceit, but in humility consider others better than yourselves.** Each of you should look not only to your own interests but also to the interests of others. **Your attitude should be the same as that of Christ Jesus.** (Philippians 2:1–5)*

Isn't this what we should be striving for anyway—the mind of Christ? In fact Paul tells us that we already have the mind of Christ, so let's walk in submission to *His mind.* Let's take a look at it. *". . . he is patient . . . not wanting anyone to perish but everyone to come to repentance." (2 Peter 3:9)* This should be precisely our desire, as well—if we love Him.

As the Bride of Jesus Christ, we could take an excellent lesson from the diligent Proverbs 31 wife. She *always* sought what was good and in the very best interests of her husband. *His desires, his interests, his purposes, and his good were her prime focus and goal.* Should we as the Bride of Christ do any less for our Lord and Savior? Remember he is faithful He is called *"Faithful and True."* How about our own faithfulness to Him? How faithful are we?

Jesus Christ is the gold that *does not* perish. Paul expressed the worth of the prize he ran to win this way.

*But whatever was to my profit I now consider loss for the sake of Christ. What is more, I consider everything a loss compared to the surpassing greatness of knowing Christ Jesus my Lord for whose sake I have lost all things. **I consider them rubbish that I may gain Christ and be found in him, not having a righteousness of my own that comes from the law, but that which*** *is through faith in Christ—the righteousness that comes from God and is by faith. (Philippians 3:7–9)*

Loving and praying for others should be a top priority in our lives. It is extremely hard to be at odds with someone for whom we are praying. Paul requested prayer,

*Pray also for me that whenever I open my mouth words may be given me so that I will fearlessly make known the mystery of the Gospel, for which I am an ambassador in chains. Pray that I may declare it fearlessly, as I should. (Ephesians 6:19-20)*

Friends, Paul shared the Gospel while in physical chains; how hard and fast we should work while we are still ambassadors without chains. Keep in mind, this liberty may not last forever. The time is at hand; let us diligently and consistently pray for each other, doing so as the Holy Spirit directs us.

As we run, pressing toward the goal—the gold that does not perish, let us do so with the mindset Paul recommends:

*Finally be strong in the Lord and in his Mighty power. Put on the full armor of God, so that you can take a stand against the devil's schemes. For our struggle is not against flesh and blood, but against the rulers, against the authorities, against the powers, of this dark world and against the spiritual forces of evil in the heavenly realms. Therefore put on the whole armor of God, so that when the day of evil comes, you maybe able to stand your ground and after you have done everything to stand. Stand firm then, with the belt of truth buckled around your waist, the breastplate of righteousness in place, and with your feet fitted with the readiness that comes from the Gospel of peace. In addition to all this take up the shield of faith with which you can extinguish all the flaming arrows of the evil one. Take the helmet of salvation and the sword of the Spirit which is the word of God and pray in the Spirit on all occasions with all kinds of prayers and requests with this in mind. Be alert and always keep on praying for all saints." (Ephesians 6:10–18)*

Church please wake up! Run! Put on the armor of God, and "go for the gold" that does not perish. The time is surely at hand!

# Chapter 18

# THE GLASSY SEA

────◦◦◦◦────

I was now permitted to view what appeared to be a huge sea. This was not a sea of water; instead it looked like a sea of beautiful pure, transparent gold. It shone like glass or crystal, and it was glorious to behold.

I wondered if this could be what John described when he heard the *"Come up here . . ."* call of (Revelation 4:1) Listen to what John had to say when he was instantly transported into the presence of the Living God. John said:

> After this I looked, and there before me was a door standing open in heaven. And the voice I had first heard speaking to me like a trumpet said, **"Come up here, and I will show you what must take place after this."** At once I was in the Spirit, and there before me was a throne in heaven with someone sitting on it. And the one who sat there had the appearance of jasper and carnelian. A rainbow, resembling an emerald, encircled the throne. Surrounding the throne were twenty-four other thrones, and seated on them were twenty-four elders. They were dressed in white and had crowns of gold on their heads. From the throne came flashes of lightning, rumblings and peals of thunder. Before the throne, seven lamps were blazing. These are the seven spirits of God. **Also before the throne there**

**was what looked like a sea of glass, clear as crystal.**
*(Revelation 4:1–6)*

The glory and beauty of this crystal sea is hard to describe in a way that will ever do it justice. The question now uppermost in my mind was why the Lord was showing it to me; so I did what I usually do; I asked the Him for understanding.

Jesus graciously explained by emphasizing to me important truths that all believers should know. The Lord said, if any person desired to earnestly contend for the "Heavenly Gold" as we have been referring to Jesus, it would necessitate nothing less than full-hearted loyalty and obedience to Him. Obedience must come with uncompromising commitment to His work on earth. This was the attitude of the first Church. Very simply, the Lord explained, *be zealous, have implicit faith, and be diligent; this is what "going for the Heavenly Gold" means.* Everyone who is diligent and faithful has this to look forward to. I could feel the heart of Jesus seeking, waiting, looking, desiring, yearning for, and demanding this kind of whole-hearted allegiance from His Bride.

You might ask, does the Lord have a right to expect such great fervor? Absolutely! Consider the price He paid to purchase His Church! He not only commands faithfulness but clearly expects it.

*If anyone comes to me and does not hate his father and mother, his wife and children, his brothers and sisters-yes, even his own life-he cannot be my disciple. And anyone who does not carry his cross and follow me cannot be my disciple. (Luke 14:26–27)*

This sounds like an overwhelming demand on the part of the Lord, but what is Jesus saying? We are to love Him and be loyal to Him above all else. There should be no comparison between our love and loyalty to Him and our love for anyone or anything else. He must come first!

Coming back to the glassy sea and my questions about what it meant, the Lord led me back to the Book of Revelation to help me to understand. John described the sea of glass before the Throne of God as follows:

***And I saw what looked like a sea of glass mixed with fire and, standing beside the sea, those who had been victorious over the beast and his image and over the number of his name.*** *They held harps given them by God and sang the song of Moses the servant of God and the song of the Lamb . . . (Revelation 15:2–3)*

John's description caused me to wonder why this beautiful glassy sea was mixed with fire and the answer to my question was found in the ones standing beside the sea. Who were they? The Bible tells us they were believers who had been victorious over the beast and his image and the number of his name.

These were tribulation saints! Yes, they were the ones who had been through the fire. Their faith had been tested by the white hot flames of persecution in the areas of obedience, faithfulness, and loyalty to Jesus Christ. They had suffered pain, shame, hatred, torture, unspeakable terror, and every temptation to disown Him, but they did not. They suffered death at the hands of the evil dictator, the antichrist—the one personally embodied by Satan himself. Yet these saints had overcome the devil *". . . by the blood of the Lamb and the word of their Testimony. They did not love their lives so much as to shrink from death" (Revelation 12:11).*

The fire that blazed upon that Crystal Sea speaks of that fervent faithfulness, the passion, the allegiance, and the obedience of every loyal believer to the Lord Jesus Christ. It is this ardent love for the Lord that blazes as a fire of remembrance before Almighty God upon that glassy sea. It is the faithfulness of saints like Stephen and Antipas, Christians like Ignatius, the apostles, and countless others whose names are known only to God. Many faithful believers were thrown to hunger-crazed animals at the Roman Coliseum. Others served as lighted torches to illuminate the gardens of the maniacal megalomaniac, Nero. Those who persevered even under the most abysmal circumstances in unbending love and loyalty to Jesus Christ are described in the Biblical Hall of Faith, as follows:

> *Others were tortured and refused to be released, so that they might gain a better resurrection. Some faced jeers and flogging, while still others were chained and put in prison. They were stoned; they were sawed in two; they were put to death by the sword. **They went about in sheepskins and goatskins, destitute, persecuted and mistreated- the world was not worthy of them.** They wandered in deserts and mountains, and in caves and holes in the ground. (Hebrews 11:35–38)*

Many of these beloved martyrs died trying to save the lives of fellow-believers. The Scriptures remind us ***"God is not unjust; He will not forget your works and the love you have shown Him** as you have helped his people and continue to help them. (Hebrews 6:10).*

The tribulation saints had only one of two choices. They could either be faithful to their Lord and Savior Jesus Christ and cling to Him even though it meant sure death, or compromise and sacrifice their souls to eternal condemnation in the fires of hell. As we can see from Revelation 15:2, that they chose to remain faithful to the Lord and overcame by the Blood of the Lamb and the word of their testimony.

It is this type of zeal and loyalty that Jesus is seeking from all of us who are called by His name. He is urging us to develop our passion for Him, so that our love and focus on Him are exclusive.

Most believers are counting on leaving this earth in the imminent and glorious event called the Rapture, which happens prior to the tribulation. Will we, however, have some challenges to face prior to that glorious event? We don't know, but we must be ready. If a time of persecution comes, will we have the same zeal, the same fire, and the same loyalty to Jesus as the ones who went through such terrifying times in the past? I believe the Lord Jesus earnestly desires to see that same fire burning brightly within each one of us, as we await the glorious day of departure.

If we continue to sit around in deep complacency we will find that we resemble the five foolish virgins instead of the five wise ones. The question regarding the condition of our lamps arises, too. Have we kept our lamps filled with the oil of the Holy Spirit and are they burning brightly as we await the Bridegroom?

Are we diligently working to show the love of God to others by helping His people? Would our works of love be ones that God will not forget? Many of us are greatly reluctant to approach a nonbeliever on behalf of our Lord and Savior. Many times we are ashamed to pray in a restaurant before we eat. We are afraid to mention His holy name in public. We are afraid that someone might be offended!

Think carefully about the disciples; think also about the tribulation saints. Faithfulness unto death was their approach. They loved others because they loved the Lord, and because they loved the Lord they shared the Gospel even if it meant certain death. What about us dear friends? What about us?

Much of the Church today might be described in what could be termed the "sandwich syndrome." The first Church was strong and on fire for the Lord. In sandwich terms, they would represent the piece of bread at the bottom—the foundation. The tribulation saints would be the strong top piece. That leaves the present-day Church in the role of the soft filling! Do we really want to be the floppy piece of turkey baloney or whatever else constitutes the mushy center of the sandwich? I think not! I pray not! It is time like never before for us to wake up and saturate ourselves in the Lord. We are to be salt and light, we must fire up in zeal, loyalty, love, and service to Jesus Christ our Lord as the first church did and as the last one will.

As we keep looking upwards, let us also keep this amazing God-given promise constantly before our eyes, in our hearts and in our minds.

*God is not unjust; he will not forget your works and the love you have shown him as you have helped his people and continue to help them. We want you to show this same diligence to the very end in order to make your hope sure. We do not want you to become lazy, but to imitate those who through faith and patience inherit what has been promised. (Hebrews 6:10–12)*

Many a Christian says, "I just don't know enough of the Bible to do that." If this is you, beloved reader, please *make* time to study the Word so that you can be obedient to the Great Commission. Time as we all know it, is fast running out! Jesus solemnly warned us,

*For false christs and false prophets will rise and show signs and wonders to deceive, if possible, even the elect. But take heed; see, I have told you all things beforehand (Mark 13:21-23)*

With the appearance of false christs, would everyone who identifies him or herself as a Christian, be able to recognize these imposters? Keep in mind we are not dealing with some naive prankster, but Satan himself! Jesus called the master of these false christs, *"the thief [that] comes to steal, kill and destroy" (John 10:10).*

There is only one way to know the true Christ, and that is through the Bible. Faith, dependence, absolute trust, prayerful study, and willing obedience come only through knowledge of the written Word of God. May we never forget John's opening statement in his Gospel!

*In the beginning was the Word, and the Word was with God, and the Word was God. He was with God in the beginning. (John 1:1–2)*

To know Jesus Christ, is to also know His Word and vice versa. Time spent in the Word is equal to a face-to-face encounter with Jesus Christ. We know that there will be much deception just as Jesus said, and we have been given every possible forewarning by the Lord to keep us from falling away from Him. Above all, we have been given the Holy Spirit to keep us on the straight and narrow, but we must know the Scriptures so that we can recognize the voice of the Holy Spirit, because His words always agree with the written Word. John explains this as follows,

*We know that we have come to know him if we obey his commands.* **The man who says, "I know him," but does not do what he commands is a liar, and the truth is not in him. But if anyone obeys his word, God's love is truly made complete in him. This is how we know we are in him: Whoever claims to live in him must walk as Jesus did.** *(1 John 2:3–6)*

Those who are ignorant of the Word will fall prey to false christs and false prophets who will lead them down the path that leads to eternal destruction. As early as Paul's time, the saints of Galatia had already started down this slippery slope, and Paul exclaimed:

**I am astonished that you are so quickly deserting the one who called you by the grace of Christ and are turning to a different gospel- which is really no gospel at all.** *Evidently some people are throwing you into confusion and are trying to pervert the gospel of Christ.* **But even if we or an angel from heaven should preach a gospel other than the one we preached to you, let him be eternally condemned!**

*As we have already said, so now I say again: **If anybody is preaching to you a gospel other than what you accepted, let him be eternally condemned!** (Galatians 1:6–9)*

A lack of knowledge of the true Gospel leaves a person vulnerable to a false one, and the dangers of this cannot be overemphasized. Remember, it only took the addition of one little three-letter word very cunningly interjected by Satan, into God's Word, to alter its meaning and bring about Eve's tragic deception and the subsequent fall of all mankind. Let's not overlook or ever take lightly the fact that *it cost God the Life of His only Son, to fix the immense problem caused by that one falsehood, which was believed and acted upon, by two of God's children.*

Seeing that we have discussed this subject rather extensively, and have prayerfully made a case for the importance of spending time with Jesus in prayer and prayerful Bible study, what will we do about it? Will we run the race keeping our eyes on the Gold that does not perish, or will we keep looking to worldly sources for comfort? Amos the Prophet tried to wake Israel up with these words. *"Can two walk together, except they be agreed? (Amos 3:3)* Joshua, when faced with a similar situation, challenged the Israelites with the following statement.

**Now fear the LORD and serve him with all faithfulness. Throw away the gods your forefathers worshiped beyond the River and in Egypt, and serve the LORD.** *But if serving the LORD seems undesirable to you,* **then choose for yourselves this day whom you will serve,** *whether the gods your forefathers served beyond the River, or the gods of the Amorites, in whose land you are living.* **But as for me and my household, we will serve the LORD.** *(Joshua 24:14–15)*

It only makes sense that if we are to agree with God, we must first know what He has to say and what He wants us to know and do. Enoch was a man mentioned in the Book of Genesis who truly knew what this meant. The Bible says about Enoch, "*Altogether, Enoch lived 365 years.* **Enoch walked with God; *then he was no more, because God took him away (Genesis 5:23–24).***

The statement, "Enoch walked with God" can only mean one thing; he was in total agreement with the Lord. This agreement was so intense that God saw fit to walk him straight into an eternity of fellowship with Himself. Enoch's sudden departure to be with the Lord should cause us to realize that this actually is a picture of the Rapture, and it is those who walk this life in agreement with God as Enoch did, who will get to go. Paul discusses this event in his letter to the Thessalonians.

*According to the Lord's own word, we tell you that we who are still alive, who are left till the coming of the Lord, will certainly not precede those who have fallen asleep.* **For the Lord himself will come down from heaven, with a loud command, with the voice of the archangel and with the trumpet call of God, and the dead in Christ will rise first. After that, we who are still alive and are left will be caught up together with them in the clouds to meet the Lord in the air. And so we will be with the Lord forever.** *Therefore encourage each other with these words.* (1 Thessalonians 4:15–18)

Friends, we must walk faithfully with the Lord everyday and be watching in all sincerity for His coming. We also urgently need to continue to encourage each other with the promise of His certain return for the church. So are we walking daily with God? Are we sincerely in agreement with Him? If so, we are doing as He commanded, and we can rejoice and encourage others with the promise of His certain and imminent return.

How tragic it would be for so many who count themselves to be faithful believers, only to get caught proverbially asleep when the Bridegroom arrives. They could be complacently enjoying a ballgame, watching a "not too bad" movie or doing whatever else they feel they just want to do. Yet they were caught lazing around because they paid little or no attention to the imminent signs of return of the Lord Jesus Christ.

This Scripture from the Book of Exodus is a magnificent portrayal of the return of the Lord.

> *On the morning of the third day, there was a powerful thunder and lightning storm, and a dense cloud came down upon the mountain.* ***There was a long, loud blast from a ram's horn, and all the people trembled.*** *Moses led them out from the camp to meet with God, and they stood at the foot of the mountain. All Mount Sinai was covered with smoke because the LORD had descended on it in the form of fire. The smoke billowed into the sky like smoke from a furnace, and the whole mountain shook with a violent earthquake.* ***As the horn blast grew louder and louder, Moses spoke, and God thundered his reply for all to hear. The LORD came down on the top of Mount Sinai and called Moses to the top of the mountain. So Moses climbed the mountain.*** *(Ex 19:16-20)*

Notice it was only Moses—the one who walked closely with God, who went up, as the Lord came down. The rest stood trembling at the bottom of the mountain. Unfortunately this will be the scenario when the Lord Jesus returns for the faithful. The ones who were complacent will have a very different experience from those who were faithful.

Suddenly there will be a loud command from the Lord Jesus, the voice of the archangel, and the blast of the trumpet, and those who were wise will depart to be with Him. The others, the complacent, like the five foolish virgins, will suddenly realize that the oil in their lamps—the Word and communion with the Holy Spirit, is at an all-time low. They will desperately want some oil now! They'll make a mad dash to buy some, to look for their Bibles, but by the time they come back, the Door to the rapture-craft will be closed. The wise will have entered and the foolish will be left behind!

The five virgins were foolish because they did not keep themselves filled up with the Word of God or walk in obedience to His Holy Spirit. Unfortunately, they had chosen to be lukewarm, or sleeping as the Bible puts it. Jesus said:

> *"**All those who love me will do what I say**. My Father will love them, and we will come to them and live with them. Anyone who doesn't love me will not do what I say. And remember, my words are not my own. **This message is from the Father who sent me.** (John 14:23-25)*

We must keep in mind that the Holy Spirit is the oil that produces light in our lives. "*So then faith comes by hearing, and hearing by the word of God*" *(Romans 10:17)*. Those who take no time for the Word of God are by their own actions declaring that they have no time for the precious Holy Spirit. Consequently, their lamps will run out of oil, and their light will be snuffed out. "Sir, Sir! These unfortunate ones will cry, "Open the door for us!" but it will be too late.

The Lord will reply, *"I tell you the Truth, I don't know you"* *(Matthew 25:11–12)*.

It is hard to think of more chilling and terrifying words to hear coming from the lips of the Lord Jesus Christ! No doubt, He would hate to speak these words, but He will say them to those who shut their ears and dragged their feet.

The good news is, there still is time, so *wake up*; but do so speedily. David prayed, "*Therefore let everyone who is godly pray to you while you may be found*" *(Psalm 32:6)*.

Do not play Russian roulette with your eternal destiny. We have not been promised a single minute; we have no way of knowing if there will be time for even another breath before our lives are gone, and we must then stand in the presence of a Holy and Righteous God.

Most people are diligent about having checkups with their doctors as a normal health precaution. Many times however, these very same people never think about having a spiritual checkup.

One way to do this is to carefully evaluate what we watch, and read. Are the sources pure or impure? Are prayer and Bible study daily priorities? If Jesus lived in your house for a while, if He was your next door neighbor or dropped by on an unexpected visit, what would He see and hear?

While we are on this subject, it might just be good to keep in mind that Jesus really does see and hear everything we do and say. The problem is, we are not usually aware of His constant presence. The Lord has a very clear view into the very core of our beings. *"The eyes of the LORD are everywhere, keeping watch on the wicked and the good" (Proverbs 15:3).*

With this in mind let's put together a simple list to evaluate our priorities. We will call it food for thought:

1. Do we begin our day with thanksgiving; in daily submission to God and putting on His whole armor?
2. Do we ask God to fill us afresh with His Holy Spirit and cover us with the Blood of Jesus each day?
3. Do we ask for His help so that we can forgive others as He has forgiven us?
4. Do we love and pray for the Church?
5. Are we faithful in our church attendance?
6. Do we make sure to spend time sharing the Gospel with the lost and dying that Jesus gave His life for?
7. Do we love the lost enough to lead them to Him?
8. Do we hate evil and love good?
9. Do we make sure we don't compromise when things get uncomfortable?
10. Do we honor the Lord, do His will, and choose His way even if it means being persecuted and having to standing alone?
11. Are we truthful in our speech, keep our word, and avoid gossip?

12. Do we watch our pride level? Choose to bless, love, and do good to those who despitefully use us?

This is not easy, you might say. Oh! You are right! This is *not* easy, beloved, but not impossible. *"I can do all things through **Christ** who strengthen me" (Philippians 4:13).* We cannot do all this in and of ourselves, but through Christ we can. Keep in mind that "practice makes perfect" as the old adage goes. So stand strong in the Lord and cheer up. God has given us marvelous promises, and He has never been known to break His Word. Simply depend on Jesus Christ, and He will be your strength.

Let's look at a few of God's very precious promises to us. The Bible tells us,

**For those God foreknew he also predestined to be conformed to the likeness of his Son,** *that he might be the firstborn among many brothers. (Romans 8:29)*

The Word also tells us that:

**His divine power has given us everything we need for life and godliness through our knowledge of him who called us by his own glory and goodness.** *Through these he has given us his very great and precious promises,* **so that through them you may participate in the divine nature and escape the corruption in the world caused by evil desires.** *(2 Peter 1:3–4)*

God's very great and precious promises are given to us for the very purpose that we might participate in His divine nature. In this way we will be able to escape the corruption in the world which obviously comes through evil desires. Every relationship is a two-way street. God, for His part, is faithful to us; we also must be faithful to Him.

If God says we may participate in the divine nature, this then means that we are able to do so, and to participate in something means to be actively involved. This puts the decision to do or not to do, right into our hands. Even though God has given us everything we need for life and godliness, we have to make a decision to be like the Lord and to prayerfully follow this commitment by faithfully walking with him. So cheer up! The Lord has made the way; in fact, He [Jesus] said, *"I am the way, the truth and the life No one comes to the Father except through me" (John 14:6).*

Life clearly has a destination—the Father, and there is only *one* path that leads to the Father—*Jesus* is His name. It is completely our choice whether we take this path or not. Link arms with Jesus; walk with Him and make every effort to keep on going in the direction He's leading, for He is leading you to the Father.

Jesus said, *"If you really knew me you would know my Father as well. From now on you do know Him and have seen Him" (John 14:7).* Jesus is pretty clear, if we choose to know Him, to spend time doing things His way by knowing and obeying His Word, we will know both Him and the Father. In doing this we will both be partaking in the divine nature and escaping the corruption that comes from the world and its evil desires. In short, to walk with Jesus means to change and purify our desires by making them line up with His.

How much time do we have left before the Lord returns for His Church? We don't know, but we can know it can't be too far in the future. John said.

> *Dear Children, **this is the last hour;** and as you have heard that the antichrist is coming, even now many antichrists have come . . . (1 John 2:18)*

If John considered his time to be "the last hour" then how very much closer must we be to the coming of the Lord? Perhaps we are down to the very final minutes or even seconds on God's clock right now.

Peter advised the church through the Holy Spirit to do the following things, and the Lord Jesus promises a rich welcome into His Kingdom for all who would do them.

*For this very reason, **make every effort** to add to your faith goodness; and to goodness, knowledge; and to knowledge, self-control; and to self-control, persever-ance; and to perseverance, godliness; and to godliness, brotherly kindness; and to brotherly kindness, love. **For if you possess these qualities in increasing measure, they will keep you from being ineffective and unproductive in your knowledge of our Lord Jesus Christ.** But if anyone does not have them, he is nearsighted and blind, and has forgotten that he has been cleansed from his past sins. **Therefore, my brothers, be all the more eager to make your calling and election sure. For if you do these things, you will never fall, and you will receive a rich welcome into the eternal kingdom of our Lord and Savior Jesus Christ.** (2 Peter 1:5–11)*

Coming back to the crystal sea with which we opened this chapter, it seems important to seek out the significant mes-sage this amazing sea has for us. I believe the answer could be found within the following Scriptures.

***Let us fix our eyes on Jesus, the author and per-fecter of our faith,*** *who for the joy set before him endured the cross, scorning its shame, and sat down at the right hand of the throne of God. (Hebrews 12:2)*

All who have diligently set their eyes on the Lord and run the race faithfully to the finish line, will receive the prize of standing beside the crystal sea that is ablaze with the inten-sity of their loyalty to the Jesus Christ, who now sits at the right hand of God the Father. Their faithfulness will glow as fire upon the sea as it is remembered before the Throne of Almighty God.

> *God is not unjust; he will not forget your work and the love you have shown him as you have helped his people and continue to help them. (Hebrews 6:10)*

At this point it might be interesting to take a quick look at the amazing arrangement of the furnishings of both the Tabernacle and the Temple. Both the Tabernacle that traveled with Moses and the Temple that Solomon built were exact copies of the Heavenly Temple.

> **They** [the earthly priests] ***serve at a sanctuary that is a copy and shadow of what is in heaven.*** *This is why* **Moses was warned** *when he was about to build the tabernacle:* ***"See to it that you make everything according to the pattern shown you** on the **mountain.*** *(Hebrews 8:5)*

So why are we going back to the Tabernacle? Because there was a piece of furnishing called the brazen laver in the Tabernacle that we would like to discuss.

> **He** [Bezalel] ***made the laver of bronze and its base of bronze, from the bronze mirrors of the serving women*** *who assembled at the door of the tabernacle of meeting. (Exodus 38:8)*

This brazen laver very interestingly was called the *sea* in Solomon's Temple.

> **The Sea stood on twelve bulls,** *three facing north, three facing west, three facing south and three facing east. (1 Kings 7:25)*

You might wonder why this is so important and where we are going. So hang on for a second. The brazen laver was made of mirrors. Interestingly, this huge sea made of mirrors was for the priests to wash their hands and feet. The importance for washing immediately speaks of cleansing. So why did the laver have to be made of mirrors? Consider, what would you do with a mirror? If you are like me, you would look at your reflection in it.

Obviously, when the priests went to wash themselves, they could also take a look at themselves in the mirrors of the laver and be convicted that they were sinful men who needed this ceremonial washing, which symbolized the spiritual cleansing they so desperately needed.

James writes:

*Anyone who listens to the word but does not do what it says is like a man who looks at his face in a mirror and, after looking at himself, goes away and immediately forgets what he looks like.* **But the man who looks intently into the perfect law that gives freedom, and continues to do this, not forgetting what he has heard, but doing it-he will be blessed in what he does.** *(James 1:23–25)*

James perfectly makes the point. The laver, or the sea, served as the means for the priests to see that they were imperfect and needed cleansing. They needed to wash so as to be ceremonially clean. This was a shadow of what was to come. The fulfillment of this shadow came through Christ.

*. . . Christ loved the church and gave himself up for her to make her holy, cleansing her by the washing with water through the word, and to present her to himself as a radiant church, without stain or wrinkle or any other blemish, but holy and blameless. (Ephesians 5:25–27)*

As we can see, Jesus loved the Church and gave himself up for her, making her holy, cleansing her by washing with water *through the Word.* As we spend time in the Word and obey it, we are being washed and purified by Jesus Himself because He is the living Word.

> *His eyes are like blazing fire, and on his head are many crowns. He has a name written on him that no one knows but he himself.* **He is dressed in a robe dipped in blood, and his name is the Word of God.** *(Revelation 19:12–13)*

We are made holy and blameless by the blood of Jesus. His name is the Word of God and through His faithfulness we become the radiant church without stain or wrinkle or any other blemish. This is the church that the Lord presents to Himself. There is both promise and warning wrapped up in this Scripture. If you choose to spend time with the Lord in the Word allowing Him to convict and cleanse you, you will be part of the radiant Church He is coming for; if not, you will not be cleansed, and so you will not be ready to go with Him.

Returning to the beautiful crystal sea of the Book of Revelation, the Lord made me understand that this beautiful sea was once again a huge mirror; but what for? Let's listen to Paul for just a second.

> **For whom He foreknew, He also predestined to be conformed to the image of His Son, that He might be the firstborn among many brethren.** *Moreover whom* **He predestined,** *these* **He also called;** *whom* **He called,** *these He also* **justified;** *and whom* **He justified,** *these He also* **glorified.** *(Romans 8:29–30)*

All who have run with endurance, keeping their eyes steadfastly on Jesus, the Author and Finisher of their faith, will one day stand together with those who have gone before, beside the beautiful crystal sea before the Throne of God. The Bible tells us:

> *But our citizenship is in heaven. And we eagerly await a Savior from there, **the Lord Jesus Christ, who, by the power that enables him to bring every- thing under his control, will transform our lowly bodies so that they will be like his glorious body.*** *(Philippians 3:20–21)*

This mighty ransomed choir of God's children will blend their voices in glorious harmony singing the song of Moses and of the Lamb in praise to God. These magnificent praises will be sung by both Jew and Gentile, one new man, establishing at last the oneness of all faithful believers, from righteous Abel to the very last one saved, in and through the Lord Jesus Christ.

> *And I saw what looked like a sea of glass mixed with fire and, **standing beside the sea,** those who had been victorious over the beast and his image and over the number of his name. They held harps given them by God and sang the **song of Moses** the servant of God and the **song of the Lamb.*** *(Revelation 15:2–3)*

Finally, mirrored on the beautiful surface of the glassy sea, all the ransomed will finally see themselves, cleansed, puri- fied, dressed in white, and holy: conformed to the very image and likeness of our beloved Lord and Savior Jesus Christ.

> *Beloved, now we are children of God; and it has not yet been revealed what we shall be, **but we know that when He is revealed, we shall be like Him, for we shall see Him as He is. And everyone who has this hope in Him purifies himself, just as He is pure.*** *(1 John 3:2–3)*

What a glorious day it will be when we hear the awesome voice of their Lord, Jesus Christ, the Bridegroom, the Messiah, the King of kings and Lord of lords, as He proudly presents the Church to God the Father: those redeemed by His blood, His own Radiant Bride, without spot or wrinkle, pure and holy, and looking just like Him in the eyes of God.

The tribulation saints sing the song of Moses and the song of the Lamb, saying:

*Great and marvelous are Your works, Lord God Almighty! Just and true are Your ways, O King of the saints! Who shall not fear You, O Lord, and glorify Your name? For You alone are holy. For all nations shall come and worship before You, For Your judgments have been manifested. (Revelation 15:3-4)*

The mighty throng John described would be all the faithful believers praising God. John said:

*Then I heard what sounded like a great multitude, like the roar of rushing waters and like loud peals of thunder, shouting: "Hallelujah! For our Lord God Almighty reigns. Let us rejoice and be glad and give him glory! For the wedding of the Lamb has come, and his Bride has made herself ready. Fine linen, bright and clean, was given her to wear." (Fine linen stands for the righteous acts of the saints.) Then the angel said to me, "Write: **'Blessed are those who are invited to the wedding supper of the Lamb!'" And he added, "These are the true words of God." (Revelation 19:6–9)***

Dear friends, what a glorious event! Please make sure to be at the Wedding Supper of the Lamb.

Awake! The time is at hand! Hallelujah! Come, Lord Jesus!

# Chapter 19

# THE SHIP

———⟨∞⟩———

For several weeks following the day I saw the slides that make up the chapters of this book, a huge ship would appear on the screen of my mind each time I prayed or worshipped the Lord. I wondered what this ship could possibly mean and why I kept seeing it over and over again.

Not thinking this could be from the Lord, I prayed fervently that I would never see it again. I even began to rebuke its appearance, claiming the Blood of Jesus, but all to no avail. Each time I entered into praise and worship, the ship would reappear.

Finally as I was in praise to the Lord one day, I saw the ship once more, but this time quite suddenly the Lord Jesus appeared, standing beside it. Then to my great amazement I saw my daughter, Carol, dressed in a beautiful wedding gown as she stood beside the ship as well. I watched in awe as Jesus suddenly walked over to Carol. He picked her up very lovingly in His arms as a bridegroom would pick up his bride. The Lord Jesus then lovingly hugged her as He easily lifted her up and placed her on the deck of the huge ship.

Fear gripped me, along with the thought that Carol was going to die. Through my fear-ridden thoughts I heard the Lord gently say to me, "Ask Me what this ship is."

Timidly I whispered, "Lord, what is this ship?"

No sooner than the words left my lips, the ship that had so far been standing very still, suddenly tipped far over to the left until the top deck almost hit the water. After a while it slowly righted itself and held still for a little while. Then quite as suddenly it tilted again; this time it went to the right, but it didn't lean quite as far over as it had done to the left.

What was all this about, I wondered. What could it possibly mean? Then slowly the Words of Solomon came to my mind. *"A wise man's heart turns him toward his right hand, but a fool's heart toward his left." [Matthew 25:31-41]. (Ecclesiastes 10:2, AMP)*

Regardless of what this ship represented at this point, if we are to make application from Ecclesiastes 10:2, then the tipping of the ship far over to the left would indicate that somehow it had been drawn into foolishness. The fact that it tilted so far over to the left, causing its uppermost deck to almost touch the water, revealed that it had reached a point of near-destruction. Had it gone over just a bit more, it surely would have capsized, taking on water and finally sinking to the bottom of the ocean. This, however, did not take place, for it appeared that a Power much greater than itself raised it up, setting it aright.

Gleaning from Ecclesiastes 10:2 once more, a swing towards wisdom was indicated when the ship tilted over to the right, even though it fell somewhat short of reaching a full measure of it.

On the day that Peter made his God-given declaration of Matthew 16:16: *"You are the Christ, the Son of the living God,"* Jesus made a very important statement of promise to the disciples, and eventually to all believers,

*Jesus replied, "Blessed are you, Simon son of Jonah, for this was not revealed to you by man, but by my Father in heaven. And I tell you that you are Peter, **and on this rock I will build my church, and the gates of Hades will not overcome it.** (Matt 16:17–18)*

When Jesus made this statement to Peter He was saying, God gave you that revelation, Peter, and My Church will be comprised of every individual who believes and makes the same confession you did, and the gates of Hades will not be able to prevail against it.

As we know, Peter was answering *the most important* question Jesus asks of every human being:

*"But what about you?""Who do you say I am?" (Matthew 16:15)* The answer we give to that all important question decides whether we will be on His right or left.

Dear reader, listen to Jesus, hear what He has to say:

*When the Son of Man comes in his glory, and all the angels with him, he will sit on his throne in heavenly glory. All the nations will be gathered before him, and he will separate the people one from another as a shepherd separates the sheep from the goats. **He will put the sheep on his right and the goats on his left.***

***"Then the King will say to those on his right, 'Come, you who are blessed by my Father; take your inheritance, the kingdom prepared for you since the creation of the world.** For I was hungry and you gave me something to eat, I was thirsty and you gave me something to drink, I was a stranger and you invited me in, I needed clothes and you clothed me, I was sick and you looked after me, I was in prison and you came to visit me.'*

*Then the righteous will answer him, 'Lord, when did we see you hungry and feed you, or thirsty and give you something to drink? When did we see you a stranger and invite you in, or needing clothes and clothe you? When did we see you sick or in prison and go to visit you?'*

*The King will reply, 'I tell you the truth, whatever you did for one of the least of these brothers of mine, you did for me.'*

*Then he will say to those on his left, 'Depart from me, you who are cursed, into the eternal fire pre-pared for the devil and his angels. For I was hungry and you gave me nothing to eat, I was thirsty and you gave me nothing to drink, I was a stranger and you did not invite me in, I needed clothes and you did not clothe me, I was sick and in prison and you did not look after me.'*

*"They also will answer, 'Lord, when did we see you hungry or thirsty or a stranger or needing clothes or sick or in prison, and did not help you?'*

*"He will reply, 'I tell you the truth, whatever you did not do for one of the least of these, you did not do for me.'*

*Then they will go away to eternal punishment, but the righteous to eternal life. (Matthew 25:31–46)*

As the ship straightened up for the second time, I felt the need to ask, "Lord where are You in relation to this ship?"

As soon as I asked the question, the deck of the ship exploded with light. In the brilliant illumination I saw the Lord Jesus standing with many, many people around Him. They were clothed in dazzling white and bathed in the radiance of His Presence. The beauty and the atmosphere of that moment of glory are hard to describe; no words could adequately do it justice. So dear reader, just close your eyes and try to visu-alize the scene as best as you can.

While I was trying to take all this in, the ship began to sail away with great speed. It raced to the horizon, and suddenly lifted off the waters like an airplane. This fabulous vessel sailed into what looked like an amazing and breathtaking sunset. Awe-struck I stared, as the brilliant glory of the intermingling colors slowly absorbed the mighty ship, obscuring it from further view.

As this beautiful ship adorned with the awesome presence of the Lord Jesus Christ sailed away, I saw a spotless white dove following after it. Effortless in its grace and beauty, the dove flew, keeping up with the speeding vessel and finally disappearing together with it into the radiant skies.

I knew that the Lord was giving me a vision of His Church going home; this was the Rapture. It was obvious now that the ship represented the sanctified Church. It also became clear to me that the Lord was making a connection between Bride of Christ and Noah and his family on the Ark. In Noah's case it was *a remnant* that was saved. Noah was faithful to God, and those who believed and obeyed Noah were saved. Again it will be the remnant—the sheep, those on His right hand, those who believe and obey Jesus Christ that will be saved and taken by the Lord when He returns for His Church.

The Lord explained, the reason I had seen my daughter Carol dressed in a wedding gown, was because I had personal knowledge that she had given her life to Him. The Lord used her to represent the Blood-bought body of believers, so that I would know quite clearly that these were the ones He was taking to be with Him forever. I saw Jesus pick her up and place her on the ship as an illustration of how He builds His Church. The Savior gathers the ones who answer His question, *"But what about you, who do you say I am?"* with the answer He so yearns to hear from the lips of every human being, *"You are the Christ, the Son of the living God."* Those who are willing to give their lives to Him receive their wedding attire—their garments of salvation and robes of righteousness, and are added to His Church.

The Lord very lovingly picks up each one who accepts His free gift of salvation, and places them into His own Blood-bought body, the Church, just as Book of Acts states: ". . .

*And the Lord added to the church daily those who were being saved" (Acts 2:47).*

I realized that Jesus had very graciously given me a glimpse of the fulfillment of Acts 2:47. He had actually permitted me to watch Him at work as He continues to build His Church with the same vital question that He asked of the disciples. His faithful, pure, and spotless Bride is comprised of only those who believe and answer as Peter did.

As we know, the Blood-bought Church, the Bride, the faithful remnant, will leave with the Lord at the Rapture, but there will be another side to this beautiful home-going picture. In the days of Noah, only eight people, a remnant, was saved on the day of the great deluge; the majority was unfaithful and faced disaster. Unfortunately, it will be so again. Only the faithful remnant will go with Jesus. This means that those who gave some other answer to the Lord's all-important question, those who believed and confessed a lie, those on His left, the ones Jesus classified as goats, the unfaithful, will not be taken by the Lord. Jesus warned us:

> *Heaven and earth will pass away, but my words will never pass away. "No one knows about that day or hour, not even the angels in heaven, nor the Son, but only the Father. **As it was in the days of Noah, so it will be at the coming of the Son of Man.** For in the days before the flood, people were eating and drinking, marrying and giving in marriage, up to the day Noah entered the ark; and they knew nothing about what would happen until the flood came and took them all away. That is how it will be at the coming of the Son of Man. Two men will be in the field; one will be taken and the other left. Two women will be grinding with a hand mill; one will be taken and the other left. (Matthew 24:34–41)*

It took Noah a hundred years to build the Ark, and it is apparent from the Scriptures that even though Noah preached righteousness to the people of his day for this whole period, they refused to pay attention. This hundred-year span speaks of a long period of preaching, paralleling the Church Age, during which the Gospel is being preached by the multiple Noahs of today.

> *. . . if he [God] did not spare the ancient world when he brought the flood on its ungodly people, but protected Noah, a preacher of righteousness, and seven others; . . . then the Lord knows how to rescue godly men from trials and to hold the unrighteous for the day of judgment, while continuing their punishment. (2 Peter 2:6, 9)*

Jesus spoke of a man in Luke 14:16–23 who gave a banquet and invited many to the feast. Of the invitees, one was real estate-minded and wanted to be excused to conduct his business. Another was steeped in livestock and had no time for the banquet, while yet another claimed marriage as the reason for his inability to attend. Likewise, everyone who had been invited had some excuse much to the anger of the host.

The Master of ceremonies was obviously not pleased. So He ordered his servants to go out to the towns and alleys and compel the poor, the crippled, the blind, and the lame to come to the banquet. The servants answered,

> *What you ordered has been done, but there is still room. Then the Master told His servants, "Go out to the roads and country lanes and make them come in so the house will be full. I tell you, **not one of those men who were invited will get a taste of My Banquet.** (Luke 14: 22–24)*

There is no doubt the Master in this story represents the Lord, and it is He who lovingly invites many. The invitees, however, are too occupied with themselves to take time to come and dine with Him. Sadly, they are all too busy to heed His generous and loving call. This story has a strange similarity to the one in which the Lord patiently knocks on the door of the hearts of the lukewarm church at Laodicea.

> *Here I am! I stand at the door and knock. If anyone hears my voice and opens the door, I will come in and eat with him, and he with me. (Revelation 3:20)*

A notable number of people who have been invited by the Lord to this beautiful occasion will once more be too busy to attend. They will have very little interest in being a part of the Marriage Supper of the Lamb. The combination of greed, indifference, materialism, and apathy, explains why so many invitees declined the honor of attending the Lord's banquet as described in Luke 14.

Jesus said:

> **Just as it was in the days of Noah, so also will it be in the days of the Son of Man. People were eating, drinking, marrying and being given in marriage up to the day Noah entered the ark.** Then the flood came and destroyed them all. **"It was the same in the days of Lot. People were eating and drinking, buying and selling, planting and building.** But the day Lot left Sodom, fire and sulfur rained down from heaven and destroyed them all. (Luke 17:26–29)

Two thousand years after Jesus spoke these words we find it to be exactly these same poor choices of the human heart that will keep many from going home with the Lord. It is also this same mindset and the identical choices of the many left behind, which will contribute to the departure of the Holy Spirit.

Does this mean that the Holy Spirit completely leaves the earth? Obviously not! The Holy Spirit is God, and God is omnipresent. However, it is apparent, that just as in the days of Noah the Lord will once more withhold His hand of protection from those who have refused to answer His call. Somehow the Holy Spirit who came to empower the Church on the day of Pentecost will now operate in ways different to that of the Church Age.

Returning for a moment to the *Rapture ship* as we will call it, the words of Paul crossed my mind as I watched the beautiful white dove leaving with the Home-going Church,

*For the secret power of lawlessness is already at work; but the* **One Who holds it back will continue to do so till He is taken out of the way.** *(2 Thessalonians 2:7)*

The "One who holds it back" surely must refer to the Holy Spirit. He is God, and it is only He who has that kind of power. The Holy Spirit empowered the Church with His presence which rested as tongues of fire upon each believer on the day of Pentecost. It is He who has sustained the Church for two thousand years. No doubt the Holy Spirit will go with the Church that belongs to Jesus Christ. Remember it was Jesus who sent the Holy Spirit to us. He said:

**But I tell you the truth: It is for your good that I am going away. Unless I go away, the Counselor will not come to you; but if I go, I will send him to you. .** *. ."I have much more to say to you, more than you can now bear.* **But when he, the Spirit of truth, comes, he will guide you into all truth. He will not speak on his own; he will speak only what he hears, and he will tell you what is yet to come. He will bring glory to me by taking from what is mine and making it known to you.** *(John 16:7-14)*

God Almighty, said once before, *"My Spirit shall not strive with man forever . . ." (Genesis 6:3).* Guess what friends; this happened in the days of Noah, but could it be that God was also referencing a different time similar to the days of Noah that would occur sometime in the future?

The Genesis 6 account of the days of Noah shows clearly the extent of lawlessness that prevailed upon the earth at the time. Paul says, *"For the secret power of lawlessness is already at work" (2 Thessalonians 2:7).* It is logical to conclude that it is this same secret power of lawlessness that raised its ugly head to cause the fall of Adam and Eve. It is also logical to conclude that this same secret power of lawlessness has relentlessly striven to destroy the all the righteous, from Abel right up to the Church that Jesus built. This power of lawlessness has continued to operate and attack the Church from both outside and from within. Jude warned:

*For certain men whose condemnation was written about long ago have **secretly slipped in** among you. They are godless men, who change the grace of our God into a license for immorality and deny Jesus Christ our only Sovereign and Lord. (Jude 4)*

The church in the dark ages, the Crusades, the spirit of apostasy and false doctrines, to mention a few, would all correspond to the ship that leaned too far over to the left. History shows us that the unwise tradition of adhering to the doctrines of men, instead of the Word of God, very nearly tipped the Church completely over. Jesus said: *"Why do you call me, 'Lord, Lord,' and do not do what I say? (Luke 6:46)* Jesus also said:

*These people draw near to Me with their mouth, And honor Me with their lips, But their heart is far from Me. **And in vain they worship Me, Teaching as doctrines the commandments of men.** (Matthew 15:8–9)*

By and large there was then and there is now a great departure from the Truth that Jesus and the apostles taught. However we can't say we have not been warned of this by the Lord.

*But mark this: There will be terrible times in the last days. People will be lovers of themselves, lovers of money, boastful, proud, abusive, disobedient to their parents, ungrateful, unholy, without love, unforgiving, slanderous, without self-control, brutal, not lovers of the good, treacherous, rash, conceited, **lovers of pleasure rather than lovers of God—having a form of godliness but denying its power. Have nothing to do with them.** (2 Timothy 3:1–5)*

We have been warned and we have been instructed what to do. We are instructed, *"Have nothing to do with them."* In other words, we are *not* to be like these people.

Except for the grace and power of the Lord Jesus, the Church might have been lost in the sea of apostasy and foolishness, but this did not happen. It could not happen, and it will not happen in the future! There remains a remnant because the Lord Jesus made this promise:

> *. . . on this rock* (Peter's confession of faith in Jesus as the Christ, the Son of the Living God) *I will build My church, and the gates of Hades shall not prevail against it. (Matthew 16:18)*

There will always be a faithful remnant; His Bride is made up of everyone who, like Peter, believes and confesses Jesus as Lord and Savior of their lives. *"Who do men say that I Am?"* Jesus asked. Thank God for Peter's God-inspired answer! *"You are the Christ, the Son of the Living God."* This confession of faith in Jesus Christ as the Son of the living God is the same one that has echoed and re-echoed in many hearts and is still daily rolling off the tongues of millions of men, women, and children.

It is these few precious words over the past two thousand years that have frustrated Satan in his unquenchable quest to destroy the Church Jesus built. Unbending faith and faithfulness to the Jesus Christ, is what sets His Church apart from the lukewarm, self-focused group that also call themselves Christians. The ones who have never chosen to get off the thrones of their own hearts or bowed to the Lordship of Jesus Christ will unfortunately have a very rude awakening—the return of Messiah for His true Church.

It is the power of Jesus Christ that keeps the Church afloat. The unseen force that kept the ship I saw from capsizing—or in other words, the power that keeps the Church from being destroyed, is Jesus Christ alone. The gates of hell can never prevail against His Church. Hallelujah!

Not unlike the account of Luke14:15–24, Matthew also speaks of a wedding banquet. Among the throngs from the street corners that were invited to take the place of those who declined to come to the feast was someone that the king took special note of.

> Then he said to his servants, 'The wedding banquet is ready, but those I invited did not deserve to come. Go to the street corners and invite to the banquet anyone you find.' So the servants went out into the streets and gathered all the people they could find, both good and bad, and the wedding hall was filled with guests. **"But when the king came in to see the guests, he noticed a man there who was not wearing wedding clothes.** 'Friend,' he asked, **'how did you get in here without wedding clothes?'** The man was speechless. "Then the king told the attendants, 'Tie him hand and foot, and throw him outside, into the darkness, where there will be weeping and gnashing of teeth.' **"For many are invited, but few are chosen.** (Matthew 22:8–14)

Who was this man and why did the king single him out? Why did he have *no* wedding clothes? Wedding garments signify the readiness of a Bride for her groom. It also indicates the condition of a person's heart. A bride's ultimate joy is to be adorned in her bridal splendor for the one she loves and is about to marry. Isaiah said:

*I will greatly rejoice in the Lord, my soul will exult in my God;* **for He has clothed me with the garments of salvation, He has covered me with the robe of righteousness,** *as a Bridegroom decks himself with a garland, and as a Bride adorns herself with her jewels. (Isaiah 61:10, AMP)*

This man had no appropriate wedding clothes. Many thousands like him who attend church have no wedding clothes, either, because they have never received Jesus Christ as Lord and Savior. Sadly they never, ever accept the free gift of salvation and so are not covered by His Blood. Consequently they have no garments of salvation or robes of righteousness.

Many will appear before Him clothed in their own righteousness, good deeds, and self-evaluation, but unfortunately, the end result for such people will be the same as for this man. They will be speechless in the presence of the Lord just as the man of Matthew 22. Frighteningly, they will hear the command of the King. *"Tie him hand and foot and throw him into the darkness where there will be weeping and gnashing of teeth."*

The Church that responds to the leading of the Holy Spirit explains the ship that tipped to the right. This is wisdom! Multitudes of every tribe and tongue and nation are turning to Jesus Christ every day. The outpouring of the awesome Holy Spirit is causing thousands upon thousands to give their lives to Jesus Christ as He moves mightily across the earth. **"A wise man's heart turns him toward his right hand,** *but a fool's heart toward his left" (Ecclesiastes 10:2, AMP).* The Bible is pretty self-explanatory; it clearly defines who a fool is. *"The fool has said in his heart, 'There is no God'" (Psalm 14:1).*

Jesus said,

*I tell you* **the truth,** *anyone* **who has faith in me will do what I have been doing.** *He will do* **even greater things** *than these,* **because I am going to the Father. And I will do whatever you ask in my name,** *so that the Son may bring glory to the Father.* **You may**

***ask me for anything in my name, and I will do it.***
*(John 14:12–14)*

This tremendous promise given to us by Jesus Christ our Lord is being fulfilled by the true servants of the Lord, who are leading multitudes to Him today. They *are* doing great things.

Has the Lord kept His promise?

When millions of people give their lives to Jesus at one gathering, this is Jesus doing a greater thing than what He did when He was on earth.

When thousands get healed at one meeting from various sicknesses and diseases, this again is Jesus doing greater things now through his followers, than while He was on earth.

When many nations are reached at one time with the Gospel message, this is Jesus doing greater things than He did when He was on earth.

This work however, is being done through just a few, but not through the Church at large. The question is, why? Why we ask again, are all Christians not doing as Jesus did? Why has the Church at large not reached the full measure of wisdom that God has made available to her?

Jesus answered this question with the first statement of His promise. *"I tell you the truth, anyone who has faith in me will do what I have been doing . . ." (John 14:12).*

The key words are, *". . . anyone who has faith in me . . ."*

Faith is the answer; but we must remember where faith comes from. Paul tells us, *"Faith comes by hearing and hearing by the Word of God" (Romans 10:17).*

Jesus said many times over, *"He who has ears, let him hear" (Matthew 13:43).*

Faith comes from hearing, which means knowing, believing, and acting upon God's Word. If we do not spend enough time prayerfully studying God's Word our faith level will be exceedingly low. When faith is low, we do not have the ability to be the conduit that Jesus needs to flow through, because we do not cooperate with Him, but operate in the flesh. Fear, doubt, and unbelief dominates, and this is why we see only a few faithful ones fulfilling this promise of Jesus.

The Church of today, more than ever before, should be earnestly looking for the return of the Lord. We should be eager, thirsty, steadfast, longing, and burning with desire to see our Lord and King.

Peter tells us how we are to get ready for the Bridegroom.

*Therefore, prepare your minds for action; be self-controlled; set your hope fully on the grace to be given you when Jesus Christ is revealed. As obedient children, do not conform to the evil desires you had when you lived in ignorance. But just as he who called you is holy, so be holy in all you do; for it is written: "Be holy, because I am holy. (1 Peter 1:13–16)*

Vine's Expository Dictionary defines "holiness" as sanctification and separation unto God. In other words we must make a decision to separate ourselves unto the Lord. Does this mean cloistering ourselves? No, of course not! Instead, we should consciously choose to keep away from everything that is displeasing to the Lord by setting aside the things of the flesh and ensuring that the Jesus Christ alone has the throne of our hearts.

Paul admonishes, ". . . *let us purify ourselves from everything that contaminates body and spirit, perfecting holiness out of reverence for God" (2 Corinthians 7:1).*

Consider the "set apart" lives the apostles lived! The Bible is replete with accounts of their holy lives, and just as they did we must do also. We must purify ourselves from everything that contaminates our minds, bodies, and spirits, out of reverence for God. This is what Paul calls the process of "perfecting holiness." This however, takes a conscious effort.

Anything we consciously choose to do becomes easier to do, and so a habit is formed. Very simply put, we should consciously make a habit of pleasing God.

Paul implores,

*Therefore, I urge you, brothers, in view of God's mercy, to offer your bodies as living sacrifices, holy and pleasing to God-this is your spiritual act of worship. Do not conform any longer to the pattern of this world, but be transformed by the renewing of your mind. Then you will be able to test and approve what God's will is-his good, pleasing and perfect will. (Romans 12:1–2)*

Offering our bodies to God as living sacrifices includes taking a close look at our hearts. Seeing that our tongues are part of our bodies, we must keep a tight rein on this little member that is so often the agent of much sin in our lives. It is also one that causes great grief to others, not to mention the Lord. While on earth Jesus was the recipient of many vile accusations, mockery, blasphemy, and rejection. The tongues of sinful people spewed out every form of vicious attack upon the pure and holy Son of God.

Jesus is coming for a spotless Bride, and He is coming soon! So how do we choose to become spotless?

The Holy Spirit takes great pains to convict us of our sins and imperfections; spotlessness can come only by constantly listening to Him and being willing to let go of the things that are unlike Christ. The Holy Spirit convicts us through the Word, which washes and renews our minds as we submit and yield to Him by making the changes that He directs us to do. As we choose to obey, the Lord looks at this humble and obedient behavior as acts of worship that set us apart and make us holy in His sight.

The Hebrew letter instructs:

**Make every effort to live in peace with all men and to be holy; without holiness no one will see the Lord.** *See to it that no one misses the grace of God and that **no bitter root grows up to cause trouble and defile many**. See that no one is sexually immoral,* *or is godless like Esau, who for a single meal sold his inheritance rights as the oldest son. Afterward, as you know, when he wanted to inherit this blessing, he was rejected. He could bring about no change of mind, though he sought the blessing with tears. (Hebrews 12:14–17)*

How easy it is to sell our own birthrights for a single meal, as Esau did! In our cases it usually happens to be a metaphoric meal. In selling his birthright, Esau compromised his loyalty to God. So what exactly do we compromise our loyalty to God for?

Most often, Christians sell their birthrights for morsels of almost anything—lust, immorality, greed, avarice, and various other forms of self-indulgence. *The Lord called Esau godless because he despised the importance of the relationship of a first-born son, with Almighty God.*

As the firstborn, Esau would have been the leader in his family—the priest, after Isaac his father had died. As the firstborn, the Messiah would have been born to Esau's lineage, had he been a man who honored God and treasured the privileged position to which he was born. Esau however, did not esteem this precious blessing and God-given privilege, so he sold his birthright for a measly bowl of beans.

Similarly, when we permit anything to become more appealing in our lives than the treasure and privilege of a right relationship with the living God, we too, in effect are despising our birthrights. We rudely interrupt our sonship, and consequently become godless as well.

It is vitally important to remember that our birthrights did not come cheaply. It cost the Son of God His life. Yet we often fall prey to Satan's thorny snares of anger, unforgiveness, bitterness, lust, and countless other forms of ungodly behavior. These things defile and destroy, and except for the gracious gift of forgiveness through that very birthright—the Blood of the Lamb—we would be as Esau, who spent the rest of his life at odds with his brother. The results of Esau's sin continue to this day.

As Paul admonished, we must take time to be transformed by the renewing of our minds. If we do, we will be at peace with each other and there will be no root of bitterness that defiles, so that like Jesus our Lord we also will be able to say, *"Father forgive them for they do not know what they are doing" (Luke 23:34).*

Stephen, the great New Testament saint, had no doubt learned to walk in the footsteps of his Master. Let's take a look at him for a moment.

> *But Stephen, **full of the Holy Spirit,** looked up to heaven and saw the glory of God, and Jesus standing at the right hand of God. (Acts 7:55)*

This happened when the people he was sharing the Gospel with, began to stone him, gnashing their teeth at him.

> *While they were stoning him, Stephen prayed, "Lord Jesus, receive my spirit." **Then he fell on his knees and cried out, "Lord, do not hold this sin against them."** When he had said this, he fell asleep. (Acts 7:59)*

This is true holiness. This is the life Paul implores us to live; he implores us to live like Jesus.

This powerful passage of Scripture from the Book of Hebrews should wake us up to the reality of God's awesome Word. Let's take a look at what it says:

> *You have not come to a mountain that can be touched and that is burning with fire; to darkness, gloom and storm; to a trumpet blast or to such a voice speaking words that those who heard it begged that no further word be spoken to them, because they could not bear what was commanded: "If even an animal touches the mountain, it must be stoned." The sight was so*

terrifying that Moses said, "I am trembling with fear." **But you have come to Mount Zion, to the heavenly Jerusalem, the city of the living God.** You have come to thousands upon thousands of angels in joyful assembly, **to the church of the firstborn, whose names are written in heaven. You have come to God, the judge of all men,** to the spirits of righteous men made perfect, **to Jesus the mediator of a new covenant, and to the sprinkled blood that speaks a better word than the blood of Abel. See to it that you do not refuse him who speaks. If they did not escape when they refused him who warned them on earth, how much less will we, if we turn away from him who warns us from heaven?** At that time his voice shook the earth, but now he has promised, **"Once more I will shake not only the earth but also the heavens."** The words "once more" indicate the removing of what can be shaken-that is, created things-so that what cannot be shaken may remain. **Therefore, since we are receiving a kingdom that cannot be shaken, let us be thankful, and so worship God acceptably with reverence and awe, for our "God is a consuming fire.** (Hebrews 12:18–29)

Holiness has got to be our way of life because it is God's way of life. Peter admonishes:

**So brace up your minds; be sober (circumspect, morally alert); set your hope wholly and unchangeably on the grace (divine favor) that is coming to you when Jesus Christ (the Messiah) is revealed.** [Live] as children of obedience [to God]; do not conform yourselves to the evil desires [that governed you] in your former ignorance [when you did not know the requirements of the Gospel]. But as the one Who called you is holy, you yourselves also be holy in all *your conduct and manner of living. For it is written, You shall be holy, for I am holy. (1 Peter 1:13–16, AMP)*

It is clearly time that the Bride of Christ wakes up to be truly purified and sanctified in Jesus Christ. We must daily renew our minds by the washing of the Word. Paul reminds us, ". . . *But we have the mind of Christ" (1Corinthians 2:16).* So let's make sure we walk in agreement and submission to Jesus Christ, keeping in mind that He lives in us.

The devil certainly brings plenty of occasions for offense. If he can keep us angry and bitter at our brothers and sisters in the Lord, he has successfully sowed seeds of division and destruction among us. Paul tells us:

*For though we live in the world, we do not wage war as the world does. The weapons we fight with are not the weapons of the world. On the contrary, they have divine power to demolish strongholds. **We demolish arguments and every pretension that sets itself up against the knowledge of God, and we take captive every thought to make it obedient to Christ.** And we will be ready to punish every act of disobedience, once your obedience is complete. (2 Corinthians 10:3–6)*

As we prepare ourselves for the soon return of Jesus, let's take Peter's advice very seriously. *"Therefore my brothers, be all the more eager to make your calling and election sure" (2 Peter 1:10).*

He urges us to do this with view to the coming day of the Lord:

*But the day of the Lord will come like a thief. The heavens will disappear with a roar; the elements will be destroyed by fire, and the earth and everything in it will be laid bare. Since everything will be destroyed in this way, **what kind of people ought you to be? You ought to live holy and godly lives as you look***

**forward to the day of God and speed its coming.**
*That day will bring about the destruction of the heavens
by fire, and the elements will melt in the heat.* **But in
keeping with his promise we are looking forward
to a new heaven and a new earth, the home of
righteousness. So then, dear friends, since you
are looking forward to this, make every effort to be
found spotless, blameless and at peace with him.**
*(2 Peter 3:10–14)*

Let us all make *every effort* to be found spotless, blame-less and at peace with the Lord and each other at His coming; being conformed to the image of our awesome Lord and Savior, Jesus Christ.

Beloved please let's get ready, for the time is at hand.

# Chapter 20

# DESTRUCTION ON EARTH

—⊶⊷—

W hat I was shown right after the glassy sea, was horrible and terrifying, and I write this with a very heavy
heart. It is with great sadness for those who would be left
behind on earth after the faithful Church of the Lord Jesus has
gone home to be with Him forever.

The scene was formidable! I saw the earth enveloped in
dense, billowing smoke and dust from multiple demolished
skyscrapers and other buildings. Every building had crumbled,
and mass destruction was everywhere. Darkness was upon
the earth, and the light of the sun was blocked out by a dense
haze of dust and smoke.

It was obvious that it would have been extremely difficult
for any living thing to breathe easily in that terrible atmosphere
of intensely acrid air. Dreadful emptiness, darkness, fearful
destruction, and devastation were everywhere. A sense of
sheer panic and hopelessness seemed predominant. There
is really no way to even begin to evaluate the emotions of any
living person who might have been trapped in that desperate
situation.

As fearsome and horrible as all the physical carnage was,
somehow a sense of even greater desolation than met the
eye seemed to prevail. This was an inescapable awareness
of the absence of God. Paul referred to this particular time,
two thousand years ago when he said:

346

*For the secret power of lawlessness is already at work; **but the one who now holds it back will continue to do so till He is taken out of the way.** (2 Thessalonians 2:7)*

God the Holy Spirit holds back evil, but once He absents His restraining power from the earth, no doubt, massive destruction, wickedness, and emptiness will be the order or the day.

A great sense of spiritual barrenness, fear, loneliness, and immense terror lurked everywhere. Hopelessness and helplessness loomed big. I could sense death in all directions, and yet somehow I also had the overwhelming perception that many people were still alive in all the wreckage and debris. Although I couldn't see any living individuals, I knew that there were lots of people who were alive and capable of moving about, while others remained trapped or buried in the rubble.

All human emotion seemed to have been shocked into dead silence on planet earth that day, and the words of the Prophet Amos came alive: *"Is not the day of the LORD darkness, and not light? Is it not very dark, with no brightness in it?" (Amos 5:20)*

Obadiah the prophet of God, warned about this many centuries ago, but his voice went unheeded at the time and now the day was upon all who rejected the call of the Lord to turn from their evil ways, to repent, and be saved. Obadiah cried out to the house of Esau because of the way they treated their brother, the house of Jacob (the nation of Israel).

*The Day of the LORD is near for all nations. **As you have done it will be done to you. Your deeds will return upon your own head.** (Obadiah 15)*

Just as in the days of Noah, people today don't even like to think about what might just be on the horizon of a not-too-distant future, and many believers continue to live their everyday lives, taking for granted that nothing will ever change.

Yet imminent changes are daily taking place before our very eyes. In adopting the mindset of willful blindness, too many choose to ignore all the Biblical warnings of the coming great and terrible day of the Lord.

Numerous Old Testament prophets such as Isaiah, Jeremiah, Ezekiel, Daniel, Micah, Obadiah, Nahum, Joel, Habakkuk, and Zechariah to name some, have trumpeted warnings of this impending day of destruction. New Testament writers, Peter, Paul, Jude, John, and certainly Jesus Christ himself, gave clear warnings and admonitions to everyone who would care to listen. More times than once, Jesus said, *". . . He who has ears to hear, let him hear!" (Luke 14:35)*

From all the great disaster and devastation that had been unleashed upon the earth, I could tell that the Rapture had already occurred, and those who had listened and obeyed the Word of the Lord Jesus Christ had been safely evacuated by Him.

Sadly, what I was seeing now, was the ensuing condition of the earth that those left behind would have to deal with. They had chosen to ignore the instructions and warnings of the Bible. Among them would be the mockers, the unbelieving, and the blasphemers. Every preacher, teacher, or evangelist God had sent their way had been ignored, insulted, made fun of, or attacked.

God had been rejected in every public arena, and the name of Jesus Christ could not be mentioned without causing offense to the very people He had lovingly been trying to warn. Every symbol of Christianity, crosses, nativity scenes, the Bible, and the ability to share the Gospel in public places had all been squelched by these godless ones who were now left to their own devices. Children had been deprived of hearing the Word of God in public schools, and they had not been permitted to pray or display anything that represented Jesus Christ and Christianity. Among them were also those who claimed to be believers but had played fast and loose with their salvation. Paul warned:

*We must pay more careful attention, therefore, to what we have heard, so that we do not drift away. For if the message spoken by angels was binding, and every violation and disobedience received its just punishment, how shall we escape if we ignore such a great salvation? This salvation, which was first announced by the Lord, was confirmed to us by those who heard him. God also testified to it by signs, wonders and various miracles, and gifts of the Holy Spirit distributed according to his will. (Hebrews 2:1–4)*

Just like the unbelievers of the days of Noah, the ones now trapped in the cataclysmic events of the day had also been too unbelieving, while others had been much too busy to heed God's loving call to turn and seek Him with all their hearts. Now, very sadly, they had arrived at the calamitous moment in time that He had warned us of innumerable times before.

Fortunately, at this moment of writing, all the destruction that we are speaking of is still only a description of a vision I was given of the fearful and terrible day of the Lord. This day is still sometime in the imminent future. If you are reading this book, obviously we have still not arrived at that day and there is yet time to seek the Lord with all your heart.

Please consider this chapter as just one more call from the Lord to all who will listen to His Voice. Perhaps you are someone who until this point has been ultracasual or free-thinking about your relationship with Jesus Christ. Will you now please take it seriously? It is my prayer that you will begin to fill your lamp with oil, by first rededicating, or giving your life to Jesus Christ, and then faithfully studying God's Word and making the changes it commands. Find a church that welcomes, honors, and obeys the Holy Spirit and become a faithful partner with them.

James gives us some exceedingly good advice.

*Therefore lay aside all filthiness and overflow of wick-edness, **and receive with meekness the implanted word, which is able to save your souls. But be doers of the word, and not hearers only, deceiving yourselves.** (James 1:21–22)*

Amos painted a rather dismal picture for those of his day who completely dismissed the Word and the call of the Lord. Amos was addressing Israel, but his words speak quite relevantly to our present times as well. He said:

*You hate the one who reproves in court and despise him who tells the truth. You trample on the poor and force him to give you grain. Therefore, though you have built stone mansions you will not live in them . . . (Amos 5:10–11).*

Many people live in this unjust manner, and they try not to believe that there is a righteous God who sees it all, but the Bible tells us:

*The eyes of the LORD are everywhere, keeping watch on the wicked and the good. (Proverbs 15:3)*

Those who think they can deal unrighteously with the helpless and poor, while they and their assets remain impregnable, have a rude shock coming. The Bible tells us, *". . . the LORD is his name—he flashes destruction on the stronghold and brings the fortified city to ruin" (Amos 5:8–9).*

Many of us remember so vividly, the horror and terror we experienced on 9/11—the attack on the World Trade Center. As heart-breaking and horrible as that event was, the day pales in comparison to what I saw in this preview, as we might call it, of the things that will transpire in perhaps the not-too-distant future. The senseless destruction of September 11, 2001, occurred in one place on earth, but what I saw was worldwide disaster.

Dear Reader, if you have never made a commitment to Jesus Christ by inviting Him to come into your heart to be the Lord of your life, I urge you to do so right now. Do not put this off for even a second longer. Your eternal future depends upon your response to this invitation from the Savior, the Messiah, the Lord Jesus Christ. The Bible instructs us, *". . . I tell you,* ***now*** *is the time of God's favor,* ***now*** *is the day of salvation" (2 Corinthians 6:2).* We are also urged, *"So,* ***as the Holy Spirit*** ***says:*** *"****Today,*** *if you hear his voice,* ***do not*** *harden your hearts . . ." (Hebrews 3:7–8).*

If you have opened your heart to the Lord and have reached a point where you are willing to obey His advice, listen to what He tells you to do, and then do exactly as He advises. The Lord says:

> *. . . if you* ***confess with your mouth, "Jesus is Lord," and believe in your heart that God raised him from the dead, you will be saved.*** *For it is with* ***your heart*** *that you believe and* ***are justified,*** *and it is* ***with your mouth*** *that you* ***confess and are saved.*** *(Romans 10:9–10)*

Beloved, I pray that you accepted the Lord's invitation to His home. If so, all Heaven is rejoicing over you and your name is written in the Lamb's Book of Life.

Now please ask the Lord to lead you to the church of His choosing, and start attending faithfully. Begin to prayerfully study the Word of God every day. Pray to the Lord and develop a warm and close relationship with Him and when He comes back for His Church, you will hear the trump of the Lord and you will rise to meet Him in the air, to be with Him forever. This promise is found in 1 Thessalonians 4:16–17.

You can be sure that the catastrophic and devastating events we discussed earlier will not be your lot. The Lord has always protected His people, and He will protect them again. Listen to Peter:

*For if God did not spare angels when they sinned, but sent them to hell, putting them into gloomy dungeons to be held for judgment; if he did not spare the ancient world when he brought the flood on its ungodly people,* **but protected Noah, a preacher of righteousness, and seven others;** *if he condemned the cities of Sodom and Gomorrah by burning them to ashes, and made them an example of what is going to happen to the ungodly; **and if he rescued Lot, a righteous man,** who was distressed by the filthy lives of lawless men (for that righteous man, living among them day after day, was tormented in his righteous soul by the lawless deeds he saw and heard)* **if this is so, then the Lord knows how to rescue godly men from trials and to hold the unrighteous for the day of judgment, while continuing their punishment.** *This is especially true of those who follow the corrupt desire of the sinful nature and despise authority. (2 Peter 2:4–10)*

It does not matter what you have done in the past, the Word of God promises us this:

**If we confess our sins, he is faithful and just and will forgive us our sins and purify us from all unrighteousness.** *(1 John 1:9)*

If you are already a believer but have grown distant and cold in your relationship with Jesus, if you have drifted from spending time studying His Word, and doing His will, I urge you also to *wake up*. Do not forget the parable of the five foolish virgins, whose lamps went out because they did not take enough oil. As we mentioned before, *oil* represents the Holy Spirit, our Lord and Guide. It is His Word that we receive when we study the Scriptures, and we must keep our lamps filled with *oil*—the Word of the Holy Spirit of God.

*All Scripture is given by inspiration of God, and is profitable for doctrine, for reproof, for correction, for instruction in righteousness, that the man of God may be complete, thoroughly equipped for every good work. (2 Timothy 3:16-17)*

We must never forget that the Holy Spirit is God. Peter reminds us:

*Above all, you must understand that no prophecy of Scripture came about by the prophet's own interpretation. For prophecy never had its origin in the will of man, **but men spoke from God as they were carried along by the Holy Spirit.** (2 Peter 1:20-21)*

Many centuries ago, the Lord instructed Amos the prophet to call Israel to repentance. These are the words Amos used:

***This is what the LORD says . . .***" "***Seek me and live;*** *do not seek Bethel, do not go to Gilgal, do not journey to Beersheba. For Gilgal will surely go into exile, and Bethel will be reduced to nothing. (Amos 5:4–5)*

Just as in Amos' day, many people still mistakenly think that they could move to different geographical locations to escape the coming adversities. At this very moment there are folks even considering the purchase of property on the moon. *Friends, there will be no place to hide.* Jesus clearly told us what people will do at this fearful time. He said:

*For the time will come . . .* [when] *"they will say to the mountains, 'Fall on us!' and to the hills, 'Cover us!'* (Luke 23:29–30)

If for some reason you are left behind, dear friend, you will have no legitimate reason to complain that you weren't forewarned. There has never been another period in history when the Word of God is being trumpeted as loudly and clearly as it is today. Radio and television have carried the Gospel to the uttermost parts of the earth. So if you find yourself left behind, it would be for one reason only; you chose to reject the loving invitation of the Lord Jesus Christ, and in doing so you also rejected Him personally.

It will not matter why you discounted the Word of the Lord; what will count is that you said "No" to Him. Unfortunately, the consequences of that action will be severe, but they would also be ones you personally chose.

The Lord hates the absence of righteousness, but what he hates even more is the lack of concern for it. God the Father said of Jesus Christ,

> **You love what is right and hate what is wrong.** *Therefore God, your God, has anointed you, pouring out the oil of joy on you more than on anyone else. (Psalm 45:7)*

Those who claim to have accepted Jesus Christ as Lord, but yet choose to remain negligent of God's standards of right and wrong, are in effect, attempting to live by their own standards of righteousness. This is a place of extreme danger. The Bible tells us: *"Hate what is wrong. Stand on the side of the good" (Romans 12:9).*

Religion will not take you in the Rapture, nor will the fact that you were a member of any particular denomination, help. It will not matter if you went religiously to church every time the doors were opened. It will not count to your credit if you were baptized, but had no relationship with Jesus Christ. If you have not permitted Jesus to be the Lord of your life and have not done your best to obey and please Him, you will be left behind. Never forget that all our own presumed righteousness and goodness, according to God's Word, is not righteousness at all. Isaiah put it this way, *"All of us have become like one who is unclean, and all our righteous acts are like filthy rags . . ." (Isaiah 64:6).*

On that day of darkness, anguish, pain, fear and total despair, perhaps you will remember the number of times you chose to disagree with God's standard of righteousness just because you liked someone; you agreed with them even though you knew they were diametrically opposed to the Word of the living God. Amos asked a very wise question: "*Can two walk together, unless they are agreed?*" *(Amos 3:3)*

It will be a terrible time for those who deceived themselves into thinking that they were doing well with the Lord, when all the time they were actually in agreement with the world's system which is ruled by Satan. Isaiah said:

*Woe to those who call evil good and good evil, who put darkness for light and light for darkness, who put bitter for sweet and sweet for bitter. (Isaiah 5:20)*

James the apostle said:

*You adulterous people, don't you know that friendship with the world is hatred toward God? Anyone who chooses to be a friend of the world becomes an enemy of God. (James 4:4)*

When Amos warned ancient Israel about their impending day of disaster they did not take it seriously. We are fast approaching this much warned of day of the Lord. This time around, unlike in Amos' day, the suffering, anguish, fear, and despair will be immensely greater. Amos drew this bleak picture for rebellious Israel:

*Therefore this is what the Lord, the LORD God Almighty, says: "There will be wailing in all the streets and cries of anguish in every public square. The **farmers** will be summoned to weep and the mourners to wail. There will be **wailing in all the vineyards**, for I will pass through your midst," says the LORD. (Amos 5:16–17)*

This sounds like economic collapse. There are many in the church who will not get their lives right with the Lord, but will continue to live under a false sense of security, trusting their finances. They will live in denial, being controlled by pride and deluded self-evaluation, until they are finally faced with the reality of the day of the Lord.

Not unlike the Israelites of Amos' day, these deceived ones will think that the day of the Lord would be a day when He would judge all their enemies and exalt them; but what a surprise it will be! Many wayward believers who walk the road of deception will have a sudden, rude awakening, like the five foolish virgins did.

Dear ones, if you want to go home with Jesus Christ when He returns for His Church, then clean up your lives the Bible way, and begin to live holy and honest lives today. When you mess up, confess your sins and ask Him to forgive and cleanse you, and be sure He will. God's grace is by no means a license to sin; His strength enables us to refuse all evil. Always ask yourself what Jesus would do in whatever situation you face, and then do what He would do.

The people of Amos' day, who remained blind to their own transgressions while looking forward to the day of the Lord as a means of revenge upon their enemies, had a rude awakening. Amos speaking under the direct inspiration of the Holy Spirit said:

*Woe to you who long for the day of the LORD! Why do you long for the day of the LORD?* *That day will be darkness, not light. It will be as though a man fled from a lion only to meet a bear, as though he entered his house and rested his hand on the wall only to have a snake bite him. Will not the day of the LORD be darkness, not light- pitch-dark, without a ray of brightness?* *"I hate, I despise your religious feasts; I cannot stand your assemblies.* *Even though you bring me burnt offerings and grain offerings, I will not accept them.* *Though you bring choice fellowship offerings, I will have no regard for them. Away with the noise of your songs! I will not listen to the music of your harps. But let justice roll on like a river, righteousness like a never-failing stream! (Amos 5:18–24)*

How important it is for us as believers in Jesus Christ, to worship the Lord in Spirit and truth. What was true for ancient Israel is also true for us. Unless we worship the Lord with all our hearts, and do our very best to be just and righteous, the Lord will not listen to our songs. He will also not accept our offerings. Remember Cain? That is a frightening thought!

*We should never sing songs of praise, or throw our offerings into the plate in a casual way.* Think how awful you would feel if someone gave you a gift by simply throwing it into some designated spot; if there is no heart connection, there is no love. Bringing an offering to the Lord should be something that is done with the utmost respect, honor, and love for Him. We should keep in mind that we only have something to bring to Him because He gave it to us in the first place. God expects us to be trustworthy. We are to have clean and pure hearts as we work alongside Him to bring as many people as possible to a saving knowledge of Him. It's time to be focused; it is time to let everything we do be an act of loving worship unto Him. Jesus said:

*Yet a time is coming and has now come when the **true worshipers will worship the Father in spirit and truth, for they are the kind of worshipers the Father seeks.** God is Spirit, and his worshipers must worship in spirit and in truth. (John 4:23–24)*

A group of people we must not forget to address, are those who have slipped back into the most chilling spiritual condition one can conceive of. These are the ones who at one point in their lives believed, accepted, and worshipped the Lord, but for whatever reason they turned their backs on Jesus. These are ones who chose to jeopardize their salvation by perhaps embracing false doctrines, idolatry, various forms of sexual immorality, evil living, doctrines of demons, and lying spirits: the occult, paganism, and ungodly ways such as new age philosophies and practices.

Some of these people continue to attend church while being actively involved in these ungodly activities. Going to church will not make you a Christian anymore than sitting in a garage will turn you into a car. You may call yourself a car all you want, but that does not make you one. There is only one way to get right with God, and that is to turn back to the Lord in humble repentance and be cleansed by the mighty power of the Blood of Jesus. The Blood of Jesus alone makes the difference between eternal life and death. Isaiah gave us a hair-raising last-day picture concerning Israel; they had been involved in pagan religions:

*You have abandoned your people, the house of Jacob.* ***They are full of superstitions from the East; they practice divination like the Philistines and clasp hands with pagans.*** *Their land is full of silver and gold; there is no end to their treasures. Their land is full of horses; there is no end to their chariots. Their land is full of idols; they bow down to the work of their hands, to what their fingers have made. So man will be brought low and mankind humbled—do not forgive them. Go into the rocks, hide in the ground from dread of the LORD and the splendor of his majesty! The eyes of the arrogant man will be humbled and the pride of men brought low; the LORD alone will be exalted in that day.* ***The LORD Almighty has a day in store for all the proud and lofty, for all that is exalted (and they will be humbled),*** *for all the cedars of Lebanon, tall and lofty, and all the oaks of Bashan, for all the towering mountains and all the high hills, for every lofty tower and every fortified wall, for every trading ship and every stately vessel.* ***The arrogance of man will be brought*** *low and the pride of men humbled; the LORD alone will be exalted in that day, and the idols will totally disappear. Men will flee to caves in the rocks and to holes in the ground from dread of the LORD and the splendor of his majesty, when he rises to shake the earth.* In that day men will throw away to the rodents and bats their idols of silver and idols of gold, which they made to worship. They will flee to caverns in the rocks and to the overhanging crags from dread of the LORD and the splendor of his majesty, when he rises to shake the earth. *Stop trusting in man, who has but a breath in his nostrils. Of what account is he? (Isaiah 2:6–22)*

Anyone who rejects the Word of the Lord and goes after any other doctrine or lifestyle is prideful. When a person chooses a path different from the Way of the Lord, they declare by their action that they believe their way is better than the Lord's. These ones fall into the category of the arrogant. Jesus said, *"I am the way and the truth and the life. No one comes to the Father except through me" (John 14:6).*

Those of the 'I did it my way' mindset will go through the terrible time of tribulation, and it will be for no other reason than that they chose their own way.

If you find yourself here on planet earth after the Rapture, one of the greatest griefs you'll suffer will be that you will remember the many times you refused the invitation of the Lord to follow Him. All it would have taken was a one three-letter word, "Yes." From that point on it would have been necessary that you remained faithful and obedient to the Lord, who loved you so much that He gave His life to save you.

Please do not allow yourself to be left behind. Get right with the LORD. If you confess your sins He is faithful and just to forgive.

Once the Church of Jesus Christ leaves with their Lord and Savior, and the precious Holy Spirit suspends His restraining power, the man who will control the earth for the next seven years will be the antichrist. He will be indwelt by Satan himself, and every form of wickedness, evil, and oppression, basically hell on earth, will prevail. The Apostle Paul says of this evil man,

*He will oppose and will exalt himself over everything that is called God or is worshiped, so that he sets himself up in God's temple, proclaiming himself to be God. (2 Thessalonians 2:4)*

Paul went on to state:

*And then the lawless one will be revealed, whom the Lord Jesus will overthrow with the breath of his mouth and destroy by the splendor of his coming. The coming of the lawless one will be in accordance with the work of Satan displayed in all kinds of counterfeit miracles, signs and wonders, and in every sort of evil that deceives those who are perishing. **They perish because they refused to love the truth and so be saved. For this reason God sends them a powerful delusion so that they will believe the lie and so that all will be condemned who have not believed the truth but have delighted in wickedness.** (2 Thessalonians 2 8:12)*

If you are left behind dear one, you will find yourself in a situation where apostasy has reached its height. Rebellion, disbelief, and hatred of God and His Holy Word will be rampant. There will be a false religious leader who agrees with the antichrist, and demands that those left upon the earth worship him.

***Then I saw another beast, coming out of the earth. He had two horns like a lamb, but he spoke like a***

*dragon. He exercised all the authority of the first beast on his behalf, and made the earth and its inhabitants worship the first beast, whose fatal wound had been healed. And he performed great and miraculous signs, even causing fire to come down from heaven to earth in full view of men. **Because of the signs he was given power to do on behalf of the first beast, he deceived the inhabitants of the earth. He ordered them to set up an image in honor of the beast who was wounded by the sword and yet lived. He was given power to give breath to the image of the first beast, so that it could speak and cause all who refused to worship the image to be killed.** (Revelation 13:11–15)*

Not only will you be facing the devastating calamities upon the earth, but you will also face physical death and torment by the antichrist if you refuse to take his mark on your forehead or your right hand.

*"**He also forced everyone, small and great, rich and poor, free and slave, to receive a mark on his right hand or on his forehead,** so that no one could buy or sell unless he had the mark, which is the name of the beast or the number of his name." (Revelation 13:16–17)*

If you decide to turn to Jesus Christ during this time of great tribulation, you will most certainly be hunted down and killed by the antichrist. Yet if you choose to take the mark of the beast, you will lose your soul and be forever separated from Jesus Christ.

The horrors of this period will not be something any person in their right mind would voluntarily choose to endure. Please heed this warning call from the Lord Jesus Christ. Do not turn away from Him. Please run to the Loving Arms of Jesus while there still is time. Don't put it off for whatever reason, we are not promised even the next breath. Jesus is lovingly reaching out to you, Please say "Yes" to Him now!

Jesus described the terrible period of the tribulation hour in the following words.

*For then there will be great distress, unequaled from the beginning of the world until now—and never to be equaled again. (Matthew 24:21)*

The Lord Jesus informs those who would be saved during of this awful period of time about what they should and should not do. He gives them clear understanding of what will be going on and also how He will appear to save them:

***If those days had not been cut short, no one would survive, but for the sake of the elect those days will be shortened.*** *At that time if anyone says to you, 'Look, here is the Christ!' or, 'There he is!' do not believe it. For false christs and false prophets will appear and perform great signs and miracles to deceive even the elect-if that were possible. See, I have told you ahead of time. "So if anyone tells you, 'There he is, out in the desert,' do not go out; or, 'Here he is, in the inner rooms,' do not believe it.* ***For as lightning that comes from the east is visible even in the west, so will be the coming of the Son of Man.*** *Wherever there is a carcass, there the vultures will gather. (Matthew 24:22–28)*

If the first three and a half years of the seven year tribulation period is bad, it only gets much worse in the second half. Jesus alerted us to the fact that Daniel's words were indeed going to come to pass.

*So when you see standing in the holy place 'the abomination that causes desolation,' spoken of through the prophet Daniel—let the reader understand . . . (Matthew 24:15)*

As we read this prophesy from Daniel, we can see that Jesus was quoting it, in Matthew 24:15–16:

*He will confirm a covenant with many for one 'seven.' In the middle of the 'seven' he will put an end to sacrifice and offering. **And on a wing [of the temple] he will set up an abomination that causes desolation, until the end that is decreed is poured out on him.** (Daniel 9:27)*

This totally evil man—the antichrist—will actually declare himself to be God! What a terrible time in which to live! False prophets will be performing lying signs and wonders, demonic activity will be at its height. Religious deceit, people betraying one another, huge cataclysmic events, and obviously nuclear war, to mention a few, will all be taking place simultaneously. Assuredly this will not be fun. Nothing, absolutely nothing, will be the same as it was prior to the Rapture, and those who choose to remain on earth will have an extraordinarily difficult time to say the least.

Perhaps the tribulation scene I was shown might have been what John described at the breaking of the Sixth Seal Judgment.

*I watched as he opened the sixth seal. **There was a great earthquake. The sun turned black like sackcloth made of goat hair, the whole moon turned blood red, and the stars in the sky fell to earth, as late figs drop from a fig tree when shaken by a strong wind. The sky receded like a scroll, rolling up, and every mountain and island was removed from its place.** Then the kings of the earth, the princes, the generals, the rich, the mighty, and every slave and every free man hid in caves and among the rocks of the mountains. They called to the mountains and the rocks, **"Fall on us and hide us from the face of him who sits on the throne and from the wrath of the***

***Lamb! For the great day of their wrath has come, and who can stand?*** *(Revelation 6:12–17)*

Keeping all this information in view, let me plead with you once more to turn to the Lord Jesus Christ and accept Him as your Lord and Savior. The only consequence of your surrender to Jesus will be eternal life with Him. You will leave this planet with the Messiah when He takes the Church home.

If you miss your final opportunity to give your life to the Lord, you will go through the tribulation period unless you pass from this life before the occurrence of that great and terrible day. However, if you were to enter eternity without ever having accepted Jesus as Lord and Savior, your situation will be infinitely worse than even that of the tribulation period we just described. So don't take the chance; you will not be able to reverse your mistake.

As I was doing a final read of this manuscript preparing it to go to the publisher, my eight-year-old grandson Micah, said to me. "Nani, I had a dream last night, I don't exactly know what it means, but this is what it was. I dreamed of a car like a PT Cruiser that was purplish blue and very sparkly. The car was in an empty dealership, but the location was not clear. The strange thing about the car was that it was named *wood* after the name a woman in my dream had called her eye.

The woman was blonde with blue eyes, and stood next to the car; she wore a white dress. On the other side of the car stood a man dressed in black; he had black eyes and black hair, even though he looked very old. Amazingly, this car was started from the back, where there were three seats. The car had only two doors but they opened very wide all the way to the front of the hood. For some reason the man in black told the woman not to start the car, but she got in the car and started it anyway. The man in black now spoke to some invisible person, commanding him to name the car "wood" after the woman's eye." Micah said, "Nani, Jesus told me the woman's name was *Deceit,* the name of the man in black was *Evil,* and the invisible person was the antichrist."

The Lord explained the dream to me, and because it is so relevant to what this entire book is about, I decided to add it to this chapter. The Lord explained that the car—a vehicle—symbolized ministry. It was purplish blue and sparkly because true ministries are supposed to be pure and holy, but this one was an imposter, posing as the real thing. The reason it looked somewhat like a PT Cruiser was merely for the name *Cruiser,* to demonstrate that these false ministries have cruised along undetected by the vast majority, gaining in strength and popularity. The empty dealership spoke of the absence of the Lord, the owner of all true ministries. The woman who stood beside the car wearing white and named *Deceit* by the Lord, symbolized the apostate churches that pose as the real thing but worship idols, false gods of their own making, whatever they may be. This was why she named her eye *Wood.* The Bible speaks of people bowing down to idols of wood and stone. They blind themselves to the true God. The man in black whom the Lord named Evil, was obviously Satan. The Bible refers to him as "that serpent of old," referencing his age.

Starting the car from the back seat speaks of stealth. The devil stealthily creeps into churches and takes over. Obviously the false church represented by the woman, is only too eager to grasp the deceitful ways of Satan. This is why she jumped in the back and started the car even though he told her not to for the moment. The antichrist, yet invisible, is obviously alive and waiting in the wings. He receives his instructions from Satan to further blind all that would be affiliated with the unholy church; hence, the devil's command to the antichrist to name the car *Wood,* after the blind eye of the woman who is the false church. Micah added that Jesus told him that many within this false church know they are in sin, which is why only one eye of the woman was called *Wood.* However, they remain there because they desire to be there. The three seats in the back demonstrate the agreement of the devil, the antichrist, and the false church working together to deceive as many as possible. Obviously the doors of the car that opened extremely wide were designed to accommodate as many as would be deceived.

Take heed; do not place yourself in any organization that does not honor the Lord Jesus Christ as the Son of God. Do not affiliate yourself with anyone who denies the death or the importance of the death, burial and resurrection of Jesus Christ. Don't agree with anyone who adds anything from any false religion to the Word of God. If you do, you will not be in the Church that Jesus built; the one He died to redeem, and the one He is coming back for. If you are already in such a place, come out at once and run to the safety of the Lord's Church.

The Lord Jesus made a beautiful promise to every true believer, He said:

*Let not your heart be troubled; you believe in God, believe also in Me.* **In My Father's house are many mansions;** *if it were not so, I would have told you.* **I go to prepare a place for you. And if I go and prepare a place for you, I will come again and receive you to Myself; that where I am, there you may be also.** *(John 14:1–4)*

As we know, it took God only six days to create the entire universe, Jesus being the One who created all things (*Colossians 1:16*) So we must wonder why it has taken Him two thousand years and counting, to prepare the mansions He promised us. What type of place must this be? The Book of Revelation gives us an idea. Jesus promised He was coming back to take us to be with Him in this glorious place He is preparing. In the meantime He gives us some advice.

*Behold, I am coming quickly!* **Hold fast what you have,** *that no one may take your crown. He who overcomes, I will make him a pillar in the temple of My God, and*

*he shall go out no more. **I will write on him the name
of My God and the name of the city of My God, the
New Jerusalem, which comes down out of heaven
from My God. And I will write on him My new name.**
(Revelation 3:11–12)*

It is interesting that we will not only have the Holy name of
God written on us, but also the new name belonging to Jesus
and the name of the city of God—the New Jerusalem. So why
is the name of the New Jerusalem to be written upon us? Let's
take a look at what John said:

*I saw the Holy City, the new Jerusalem, coming down
out of heaven from God, **prepared as a Bride beautifully dressed for her husband.** (Revelation 21:2)*

Very interestingly the Holy City—the New Jerusalem—is
prepared as a Bride, beautifully adorned for her husband.
Isn't the Church the Bride of Christ? Again, isn't the Church
made up of believers in Jesus? Peter had an awesome thing
to tell us:

*As you come to him, the living Stone-rejected by men
but chosen by God and precious to him- **you also, like
living stones, are being built into a spiritual house
to be a holy priesthood, offering spiritual sacrifices
acceptable to God through Jesus Christ.** For in
Scripture it says: "See, I lay a stone in Zion, a chosen
and precious cornerstone, **and the one who trusts in
him will never be put to shame.** (1 Peter 2:4–6)*

From what Peter just told us, we note that *we like living
stones are being built into a spiritual house to be a holy priesthood.* So let's look once more at the New Jerusalem.

*. . . one of the seven angels who had the seven bowls
full of the seven last plagues came and said to me,*

*"Come, I will show you the Bride, the wife of the Lamb." And he carried me away in the Spirit to a mountain great and high, **and showed me the Holy City, Jerusalem, coming down out of heaven from God.** It shone with the glory of God, and its brilliance was like that of a very precious jewel, like jasper, clear as crystal. **It had a great, high wall with twelve gates, and with twelve angels at the gates. On the gates were written the names of the twelve tribes of Israel.** There were three gates on the east, three on the north, three on the south and three on the west. **The wall of the city had twelve foundations, and on them were the names of the twelve apostles of the Lamb.** (Revelation 21:9–14)*

The twelve gates had the names of the twelve tribes of Israel, and on the twelve foundations of the city were the names of twelve apostles—the first Church. So that leaves the walls of the New Jerusalem; what are the walls made up of? Peter said we as living stones are being built into a spiritual house.

I suggest to you that the reason it has taken the Lord Jesus Christ two thousand years thus far and counting, to prepare a place for us, is because He is building the walls of the New Jerusalem with living stones—*every true believer in Him.* He daily adds to His Church those that would be saved, until the building is complete.

We have no idea how much longer it will be before the final living stone is in place, but all evidence points to the fact that it is imminent.

Will you be one of the beautiful living stones that shines with the glory of God; with brilliance like that of a very precious jewel, like jasper and clear as crystal? Will you have the name of God, the Lord Jesus Christ and the City of God written upon you? You might even be the very last stone needed, before Jesus returns for the Church. So please surrender to Jesus and make sure this awesome blessing is yours for eternity.

At this time I want to take a moment to plead with every born-again believer to reach out with the Gospel to as many as you can. Please do everything within your power to persuade someone to receive the Lord. You might be the one to lead the very last person to Jesus, this side of the tribulation. There is very little time left, so please make every moment count for the Lord. Lead as many as you can to the Lord and never forget this great and wonderful promise from Him.

*Those who are wise will shine like the brightness of the heavens, and those who lead many to righteousness, like the stars forever and ever. (Daniel 12:3)*

Rise up beloved, and shine for Jesus. Let the light of the Holy Spirit shine through you. Don't forget what Jesus said to us:

*You are the light of the world. A city on a hill cannot be hidden. Neither do people light a lamp and put it under a bowl. Instead they put it on its stand, and it gives light to everyone in the house. In the same way, let your light shine before men, that they may see your good deeds and praise your Father in heaven. (Matthew 5:14–16)*

Dearly beloved of the Lord! Rise up and serve your God and King, and live with Him forever.

The time is at hand! Amen! Come, Lord Jesus!

CPSIA information can be obtained at www.ICGtesting.com
Printed in the USA
LVOW07s0836180813

48371LV00005B/43/P